A LIFETIME
OF OBSERVATION IN THE
POLITICAL COMBAT ZONE
HAS PRODUCED THIS AMAZING
AND REVEALING BOOK!

"O'CONNOR DOES A BRILLIANT JOB . . . Few have seen Daley as clearly. O'Connor has listened at enough keyholes to know as well as anyone why Chicago ticks to the rhythm of Daley's heart . . . A solid biography . . . A fascinating tale . . . We get inside the high stakes game where it is much more important to be feared than loved."

Chicago Magazine

"CHICAGO FROM THE INSIDE . . . Fascinating and extremely well written! A masterful chronicle of how a political machine works!"

John Chancellor
NBC News

"THE STORY AS IT SHOULD BE TOLD . . . It's good to see a book like CLOUT. O'Connor, himself a gritty Chicago survivor, is a long-time television reporter who knows his politics. He dissects the Daley myth with straight, detail̶e̶d̶ ̶w̶r̶i̶t̶ing. A valuable and enjoyable histo̶r̶y̶ ̶ ̶ ̶ ̶ ̶ ̶a̶ ̶ remarkable, enigmati̶c̶ ̶ ̶ ̶ ̶

̶ ̶ ̶ ̶ ̶ ̶ ̶ ̶ ̶atricia O'Brien,
̶ ̶ ̶ ̶ ̶ ̶icago Sun-Times

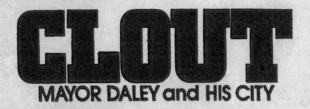

CLOUT

MAYOR DALEY and HIS CITY

LEN O'CONNOR

 AVON
PUBLISHERS OF BARD, CAMELOT, DISCUS, EQUINOX AND FLARE BOOKS

AVON BOOKS
A division of
The Hearst Corporation
959 Eighth Avenue
New York, New York 10019

First Avon Printing, March, 1976

Printed in the U.S.A.

For the gifted Don H. Reuben

Contents

Preface

Chicago is a special-situation city, resting on an unlikely base of provincialism and deceptive sophistication. For almost half a century, Chicago has been ruled by a self-disciplined band of rogues who proudly call themselves Democrats—those belonging to the nonpolitical financial sectors of the city having little knowledge of how the city is run but being reasonably satisfied with the end product.

This book had its beginnings at a time when few Chicagoans had heard of Richard J. Daley, and many of those who knew him had little basis for believing that he would prove to be a classic overachiever.

Like Chicago itself, the man who has set the U.S. record for serving as a big city mayor is enigmatic. Like the city he rules in autocratic fashion, Mayor Daley has hitherto defied definition. The outward signs of his strengths and weaknesses are there for all to see, yet he remains elusive, and it is with caution that one must approach the tricky business of attempting to capture the real Daley in the pages of a book.

Nonresident writers have not infrequently tried to run him down and exhibit their prize, but the chase leads over a slippery urban landscape, and it is with an impudent Irish smile that Daley seems always to escape them. How could it be otherwise, when those of us who think we know him and understand the chronology of his rise to power are never quite certain what manner of man he is?

There are some who view Daley as a man whose blood flows through arteries of refrigerated granite. This would seem to be true if one considered only the moments when he has coldly spurned someone who has displeased him or the times when he has petulantly turned icy and imperious.

Unpredictably, however, his emotions sometimes take charge and he swings to the opposite extremes of sentimentality and indecision.

As a political animal, Daley is king of the pride. As an ordinary mortal—taking his place in the penitential line leading to the confessional at, say, the funeral mass of Jennie Bauler—it is a self-effacing Daley that we see.

It was quite a human Daley that some of us saw when, in 1954, it appeared that he had been frustrated by his enemies within the Democratic party when he first aspired to be leader of the pack. It is difficult to accept the finding that Daley is a cold and unfeeling man when you have seen him standing on the fringes of a scene of tragedy in his city where innocent persons have perished or been left in misery—a holocaust at a school, a commuter train wreck—with the bewildered look of a man who wonders why God has forsaken him.

There has been frequent allusion by those who have scurried into Chicago to have a look at Daley, racing away to write about him as if they understood him, about the clumsy style of his speech and his unpolished manner; it is an error to judge him by these externals. It is equally inaccurate to hail him as a political genius—because he is more of a tradesman than an artist.

Daley might well be described as the ultimate pragmatist in the sometimes bawdy and sometimes cruel world of politics. But this conclusion leaves unanswered the question of how such a big city boss can function amid all the favoritism and corruption that swirls about him while wrapping his life in the daily devotions of Roman Catholicism. What kind of man can this be, so strong in practicalities and so seemingly short on charity?

On his seventieth birthday in 1972, he responded to the gush of a City Hall secretary that he would always be mayor with a statement that seemed to rebuke the woman—reminding her that, great as he was, there was yet a higher order of clout than any he possessed. "The future belongs to the Lord Himself," Daley had said. "Where I go, and how long I am able to serve the people of Chicago, depends on Him."

When, in December of 1974, he offered only a polite resistance to the idea of running for his sixth four-year term, he characteristically said that it would be with the "help of God" that he would face and conquer the problems of Chicago and serve out his four final years. Simultaneously, though, when asked to estimate his chances in the 1975 election, Daley curtly replied, "I always win."

An undefinable man, Richard Daley; complex. Unmovable as a bucket of ten-penny nails in one set of circumstances, sentimental to the point of being maudlin in others.

To portray accurately so mystifying and paradoxical a man is perhaps too much of an undertaking; the political mountain that is Daley is all too often obscured by the mist of doubt as to whether anyone outside his own family really knows him. Yet, perhaps each of us who knows something of him should make an effort to define him. Surely, the nation has never seen his like before—nor is it likely to see anyone quite like him again.

Chicago
December 29, 1974

visitors—yet a city abounding in night spots specializing in vulgarity and lewdness at exorbitant prices.

One need not go back to Jacques Marquette, a Jesuit priest, paddling up the river in his canoe in the seventeenth century, gazing at the unexplored place that was to be the site of a major city. One can skip over the first bootleggers who hustled the Indians. One need not tarry over Chicago's incorporation in 1833 nor dwell on the election of Chicago's first mayor, William B. Ogden, in 1837—except perhaps to note that the city's population then was 4,170 and that Ogden was a Democrat. One need not bother with the oft-repeated line that Chicago is a place where the folks take secret pride in their wickedness or with the so-called Great Fire of 1871—which was in some ways a blessing, since it cleared out the haphazardly constructed center of town and allowed more substantial rebuilding.

Closer to a real beginning is the Chicago of Lincoln Steffens. The Chicago of Richard J. Daley's time is remarkably similar to the evil city that muckraker Steffens set out to discover three-quarters of a century ago. Yet Chicago cannot simply be dismissed as "evil," the conclusion that satisfied Steffens in his disquisition on what set Chicago apart from the other major cities he had explored for the enraptured readers of *McClure's* magazine, if only because along with its corruption Chicago has long manifested an unrequited yearning for reform.

Steffens, a competent newspaperman who cut his investigative teeth on Wall Street's greed and the graft and villainy of such cities as Minneapolis, St. Louis, and Philadelphia, came to Chicago because of the never-ending search by his brilliant editor-publisher, S. S. McClure, for more shocking stuff than Steffens had yet uncovered. Steffens had tilted his lance during his Wall Street days at such unapproachable despots as Andrew Carnegie, founding father of U.S. Steel Corporation, the head of J. P. Morgan and Company, and other New York principals in the unconscionable world of big business and finance, but there were plenty of targets waiting for him in Chicago. He might have zeroed in on the meat packers, the grain market manipulators, the traction magnates, the industrialists who clung to the twelve-hour work day as if it were a precept of holy writ. He might have directed the light of his investigative lantern at the Chicago financiers who had the foresight to recognize that the profits of having a monopoly on such utilities as gas and electricity would be well worth the enormous bribes that had to be paid to acquire it. Steffens might have searched out the possible connection between the subsistence wages paid to sales girls in the fashionable stores on State Street and the inexhaustible supply of female flesh in the fashionable, and not so fashionable, brothels in downtown Chicago and the Near South Side "amusement" area—the political domain of the amoral and unsavory "Bathhouse John" Coughlin and Michael ("Hinky Dink") Kenna, who held sway for forty years as the Democratic bosses of the First Ward.

In short, there were any number of alleys of investigation beckoning to Lincoln Steffens. Yet he does not appear in retrospect to have ventured far into any of them. Perhaps there was just too much corruption for even Steffens to pin down and identify.

And then there was the question of reform. The present-day journalist surveying Chicago in a quick study would wind up in the offices of the Chicago Crime Commission or of the Better Government Association. Lincoln Steffens's source for what was being done in the name of reform seventy-five years ago was the Municipal Voters League.

Chicago has never been short on fiery reformers or organizations seeking reform—any more than it has ever been short of rogues who need it. The evangelist who headed up the Voters League was a squat, audacious businessman named George E. Cole, who openly charged that twenty-six of Chicago's aldermen were crooks and that the league intended to run them out of office. "Chicago," Lincoln Steffens wrote, in admiring reference to Cole, "likes audacity and is always willing to try anything once; no matter who you are, where you come from, or what you set out to do, Chicago will give you a chance."

Then, as now, it was only partly true that Chicago enjoyed audaciousness; the masses have always loved it, and those in jeopardy of exposure fear it and grimly abide it. In the areas where power of whatever persuasion exists, there is brooding resistance now, as there was three-quarters of a century ago, to the reality of reform. In the words of the Honorable Richard J. Daley: "Indictments don't mean anything; men are entitled to be innocent until they are proved guilty"—this while federal grand jury droppings charging conspiracy, malfeasance, and income tax evasion were soiling the reputations of about a dozen of his best people.

The events of 1972-1974 amply demonstrate the reformers' enthusiasm for reform; likewise, Daley's reaction to each reform success demonstrates his abhorrence of reforming zeal. For example, Daley was sick during the many months that the man he made governor, Federal Judge Otto Kerner, Jr., of the Seventh Circuit Court of Appeals, was under investigation for conspiracy and tax evasion in connection with his purchase of racetrack stock—and utterly depressed when Kerner was indicted on December 15, 1971, found guilty on February 19, 1973, and sent to prison on July 29, 1974 for these and perjury charges as well. Daley was saddened when U.S. Attorney James R. Thompson secured the indictment on September 28, 1972 and conviction on March 7, 1973, of Cook County Clerk Edward J. Barrett for soliciting a $187,000 bribe as a condition of purchasing voting machines. Daley's sadness turned to anger on October 5, 1973, when his chief of traffic and eighteen vice detectives were nailed by Thompson, in connection with extortions in the Near North Side police district. Daley was crushed when his neighbor and closest confidant, Matthew Danaher—Daley's Cook County Circuit Court clerk—was indicted on April 10, 1974 for his part in a suspicious $400,000 real estate scheme. Daley was numb by May 10, 1974, when District Attorney Thompson got around to indicting (and on October 9 securing the conviction of) his City Council leader, Alderman Thomas E. Keane, on charges of conspiracy and mail fraud in a million-dollar real estate deal that involved public bodies.

During 1972-1974 something like half a hundred policemen, including two district commanders, were sent to prison by Thompson for extortion and tax evasion, and scores of others were under investigation; two Daley-loyal aldermen and one ex-Daley alderman were convicted of soliciting bribes to approve zoning changes in their wards; Daley's onetime press aide was convicted of federal offenses; and various other Daley loyalists were put under indictment or sought to escape it in enforced appearances before the federal grand jury. In all, it was no small reform victory.

But if such zealous reforming goes on, how can Daley and all the other leaders of Chicago get away with it? Simply because now, as was the case seventy-five years ago, while the people of Chicago applaud the spray of sparks as the reformer sharpens his ax, Chicagoans just as cheerfully grin if the reformer loses his grip at the grinding wheel and gets cut. True, Chicago is delighted by audacity, but the city now is conditioned to expect little to come of it. If, perchance, the reformer accomplishes a little something, the taxpayers have learned from experience that politicians will methodically repair the damages when the reformer is gone or his fury has been abated. In short, a reformer should be careful not to provide Chicago with more reform than Chicago wants—not least because Chicago knows that those under attack fight back.

And when Chicago's powerhouse fights back, everything is fair. Thus, in an effort to neutralize public acceptance of the damage U.S. Attorney Thompson was doing to the Democratic Machine and to Daley's image as the totally honest man, in the fall of 1974 the Democrats encouraged speculation regarding Thompson's personal political ambitions. With typical Chicago logic, the Democrats slyly insinuated that a federal prosecutor who would bluntly say that Spiro Agnew was a crook—which is precisely what Thompson had said, returning from the proceedings in Washington where Agnew got off the hook—had to be seeking advantage for himself out of someone else's misery. Secondly, and more deplorably, a vicious rumor was spread in Chicago that Thompson was not so clean—that he had a skeleton in his closet. (It is noteworthy that those who said this carefully avoided specifying what Thompson's secret might be.)

How reform, with all its limitations, works in Chicago is well illustrated by George Cole's campaign against Bathhouse John Coughlin, alderman with Hinky Dink Kenna of the First Ward (in those days each Chicago ward was represented by two aldermen). Coughlin simply and blithely retorted to his accusers that he had the backing of the Loop bankers and the State Street merchants and, his boast being true, sailed safely through the storm stirred up by the Municipal Voters League and subsequent storms as well.

This is not to say that the league was ineffectual; on the contrary, it succeeded in drumming many of Coughlin's colleagues out of office, and for a dozen years or so, under the direction of Walter L. Fisher—George Cole having been forced into retirement because of poor health—it appeared to Lincoln Steffens that the league was having "astonishing" results.

Fisher, a capable man who wound up eventually in the cabinet of President William Howard Taft, was a reformer to be reckoned with. The bosses referred to him in time as "that sonofabitch!"—which is of course the choicest accolade a politician can bestow upon his enemy. Fisher's modus operandi was to compile in each ward every shred of information about the candidates and lawlessness—the ward's political center of power, the extent of the graft, the pattern of vote-control, *everything*. Through publicity and dealing directly with residents of the ward—appealing to their good judgment—he sought to force the election of aldermen who would work not for themselves but for the citizens. Simultaneously, Fisher applied pressure to people of his own class, socialities, and the business community to deal honorably with the city.

The same methods were employed two generations later by another Chicago reformer, the witty, wise, and ingenious Saul Alinsky, now dead: get to the people with the facts of what is going on, serve notice on the business world that its members will have no peace until they cease to cheat and lie.

Yet for all his success Fisher—like Alinsky—ultimately failed. Reform cannot survive in a contest with greed, unless, that is, it enjoys the absolute backing of the majority of the citizens. And Chicagoans are so conditioned to seeing the reformers fail, sooner or later, that they stand on the sidelines until the battle is over—when life always goes on as usual.

The business community, naturally, saw to its own interests. In Chicago these interests were clear. As Steffens confessed in his autobiography, Chicago businessmen *say* that they pine for good government—yet, in his experience, "businessmen hated and fought and clamored and wriggled and bribed" to outwit the reform government of Chicago. "And finally," Steffens said, writing in 1931, "they killed it as literally as the gunmen of Chicago now kill one another." Why—when the Municipal Voters League was striving to give them the kind of government they had asked for? "They said what they wanted was not *this*, but 'good' government."

Ultimately, in fact, it is with the establishment that responsibility for continued political corruption rests. Simply put, monied people stand by those with political ambition who show, when they are elected, that they operate the machinery of government in such a way that the monied folks get the kind of government they want. This identification is not openly acknowledged, of course, but the kind of government they want is the Richard Daley kind—the kind that provides opportunities to grab up public property at bargain prices, zoning changes to accommodate the development of these properties, tax "considerations" when the structures are built. What they want is freedom from harassment by city departments, adequate police and fire protection in establishment neighborhoods, a confinement, insofar as it is possible, of militant minorities—all of this carried out behind the icon of a God-fearing family man who is mayor.

As in the past, when people of position and affluence today claim to face up to what they regard as their "civic responsibilities" by, for example, supporting as a worthy cause the Better Government Association—which tries to keep a beady eye on politicians—this carries with it no commitment to stand with the BGA politically. Thus when, in 1971, the executive director of BGA, Richard Friedman, decided to run against Daley for the office of mayor, those who had helped finance Friedman's considerable number of exposés of waste and payroll-padding in the Daley administration wanted nothing to do with him. Consequently, having deluded himself into believing that the better element wanted honest government, Friedman must have been shocked when he received less than 30 percent of the vote. He was defeated by Daley, 740, 137 to 315, 969.

It had been emphasized to Friedman, when he confided to a few well-informed people that in the interests of public discussion of important issues he felt obliged to run, that he must constantly remember that he had no chance of winning. How could a Republican candidate for mayor win when diehard Republican business people were holding Daley upright, stuffing campaign money into his pockets? Like many underdog candidates, Friedman made the grave error of translating into votes the not-friendly reception he got as he walked the neighborhoods, preaching his gospel.

With a new executive director—Friedman was disqualified by reason of his political identification—the BGA got back to the task of rooting up evidence of deceit and corruption in the Daley administration—again with the aid of fresh donations supplied by respectable citizens, who reassured each other that they could rest easy for another four years, knowing that Dick Daley, God love him, would remain in charge of things.

If it seems incongruous that the better element of Chicago would pamper, much less tolerate, a political machine that requires constant watching, in Chicago it has always been the practice for the monied crowd to work for a *balance* of progress and corruption.

Outsiders simply do not understand that in Chicago you are expected to pay for what you want—a mooring for your yacht in lakefront harbors, permission to block off streets during construction work, a dispensation from the legal closing hours if you operate a place that caters to late-night drinkers. Chicago is the place where motorists who get pulled over for speeding adopted the habit of having their driver's license protectively wrapped in a ten dollar bill. In Chicago it is considered to be well-nigh impossible to promote successfully a fund-raising dinner for a worthy cause without the support of City Hall. For example, P. J. ("Parky") Cullerton, for decades Cook County assessor, was an invaluable ally if you went seeking generous contributions for some charitable purpose. A mere phone call by Parky Cullerton to the owner of important real estate, the tax assessment of which was in Parky's control, seemed to work wonders. Indeed, in Cook County almost every holder of valuable real estate has his own man whose job entails "working things out" with the assessor's office.

There has always been in Chicago a high tolerance for sin and scandal; the imperative conditions imposed on the politicians are (1) that the city must function in an orderly way and (2) that it must always be possible for an enterprising man to make money in the city. And it has always been that way. Personal behavior is pretty much a matter of one's own conscience in Chicago, conditioned only by a need to be discreet. For example, some of the city's most famous people are delighted to receive invitations to frolic in the North State Parkway hutch of Hugh Hefner, the local Christopher Columbus of soft porn. It is a not uncommon practice in the Chicago business community to supply important out-of-town clients with high-priced hookers, the madam customarily sending over one of the girls on the first of the month to settle the firm's account. The transaction is carried out as efficiently as Illinois Bell collects its phone bills.

Structurally, Chicago is, of course, different from the city that Lincoln Steffens investigated; philosophically, in that the debauchery of today coexists with thoughtful planning for tomorrow, Chicago is the same.

Curiously, the natives, along with patiently accepting the calumny that whorehousing and gambling and killing people are the natural endowments of people who live in Chicago, have manifested little objection to the city's existence as a breeding ground for political bosses. As Richard J. Daley would say, arching his brows, "Do you have a better plan for runnin' a city?"

The first recognizable boss was Michael Cassium Mc-Donald, who came on stage early and stayed late. McDonald, a gambler-saloonkeeper by profession, was the first to detect the common bonds of interest of the criminal element and politicians and introduce one group to the other. He went to work as matchmaker shortly after the fire of 1871, prospered, and lasted until 1907. As he lay on his deathbed, broken by the shock of his wife's having murdered her paramour, the *Chicago News* remarked editorially:

> When the City had a scant half-million, this man ruled it from his saloon and gambling house. . . . During many succeeding years, bad government was accepted as a matter of course. Vice sat in the seats of power. Wretched conditions were excused on the theory that "vice made the town lively."

The newspaper's premature eulogy gave the dying McDonald credit for electing aldermen who lorded it in city council and county commissioners who stole everything in sight, and for providing contracts for public works that had "thievery written between the lines."

Yet, for all his innovations, the one element that McDonald did not hit upon was the idea of political *organization,* an obvious device that also escaped the attention of subsequent political bosses. McDonald's vision, and that of the bosses who followed him, was limited to looking at the game one play at a time. And, of course, this is what politics is all about. Richard J. Daley attacks each election, his own and that of any of his people, as if it were the only election that mattered; and it is, for the boss who slips up quickly loses all authority. But winning elections is only part of the story. Daley would abhor a loosely knit, carelessly disciplined political organization—the kind, until Anton J. Cermak's time, that was accepted as good enough, allowing for each fellow to have varying degrees of autonomy.

Cermak was, undeniably, the political precursor of Richard J. Daley. Daley was just another precinct captain, pushing doorbells in search of votes for candidates on the Democratic ticket when Cermak was fashioning the organization along a ward-boss chain of command that he, in the manner of a Mafia chief, could control. Despite his weakness for isolating himself in a circle of inferior bootlickers, Cermak was the ultimate politician. He made all the rules, dealt all the cards, and destroyed any rebellious ward boss who dared to seek larger portions of the loot than he "deserved."

Cermak was an innovator with a none-too-popular new idea. Proof of this can be seen in the scramble for restoration of war-boss power after Cermak's death, in 1933, when the ward bosses immediately resumed pushing for more elbow room. The problems that arise from diversified control are obvious. Indeed, Edward J. Kelly, chosen to succeed Cermak, is frequently quoted to the effect that if a Chicago boss does not run the Machine, the Machine will damn well run the boss. The irony of this is that, whereas Ed Kelly learned the *principle* from Tony Cermak, Kelly could not make it *work*—as witness the Machine's eventual decision to get rid of him.

The difference between Kelly and Daley is that Daley knows the basic order of things in the doctrine set forth by Cermak, and he likewise knows how to lock up the principles in a political approach that does work. Daley has always understood that for a man to get where he is going, he must seize power before he can exercise that power. More than that, to retain power, Daley has intuitively known from the beginning, a man must surround himself with servitors, people who are totally loyal and utterly dependent upon the man, Daley, for their own well-being.

If Cermak had a political weakness, it was his eagerness to expand his influence across the city, profiting from the contention among his rivals. But he underestimated his need for a palace guard comprised of faithful followers who needed him. Kelly's weaknesses were his lack of a personal power base and his failure to estimate properly his ability to maintain party discipline. Daley's strength lies in the fact that, born of a working stiff, schooled in the tough streets of big city politics, he recognized from the beginning that the unwavering loyalty of one's personal associates is *the* requirement in Chicago for gained control, he had the wisdom to place people he could trust—people he could count upon to protect him—in charge of virtually all sensitive departments of city government. The simple truth is that had it not been for his deliberate steps to dictate and rule through the process of inbreeding, his boyhood friends and the sons of his boyhood friends getting the key jobs that he could dispense, it is unlikely that he would have landed on anyone's list as Greatest Mayor Chicago Ever Had. In the interests of their own well-being, those outside his circle would have finished him off ere he could reach for the scepter he has carried for twenty years.

At their first sighting of Richard J. Daley, candidate for mayor, the commerce, industry, and social register crowd put him down as a lout—proof, if any were needed, that they are not so smart, either. Only his Bridgeport neighbors, hungry for a taste of payroll pie, licking their lips in anticipation of the grand opportunities that the election of Daley would bring, had an accurate measurement of the man. Only a few of the old pros who had "seen 'em all" since Carter Harrison's day—such pre-Cermak and pre-

Kelly ward bosses as Paddy Bauler and Charlie Weber, for example—recognized that Daley would prove worthy to stand in the exclusive company of Carter Harrison II and Tony Cermak as Chicago mayors who possessed brass balls.

To rule Chicago, a truly strong mayor must never for a moment forget that Chicago, like Holy Mother Church, is a congregation not of saints but sinners. The genius of Tony Cermak built the Democratic Machine of Chicago along lines that are remarkably similar to those of Rome, and it is upon this structure, polished and refined throughout the twenty years that he has reigned, that the power of Richard J. Daley rests.

Daley is not a pope, but in the political sphere he is the most reasonable facsimile that big city politics has ever seen. The powerful men on the Democratic Central Committee of Cook County would guffaw at a suggestion that they are Daley's College of Cardinals, yet these are the men—the fifty ward committeemen from the city and thirty from the "dioceses" of Cook County that lie outside of Chicago—who decide, in secrecy, who is to be elevated when the reigning pontiff is gone. In the meantime, of course, they do Daley's bidding. Below them, the Cadillac monsignori are those who reign over precincts that deliver a big vote. And so on, down the line to what could be considered the rosary-bead faithful—the common folks who were born Democrats or who were fortunate enough to be converted to the true political faith, thus obtaining sustenance and favors (in exchange for unswerving political loyalty).

Outsiders are sometimes befuddled by the overlapping areas of Daley's authority. Just as the Holy Father is Bishop of Rome, the seat of Daley's power is Chicago and he runs it with a hierarchy of the fifty ward committeemen. This group is known as the Democratic Central Committee of Chicago, but only about one third of the fifty are permitted any voice in decision-making. Additionally, there is a Democratic Central Committee of Cook County—likewise run by Daley—which is comprised of the fifty Chicago committeemen and the thirty county committeemen who are elected to four-year terms by the registered Democrats of the wards and thirty townships located outside the city limits of Chicago. The

number of registered Democrats in the areas outside of the
city has steadily increased, as whites pull up stakes and
flee to the suburbs; yet, because the Democratic vote in the
non-Chicago areas is hardly two-fifths of the total in all of
Cook County, the leverage is retained by the Chicago
organization—the ultimate power remaining in Daley's
hands, Daley deciding, for example, which of the thirty
township committeemen can safely be included on the
inner circle, or curia, of those who are allowed some say
in political decisions that affect all of Cook County.

By state statute, Chicago is defined as a strong-city-
council, weak-mayor form of government. Since 1870 it
has been the state legislature's intention to concentrate
authority not in the mayor but in the city council. Yet,
as Daley has shown, the intent of the 1870 Municipalities
Act can be easily circumvented—a "weak mayor" can
rule as a dictator if he acquires *political* control of the
"strong council." As Ed Kelly said, "You run them or
they'll run you." Daley, perhaps, explained it better in
answer to the question of how he could be a good mayor
and, simultaneously, political boss of the Democratic
party: "I figured it out real early: How can you control
the city *unless* you're the leader of your party?"

There is no question as to who presently holds the
power in Chicago; it is the mayor, not the City Council,
and he controls the council by virtue of controlling the
ward committeemen that run the ward organizations that
elect a very high proportion of Chicago's aldermen. In
many cases, the committeeman is also elected alderman—
but the place of power is in the party office, not in the City
Council, for it is from among the fifty ward committeemen
that some fifteen members of the Central Committee
who sit on the policy-making body of the Cook County
Democratic party under its long-time chairman, Richard
J. Daley, mayor of Chicago, are chosen; and if sometimes a committeeman makes it on the strength of the
votes he can produce and sometimes merely at the pleasure of Chairman Daley, it all amounts to the same thing.
Political control in Chicago rests absolutely in Daley, who
decides who will be voted in.

The major hurdle, therefore, to Daley's becoming a
strong mayor was not the "strong" City Council provided
by statute but rather the need to win acceptance as

chairman by the Central Committee. The secret of Daley's long reign is that, in exploiting his opportunity to be a strong mayor, he acquired not only the power to dictate to the City Council but also the power of patronage, with which he has quite nicely controlled the party organization.

Another reason for Daley's success is that he always learned from the mistakes of others. For example, one would imagine that the all-powerful leader of so important an organization as the Democratic Machine in Chicago would live in the finest house in the most exclusive area of the city. But Daley still lives in his old Bridgeport neighborhood. When Tony Cermak was mayor, he forsook his Bohemian neighbors and their drab section of the West Side to take up residence in the Congress Hotel on Michigan Avenue. Ed Kelly was, like Daley, a Bridgeport boy who grew up in the stench of the Union Stock Yards, but he moved out and settled down on Chicago's Gold Coast as quickly as he could afford to do so. Martin H. Kennelly, Daley's immediate predecessor, was likewise a child of Bridgeport, but when Kennelly hit it big in the business world, he was comfortably housed in the fancy Edgewater Beach Apartments, at the extreme northern end of the city's Lake Shore Drive, with a nice view of Lake Michigan.

With Daley there was an understanding, shared by the man and his neighbors, that it would be unseemly for him to locate in a more desirable place. Politically, Cermak, Kelly, and Kennelly cut from underneath themselves their home base. Daley knew better. He has a neatly groomed Castel Gandolfo at Grand Beach, Michigan, to which he can escape—seven acres, with a large house that faces on Lake Michigan. For the most part, though, he is content to live in a brick bungalow in the place of his birth. It is not, the privileged few who are invited there will tell you, so plain a residence as Chicagoans have been led to believe; even to the casual observer, touring the neighborhood, Daley's house is beyond question the best-looking one in the area. But it is no palace.

Conceivably, there might be times when Daley strides down the walk in his dinner jacket and climbs into the rear seat of his black limousine to go back downtown for some function, detectives in the tail cars watching his every move, that he might yearn to live in better style, as Kelly and Kennelly did. But his predecessors never identified with Back of the Yards; they did not achieve eminence because of any connection with it. Kelly and Kennelly were "from" the neighborhood, but never part of it. And Daley knows that Ed and Martin paid for this, for moving out, when they needed devoted friends and didn't have any.

Daley protests that he likes living where he does. Perhaps he does, but he stayed because he felt he should never relinquish his base. Now it is too late for Daley to have a choice in the matter; it would be ludicrous for him to make a move now, now that he is seventy-two, having lived his entire life in the space of a few blocks, worshiping all through the years at the same church. It hardly matters now that Richard Daley, preeminent authority of a great city, with power to smite the mightiest forces that confront him, is a Gulliver in a neighborhood of Lilliputians—pinned down in plain-jane Bridgeport. All that matters to Daley, perhaps, is that he set his sights as high as any boy in Bridgeport dared—and that he got what he wanted.

CHAPTER 2

Up from Bridgeport

"A Government is nothing more than a gang of men, and as a practical matter most of them are inferior men."
—*H. L. Mencken*, Minority Report

Richard J. Daley is living proof of the frayed American tradition that the United States is a land of unlimited opportunity, no matter how humble might be an ambitious man's beginnings. Daley's special advantage was that fate continually located him no more than a step behind the man whose place in the sun he coveted. Otherwise, he was an unlikely prospect for a rise to power, born as he was of simple stock in a quite ordinary section of Chicago, endowed with no apparent inclinations toward scholarship.

Daley was born in a two-flat at 3502 South Lowe on May 15, 1902, baptized at nearby Nativity of Our Lord Roman Catholic Church, and has spent his life in Bridgeport, a grubby white enclave in an otherwise largely black section of Chicago. The community, about four miles south of downtown Chicago, was settled almost exclusively by immigrants of Irish, Polish, German, Lithuanian, and Italian extraction. These people put down in Bridgeport because of its proximity to the Union Stock Yards and industrial plants where jobs were available. They were low-income people, frugal and exceedingly clannish despite the polygenesis of their origins. Bridgeport was from its formulation an area of low literacy, where only the fortunate few boys got to attend De La Salle, the Catholic neighborhood high school, the tuition, while moderate, requiring too big a dip into family budgets. Until relatively recent times, only a very rare few got to college. It followed, of course, that those living in Bridgeport took shelter in prejudice toward all outsiders.

Daley's mother, née Lillian Dunne, was an exception among Bridgeport women; she busied herself in the cause of the suffragettes, for example, and she recognized the need for education and for the perseverance a lad would have to have to make something of himself. Moreover, having been thirty years old when Richard was born and having no other children, she could afford to enroll young Richard at De La Salle, where he learned commercial subjects—bookkeeping, typing, and such like—and she could afford to dress him more neatly than the sons of most other families in the neighborhood.

An only child, Richard was on the shy side, as most only-offspring are—and the lad had the example of his taciturn father, Michael, to guide him in the advantages of keeping one's mouth shut. However, this worked to young Daley's advantage; holding one's tongue is a valuable talent if one wants to move forward in the world of politics. And he has made good use of his childhood habit. Part of the mystique of Richard J. Daley still is that no one ever seems to know precisely what it is that he is thinking.

Old-timers say that young Daley was reluctant to precipitate a fight but that he was good with his fists if goaded into one. He was stocky and strong, which was lucky because, as the best-dressed kid in Bridgeport and the only one known to carry a clean handkerchief, he probably had to defend his honor not infrequently. Young Daley's father, a slight man—a sheetmetal worker, born in County Wexford—must have been pleased to see that his son could take care of himself, but he was not the sort who would say so. Michael Daley did, however, give his only son solid religious example, the three members of the Daley family going off together daily for mass and communion at nearby Nativity of Our Lord Church, where young Richard also attended grade school—graduating, at age thirteen, in 1915.

There was a true affinity between father and son; perhaps the eight-year difference in age between husband and wife, Daley's father being the younger of the two, had something to do with it. In any case, the father lived to see his boy become mayor of the city whereas Daley's mother died at an early stage of his rise to power, though not so early that she could not see that her dreams that Richard would make something of himself were not in vain.

The homogenizing agent of the conglomeration of nationalities in such neighborhoods as Bridgeport was the neighborhood gang. Lads of vastly different origins hung together, played together, and zealously fought together to repel intruders who swaggered in searching for trouble. The hero figures of an area such as Bridgeport were the ward politicians, because they were symbols of affluence and they were the ones who could work such miracles as getting someone out of jail, getting an ailing grandmother into Cook County Hospital, or finding some lad a job. Modeling itself on its political superiors, a neighborhood gang, to amount to anything, had to have an organization —with elected officers, a headquarters, and a close identity with the ward politicians who ran things.

In the natural order of things, the gang member who kept his nose clean—that is, did not fall out of favor with the local politicians and yet preserved the integrity of his manhood and community by fighting lustily against all would-be intruders—graduated from the gang of lads to the gang of men known as the social club, which was a gang of rough lads grown older and, when necessary, more violent.

In Bridgeport, the only organization of consequence was the Hamburg Social and Athletic Club. The roster of Hamburg Club alumni includes an extraordinary number who have made it big in local government and the judiciary—solid proof that having powerful friends is a valuable asset, if not a prerequisite, for those who seek success in these fields of public service. In 1924, at age twenty-two, with one year of experience as a Democratic precinct captain, Dick Daley—the paid secretary of the Eleventh Ward office by reason of his being able to type and keep his mouth shut—won his first election: by acclamation he was chosen to be president of the Hamburg Social and Athletic Club. He held this post for fifteen years, early evidence that when Daley got a job he kept it.

Daley's fellow Hamburgers, who prided themselves on a

proven ability to get out the vote, although they soft-pedaled the idea that they were, at base, a political organization, figured that Dick Daley was on his way. In addition to his typing talent and talent for keeping his lips buttoned, Daley avoided a common Bridgeport practice of bad-mouthing others, was eager to please everyone, and seemed keen to learn whatever anyone else might teach him. On top of everything else, Daley was Irish, and while ethnic background was not a bar to membership in the Hamburg Club, any more than it was a bar to living in Bridgeport, by common consent the leadership role fell to the Irish. In any case, it could not have been otherwise when Daley was elected chief Hamburger, because the biggest man in the neighborhood, in all ways, was a boozy, conniving, gluttonous three-hundred-pounder named Joseph ("Big Joe") McDonough, who was both Democratic committeeman and alderman of the Eleventh Ward.

Joe McDonough, a college football star who was elected alderman in 1917, at age twenty-eight, and ward committeeman in 1918, was a ferocious man to have as an enemy, but he devoutly followed the rule that a good ward boss must be ever mindful that his constituents get a fair share of things. McDonough, while at heart a true pragmatist, was without question a man who took no nonsense from the boys downtown.

Daley's election as Hamburger president confirmed in the minds of the Eleventh Ward the feeling that Big Joe had taken a shine, as they say in Bridgeport, to young Daley, who was already McDonough's ward secretary, and great achievements were being predicted for the ever-smiling Dick Daley before he was far out of his teens. About all that Daley, with such a powerful patron, had to do to nourish his ambitions was to stay out of trouble and to make certain that the Hamburg Club worked diligently to get out a vote for Joe McDonough and such other Democratic candidates as McDonough had a personal interest in getting elected.

Daley, all of his life, has had a knack when it comes to keeping out of trouble. Indeed, so skillful is he that it seems that he can associate with the worst of the breed in any enterprise and come out of it smelling like an Irish rose, no matter what happens to the reputations of the others. When Daley was picked to be president of the Hamburgers, for instance, it was widely believed in Bridgeport that the older Hamburgers had been in the front line of violence in Chicago's worst race riot, in 1919, one month after Daley graduated from high school. The riot began when a black put his feet on an all-white beach—and was beaten to death for his temerity, the first of thirty-eight to die, white as well as black, in four days and nights of horror that left five hundred persons injured and a thousand homes charred wrecks. Yet Daley, then only seventeen, escaped involvement in any of this— although he almost certainly had been on the fringes of the Hamburger crowd, because "being there" would have been a point of honor.

Hatred of blacks, of course, is a native condition of those who live in Bridgeport. Daley's racial consciousness was hardly raised by the 1919 riot or by having had to confront many blacks on his way to and from De La Salle, which, though its enrollment was solidly white, was in an adjoining black neighborhood. Thus it has always grated upon Daley, though he has hidden his feelings as well as he can, and other Bridgeport whites, who have not hidden their feelings, that political expediency requires him to socialize with the likes of the late William Levi Dawson, the black congressman who ruled the South Side ghetto.

Bridgeport being largely Roman Catholic, attendance at Sunday mass was a condition of social acceptance during the years that followed the settlement of immigrants in this area. This was but one place of many, of course, where the preachment of loving one's neighbor as an equal child of God never got through to the worshipers. In Bridgeport, indeed, blacks were customarily referred to as "the savages," which provides a measurement of the area's racial attitude. Moreover, while it was not the Irish alone who harbored these non-Christian prejudices, it was the Irish who provided leadership to the gangs that patrolled the neighborhood, ever eager to smash the heads of blacks or of others who had the poor judgment to enter it. There is not a trace of evidence that young Daley participated in the brawls that ensued; characteristically, he would have been occupied with his studies, family affairs, or Joe McDonough's business. Yet these were his friends, and at least by passive acceptance of what they were up to, Daley's sentiments were with them.

The irony of militant prejudice on the part of the Bridgeport whites is that as the children of immigrants who had suffered so much from intolerance they yet could practice it so willfully. But they were a tough bunch, the first-generation whites whose people had fled the homeland and clustered in Chicago in modest dwellings back of the yards, and the toughest of all, if one can judge by their determination to become leaders, were the Irish. Escaping from British persecution often at great personal sacrifice, they had arrived exhausted at Chicago's Dearborn Street railroad station, with identification tags tied to their outer garments, tin boxes of their personal belongings in hand, waiting to be claimed by relatives or friends who previously had made the journey and who were sufficiently settled to provide the arrivals with a five-cent street car ride to Bridgeport, a bed to sleep in for a few days, something to eat, an earful of employment possibilities, and a bit of money to tide them over until they could get started.

The patron saints of Ireland—Patrick, Bridget, and all of the others—probably looked down approvingly upon these threadbare Irish people who endured so much to prospect, under the odoriferous pall of Chicago's Union Stock Yards, for the right to worship God in their own way, building churches and parochial schools, scraping up money to import priests and nuns, who grimly conveyed a warning of hellfire and damnation in brogues that flowed as softly as the River Liffey. Patrick and Bridget and all of the others might not have been so pleased, however, at the arrogant, bigoted, overly ambitious breed the immigrants foaled. The offspring, as we have seen, cut up into raucous, brawling, rough-mouthed gangs—hastily blessing themselves as they swaggered past the parish churches of their ethnic enclave.

In need of contact with people from the old country, immigrants customarily banded together, in Chicago, Boston, New York, and elsewhere—"taking care of one's own," as the Irish say. Equally inevitably, Greeks immediately began to take advantage of Greeks, Italians and Sicilians developed the art of intra-ethnic assassination, Jews succumbed to the temptation of outsmarting Jews—

for in the struggle to "get ahead" it followed that the different groups found in their own ghettos the first targets of opportunity. The Irish were no exception in this, but what made the Irish different from any other group was that—whereas most of the others drifted generally into commerce, industry, and art—from the very beginning the Irish made a determined effort to seize *political* control, especially in such places as New York, Boston, and Chicago.

Perhaps there is a subconscious remembrance among the Irish, based upon hundreds of years of oppression and religious persecution "back home," that it matters not how large your share of the population might be, nor who milks the cows; the only thing that matters is the question of who is in charge of the whole affair. In any case, Daley's Bridgeport people understand all this perfectly well. They and their fathers before them—the Irish of Chicago—did not merely *hope* to gain political control of the city; the Irish-Americans of Bridgeport had long dedicated themselves to producing the Man. What Bridgeport always wanted was a tough, smart son of its own who could take Chicago by the throat and hang on, taking good care of his Eleventh Ward pals in the bargain. By virtue of the great Joe McDonough's anointment, and his own recruits, young Daley seemingly was the Messiah —to Bridgeport if not, at first, to anyone else.

Long before anyone else realized it—long before Adlai E. Stevenson, who saved Daley from political oblivion (and lived to be double-crossed by Daley in 1960), before such wise old Irish professional politicians from other areas as the Bobbsey Twins of the anti-Bridgeport Irish, John J. Duffy, who wound up running the Cook County Board, and James McDermott, who died as a circuit court judge, were aware of him, before Democratic king-maker Jacob M. Arvey was saying, "There is no office within the power of the people to bestow upon a man that Dick Daley cannot attain"—Bridgeport was placing its bets on Daley.

There were other young men in Bridgeport, brighter than Daley, who envied the status he had with Joe McDonough. But all the others were flippant, whereas Daley was reserved, and all had other disadvantages, too. Some—Daley's best pal, William J. ("Billy") Lynch, for example—were too bright and made McDonough uncomfortable, if not wary. Some were too argumentative for their own good at the Hamburg Club and at Eleventh Ward Democratic Organization meetings. Some got too much of a reputation for drinking, and in a neighborhood that is given to peeking through the curtains, a young Bridgeporter who spent a good deal of time in the Halsted Street speakeasies couldn't expect to keep this secret. Some who might have emerged as Daley's rivals were too vocal in presenting their ideas of how the Eleventh Ward should be run, falling by the wayside as they created an impression that they would keep all the benefits for themselves and a chosen few. It was the judgment of Bridgeport, in short, that whatever Dick Daley's limitations might be, he was trustworthy and not too smart, he *was not* a heavy drinker or a big talker, and that he *would be* fair to one and all—all invaluable credentials for a young man who is politically ambitious.

Then, too, Daley was reputed to be studious, no scandal was attached to him, and he was known as a lad who applied himself to whatever the task at hand might be— working a precinct, keeping the books at ward organization headquarters, collecting organization dues from people Big Joe had put on the city payroll, quietly forcing McDonough to do something about the plea of a constituent who was in a jam of some kind and needed help. All through his public life, in fact, Daley has held that politics is the business of doing things for people. If this latter quality is the criterion of successful politics, there are few in Bridgeport who could say that Daley is not good at his business.

So it was that when Daley came along in the mid-1950s as a candidate for mayor and subsequently proved that he knew what kind of service the voters wanted—exhibiting his talent for keeping quiet when he had to, for compromising when he had to, for waffling on controversial questions when the making of a decision would create enemies—Chicago as a whole did not know there was such a man, but Bridgeport had seen signs of Daley's expertise as far back as the early 1920s.

As a boy out of De La Salle High School, Daley worked in the nearby stockyards—a matter which, in his early years of public life, he avoided mentioning, presumably

out of embarrassment at having had such humble employment. In later life, in keeping with the custom of self-
made men who boast of how they had had to peddle
newspapers in their impoverished early days—and Daley
actually did a little of this, also, hopping onto Halsted
Street cars of the Chicago Surface Lines to walk the cars,
selling a newspaper or two—Daley began boasting of how
he had been willing to do anything honorable to get a
start.

The start when it came was getting himself appointed
Eleventh Ward secretary. It was not much of a start, but
it began to open his eyes and show him how things worked.
Simultaneously, he attended night school—four nights a
week—at De Paul University. His mind set on getting a
law degree, he started night school in 1923 as soon as
Joe McDonough brought him down to City Hall. (It took
Daley eleven years to get his degree, the first several of
which were spent repairing his scholastic credentials for
admission to law school; it can be noted, in passing, that
it is characteristic of Daley's life that he spent a lot of
time, if necessary, to get where he wanted to go.)

When McDonough was elected alderman for the first
time, in 1917, he found himself caught in a power struggle
of two groups of Irish politicians. As he considered the
question of which group to cast his lot with, he was
propositioned by a cunning West Side Bohemian, Anton J.
Cermak, to put in with *him*. That was enough for Big Joe.
Cermak, who had gone to the City Council from the
Lawndale ward in 1909, was now, with a few powerful
non-Irish cronies, the man who held control of such graft-
laden committees as those that dealt out franchises to the
Chicago transit companies and the public utilities, and that
was where Joe McDonough wanted to be. It did not con-
cern McDonough that Alderman Cermak openly hated the
Irish because they had the nasty habit of ganging up on
Tony Cermak to deny him slating for higher office.
However, if Big Joe had any qualms, he was reassured by
Cermak, who pointed out that the Irishmen high in the
party who hated Cermak also disdainfully put down the
Back of the Yards citizens as "pig-shit Irish."

As McDonough's man, Daley had also become a
Cermak man, though at a distance. It was not until 1923,
when the Democrats elected a reform mayor, William E.

Dever, to replace the incorrigible William Hale Thompson and Daley was brought downtown by McDonough, that opportunities opened up.

At best, Daley's job as a back-room flunky in City Council was menial work, with a good deal of aldermanic abuse tied into it. But at least the pay was better than anything young Daley had been earning, and that helped to ease the humiliation of being ordered to fetch coffee, cigars, and racing forms for the aldermen. Then, too, working in the area directly behind the council chambers, Daley found that the educational opportunities for the study of wheeling, dealing, and skulduggery were unlimited. Indeed, though the job at City Hall also gave Daley ample time to attend his night classes at De Paul University, considering what his future was to be, he got a more valuable education by day than he got at night. Finally, as it developed, this was only the undergraduate schooling that Daley's association with Big Joe was to provide. He was to learn much more than the connivance and shared-bribes technique of how big money passed into fat aldermanic hands. And Joe McDonough's accommodation with Tony Cermak was the key.

Cermak hated the Irish because, as we have seen, the Irish, headed by men of the like of Roger C. Sullivan, George E. Brennan, and Alderman John Powers, thwarted his desire to run for higher office. True, Cermak had been able to seize control of the City Council, but Sullivan was party chairman, Brennan and Powers were the heirs apparent, and the troika had no empathy for Cermak's ambition to run for mayor. "That Bohunk wasn't even born in this country!" they commented on more than one occasion with more accuracy than grace.

Sullivan died in 1920, but Brennan immediately grabbed the chairmanship of the party, and the controlling fraction's disdain for the man they referred to as "Pushcart Tony" remained the same. Cermak continued to press for further honor, and Big Joe was at Cermak's side—and Dick Daley could not have avoided knowing all of this—when Tony stormed out of a Chairman Brennan slate-making session in the Sherman Hotel in December 1922, furious that he had been denied a chance to run for mayor, loudly voicing the vow: "I will fuck those Irish some day!"

Actually, common sense dictated the denial of Cermak's

bid to run for mayor. To unseat the abominable Mayor William Hale Thompson, Brennan figured he needed a thoroughly respectable candidate and, since Cermak's reputation already was somewhat unsavory, handed the nomination to a respected member of the superior court, William E. Dever. Besides, Cermak had just been elected president of the Cook County Board, and aside from the fact that the Democrats would lose vast patronage to the Republicans if he now relinquished that office, it would have been unseemly for Cermak to switch jobs so quickly. So Dever got elected mayor, Cermak remained "Mayor of Cook County," allowing the newly formed crime syndicate to transfer the base of their vice and gambling operations to such places as suburban Cicero, and Joe McDonough as a reward for his support got to give out county jobs to many Bridgeport people. Daley, for his part, had much to do with doling out Big Joe's patronage, and that grew, too, as Cermak ran successfully, in 1926, for a second term as president of the County Board and finally succeeded to the party chairmanship when Brennan died, in 1928.

At that point Cermak did a little something for Big Joe, personally. When he ran a third time, in 1930, for president of the County Board—successfully, despite growing evidence that he was in league with the Johnny Torrio-Al Capone gang—he slated McDonough for county treasurer. The Great Depression having set in, the Republican party getting the blame for it, the Democrats swept the county vote. As a result, Big Joe shifted his office to the County Building; Richard J. Daley naturally went along. Daley was on his way.

What happened was that, at age twenty-eight, Daley, McDonough's secretary, found himself functioning as a de facto county treasurer because Big Joe was not disposed to do the work he had been elected to do—actually had no time to do it, putting in the hours that he did in speakeasies, eating places, and racetracks.

The arrangement—Daley doing the work, Big Joe getting the credit—was naturally not without real advantage for Daley. He not only discovered how tax money was extracted and moved around, but he learned a great deal about how political jobs were passed out and what a precinct captain or his ward committeeman expected in return for a good effort on election day. Of course, Daley had already picked up a lot of useful experience and knowledge while working for McDonough in the back rooms of the City Council. He knew all about the whispering that went on among aldermen when a "money ordinance" was up for passage; he had learned that, in zoning matters, it was as unseemly for an alderman to interfere in the internal affairs of another man's ward as it was for a bishop to start handing out ecclesiastical orders in another man's diocese. Probably, in fact, Daley was not even startled by the high stakes wagered at the crap game that seemed to be frequently in progress in the antechamber of the City Council. Certainly, it could not have taken him long to realize that without the income of their illegal saloons and bookie joints, the lowly paid aldermen could hardly have been able to take a hand in the game.

In fact, Daley, being shrewd and a quick learner, had absorbed a great deal by 1934 when Big Joe McDonough, at age forty-five, having reached the limit of the eating and carousing a man can stand, died. There is a saying in the mortuary business that you hardly ever see a fat man in the casket, but Big Joe was an exception. Daley knows. He was one of the pallbearers who hauled McDonough into the Roman Catholic Church of the Nativity of Our Lord, religious mother house of the Eleventh Ward, and thence to the cemetery. Breathing hard under part of the load on the other side of the casket, opposite Daley, was a fellow named "Babe" Connelly, who, step in step with Daley as Big Joe McDonough was carried to the grave, was politically one step ahead of his fellow pallbearer. For a start he figured to be the new Eleventh Ward alderman and political power.

Connelly, who had made money through ownership of a blind pig during Prohibition and in the horse book business, was, in 1934, with Prohibition as dead as McDonough, proprietor of a prospering saloon. He also was unpopular with Daley and his friends, not because of booking bets on the horses or having operated a speakeasy—no one ever lost social stature in the Eleventh Ward for this—but rather because he had no clout downtown, no jobs to hand out. Not unexpectedly it was deemed futile to hitch one's wagon to so dim a star, especially with Daley around—moreover a Daley who, at age thirty-two, was finally getting his law degree, which was considered to be a big plus in his not-so-secret ambition to become mayor one day. Additionally, Daley was in favor with Boss Cermak and with the other bosses downtown—a unique achievement given the hatred between Cermak and his associates. The evidence was there for all to see. For example, Daley was kept in his post in the county treasurer's office when Thomas Nash, a cousin of Patrick A. Nash, who had succeeded to the party chairmanship when an assassin's bullet eliminated Mayor Cermak in 1933, was selected to take Big Joe's place. Still living in the block where he had been born, in a flat at 3502 South Lowe, less than a full block from where he was to live as mayor, Daley had greater rapport with the young bloods of Bridgeport than Connelly could ever hope to have. Yet Connelly, by reason of seniority, stood in Daley's way.

There could have been a pro-Daley putsch following the death of McDonough, but patience is one of Daley's most important natural assets. Thus, although Daley was considered to be the legitimate heir of Big Joe, he deferred to what seemed to be the wishes of the bosses downtown—Pat Nash and Edward J. Kelly, who had been picked to take Cermak's place as mayor. The Kelly-Nash decision was to let Babe Connelly be committeeman of the Eleventh Ward but to neutralize him by calling home from Washington a hard-drinking congressman named Thomas Doyle, a hero of the Hamburgers, to take McDonough's seat in the City Council. This seemed to put Daley in third place, but if so, it was not for long. He was Number Two again one year later when Tommy Doyle died. However, Connelly then put himself in as alderman, combining that post with his committeemanship and confronting Daley with a great increase in power. In the circumstances, Daley needed a big break—and got one.

In October, 1936—two years after McDonough had died, one year after Tommy Doyle had died—a state representative of the district, an elderly Republican named David Shanahan, died. It was a short two weeks before the 1936 state biennial election, and Bridgeport was titillated by the announcement that the seventy-five-year-old Shanahan, five-term speaker of the Illinois House, was an honorable man to his last days, exchanging, on his death-bed, marriage vows of Holy Mother Church with one Helen Troesch, forty, who had served him faithfully for two decades as secretary and amoretto. Bridgeport followed with interest the Widow Shanahan's successful struggle in probate court to retain the $500,000 or so that the speaker had managed somehow to put aside during his years in the public service. Shanahan's body was hardly cold, however, before Bridgeport also realized that his timely departure for possibly a better world had provided a lovely chance for Daley to improve his lot in this one.

Here, clearly, was a double opportunity for Daley: he could run as a write-in candidate for the seat reserved for Shanahan, whose name was already on the ballot, and simultaneously demonstrate to the boys downtown that the Daley crowd could get out the vote—actually the Daley workers brought in 8,500 write-in votes for their candidate —when the pressure was on.

The city at large was briefly intrigued by the sight of a Democrat running for office as a Republican party candidate. Still, the results were predictable, and the intriguing part of this affair was not that somebody named Daley had been elected to his first public office but, rather, that somebody named Shanahan had got elected out there as a Republican in the first place. (The explanation was that three representatives were elected from each district, two from the majority party and one from the minority, and Shanahan was as likely a name to get Republican votes in Bridgeport as any other.) At his swearing in, in Springfield, Daley promptly opted to sit with the Democrats and thus, for that biennium, Bridgeport was represented by three Democrats.

Death continued to haunt those who stood in Daley's way. In 1938, for example, death took Patrick J. Carroll, a Democratic state senator whose district locked in on the Eleventh Ward. Once again, it was the ubiquitous Richard J. Daley who filled the breach, winning renown as Mayor Ed Kelly's man, stepping up from the state house to become a state senator, and a Democratic one *officially,* too.

A carnival spirit prevails at the state capital during the legislative sessions, with considerable emphasis on booze, women, and poker playing. The virtuous were those who got the work done. Daley broke all the state customs.

Newly married in 1936 to twenty-five-year-old Eleanor ("Sis") Guilfoyle and driven by the compulsion to make good, Daley was exceptionally well behaved for a legislator. What free time he had, for example, he spent in study —and in making good.

And life was good. The thirty-four-year-old new bridegroom was busy in Springfield. In Chicago, where he and his wife built their present home at 3536 South Lowe, he became in 1936 a partner in a modest law firm with his friend William Lynch and one Peter V. Fazio. The partners took care of the clients that Senator Daley helped provide, attorneys who happen to be legislators enjoying very good luck in meeting people who need their services.

If marrying Sis Guilfoyle was the greatest moment of his life, as he claimed, Daley's greatest accomplishment as a senator was engineering for Mayor Kelly the phasing out of the two bankrupt public transportation facilities, the Chicago Surface Lines and the Chicago Rapid Transit System, Kelly's bill setting up the Chicago Transit Authority and providing $87,000,000 for the bond holders of the two predecessor systems. Kelly had come to know Daley by observing his trustworthiness as chief deputy comptroller of the county treasurer's office—a post that he had been accorded to regularize his position and that he continued to hold while he served in Springfield—and it came as no surprise to anyone when the mayor designated Daley to be his man in the state senate. The Chicago Democrats knew that by training, Senator Daley could be counted upon to work out passage of the transit deal that Kelly and his friends had contrived.

Ironically, the work Daley did to create the CTA— helping to saddle it with heavy debt—was to haunt him in later years when, during his long reign as Mayor, the financial plight of the CTA was constantly to bedevil him.

Otherwise, Daley's career was uneventful. Lynch took care of his interests in the city, and in Springfield Daley was industrious and largely unseen. What was not obvious at all was the education in state and political affairs he was getting for himself—which makes his decision to allow himself to be slated to run for sheriff of Cook County, in 1946, all the more strange.

The sheriff's campaign of 1946 was Daley's only cropper in his slow ride to high office. The initial decision was made by party chairman Jake Arvey, and the upshot was that Daley took a lacing at the hands of an unknown Republican named Elmer Michael Walsh.

There had been great anticipation in Bridgeport when Daley was slated for sheriff. The only person with an intuitive understanding that this was a deplorable development was Daley's mother; she died, however, between the time that he was put on the ticket and his defeat in the election many months later. At least she was spared the blow of seeing her son humiliated. The Daley crowd was stunned by the loss. There was a story that the only fellows in the Eleventh Ward seen smiling that election night were the friends of a saloonkeeper named Babe Connelly, and there were inside jokes that, for once, the guy in front of Dick Daley had forgotten to die. But the shock was only temporary. Wise heads knew that getting beaten for sheriff was probably the best thing that had ever happened to Daley.

Cook County was running wide open in 1946. Not only were the horse books operating in the city under the blinded eyes of Mayor Edward J. Kelly, the books were operating in all parts of Cook County. No fashionable country club was properly equipped without its roomful of crime syndicate slot machines, vice was widespread in Cicero, and the syndicate had transformed the main street of an innocuous little place called Calumet City, at the extreme southern limits of the county, into a latter-day replica of Gomorrah. Knowledgeable people had a rule of thumb at that time that if a sheriff couldn't step out of office four years later with a clear $1,000,000 in his pocket, he just wasn't trying.

At the same time, and for the same reasons, getting elected sheriff of Cook County in those days was like writing out your own political death certificate no matter what you did, as Elmer Michael Walsh and other persons who have occupied the office both before and after him, discovered. Had he been elected sheriff of Cook County in 1946—and one must wonder if Arvey and Kelly were setting him up—the odds overwhelmingly would have favored the proposition that, politically, that would have been the end of Richard J. Daley.

Still, a loss of status necessarily ensued from the loss to Elmer Walsh. Moreover, to make the race for county

office Daley had had to forsake his place in the state
senate. Of course, that did not leave Daley jobless. As a
reward for allying with the Kelly-Nash Machine, Daley
continued to hold the highly sensitive, well-paid, nonelec-
tive post of chief deputy Cook County comptroller—
which meant, actually, that he functioned as county treasurer, which was an elected office, without the higher pay
and title. It was in this office, awarded to Daley by the
party bosses, that he honed the knife that slices the sirloin
of political patronage. There is *no one* in Cook County
government who is more knowledgeable than the comptroller in the matter of knowing who is on the payroll,
who put him there, how much he gets paid, and what
services he rendered to get the job. The comptroller knows
where the big money is spent, who holds the contracts, and
who fronts for the contractors when they change the original specifications on which they bid to fleece the taxpayers
out of sizable adjustments. Daley learned his lessons well.

It might strike even politicians in other parts of the
nation as bordering on the unethical for a man to draw
paychecks from two governmental bodies simultaneously
—which is what Daley did, getting paid by the state for
serving in the senate and getting paid by Cook County for
keeping track of the books. Even in Illinois riding two
payrolls is referred to not unrealistically but matter-of-
factly by politicians as "double-dipping." But it was and
is an Illinois practice, and Daley had reason in 1946 to be
pleased that it was. Even though he took a pasting at the
polls and had surrendered his seat in the senate, he still
had the better-paying job in Cook County with all of its
educational advantages, to fall back upon.

The greening of a political tree takes time, and yet
another man had to die—*two* more, in fact—to provide
Daley's tree with space to grow and flower. The evidence
seems to be—and even Elmer Michael Walsh would testify
to this if he could speak from his grave—that the hazard
of getting politically involved with Daley consisted of having the bad luck to be the man directly in front of him.

CHAPTER 3

Doing Time

"Modern politics is, at bottom, a struggle not of men but of forces."
　　　　　　—The Education of Henry Adams

Success in politics is largely a matter of manipulating one's enemies and rivals, of neutralizing their tricks and ambitions, and this is especially true at the local and state levels.

In Illinois there are three basic concentrations of political power, the offices of mayor of Chicago, governor of Illinois, and president of the Cook County Board—in that order of importance. For nearly half a century, the Democrats have controlled Chicago's City Hall and, except for the election of two Republicans, the County Board. Control of the Governor's office fluctuates, depending principally on how Illinois votes in national elections —consistently voting for the winner.

The prize to be won in each case is vast patronage— about sixty thousand state jobs, thirty thousand Chicago jobs, and fifteen thousand Cook County jobs—the foundation of any successful political machine, in the First Ward of Chicago or in Mother Russia, being an ample supply of places on the payroll for the faithful. Outmanned in the number of jobs he has available, the mayor of Chicago is nonetheless a more powerful figure than the governor because the political impact of a smaller number of jobs in a smaller area is much greater than the impact of a larger number that has to be spread over the entire state. Similarly, political favoritism in the awarding of contracts produces more effective benefits when limited to the city, rather than spread over the state; additionally, a strong mayor of the Richard J. Daley type is less constrained than a governor in the spending of public dollars because it is much easier to work one's will on a weak City Council than on a contentious legislature. With far less money to spend, the mayor has a dominant voice in how it is spent.

The mayor of Chicago and the governor of Illinois are natural political enemies, forever engaged in a subtle game of upsmanship. The contest for influence and public acclaim intensifies if, as at present—with the entrenched Mayor Daley continually ragged by the unorthodox ploys of the evangelistic, non-organization Governor Walker— they are rivals in the same political party. In many matters of common interest the rivals will grudgingly work together, as they did for passage of a regional transportation act in 1974, for example, when both Daley and Walker recognized the imperative need for a new six-county agency to rescue the Chicago Transit Authority, the commuter railroads, and various independent bus lines from imminent insolvency. Daley and Walker were forced to work for the creation of a $500,000,000 agency that would ensure reasonably good public transit for the economically vital northeastern corner of the state. Even in such unavoidable cooperative efforts as this, however, a conflict inevitably arises as to who will be put in charge—Daley's man or someone who inclines toward Walker. The public sees this confrontation because it is played on an open stage; the public is not aware of the constant maneuvering for advantage in other areas of conflict, and there are many, between a Walker and a Daley.

To take yet another view of the political structure of Illinois, one must understand that the continuing struggle for control involves a contest between Cook County, with about half of the state's population, on the one hand, and 101 other counties, referred to in toto as "downstate," on the other. The prizes that are fought over here are control of the governor's office and control in both houses of the legislature. To be an effective mayor of Chicago, it is necessary to have sufficient strength in both House and Senate to get bills approved, because the state constitution vested power over all municipalities in the legislative body. In consequence, an antagonistic legislature can strangle the mayor. In practice, the Democrats generally control the House by a narrow margin, and, likewise by a bare majority, the Republicans run the Senate, although infrequent lopsided elections, such as the anti-Nixon Democratic sweep of November 5, 1974, result in one party's having numerical control of both chambers. Generally, though, control is divided, and the situation leads to wheeling, dealing, and compromise, since each side depends upon defections or concessions from the other side to get its bills passed. All of this would work to the detriment of Chicago, of course, were it not for the fact that the Democratic leaders in Springfield are Mayor Daley's mouthpieces. As the most powerful Democrat in the state, Daley can and does call the Democratic shots in Springfield, frustrating Walker's desire to share this authority, and, as a result, obtains for Chicago much of what he wants. Conversely, without a strong mayor like Daley, Chicago could legislatively be strangulated.

Control of the Cook County Board is conceded to the Democrats, although now and again the disenchanted voters elect a Republican to head the board. The Democrats' advantage traces back to the time when Chicago was the population center of Cook County and was deemed to be entitled to two-thirds of the fifteen (now sixteen) county commissioners. And while, with multimillion-dollar county highway projects to let and zoning control over expansive unincorporated areas, such as those around O'Hare International Airport, where industrial and residential complexes have mushroomed, the county commissioners have gained in responsibility in direct ratio to the departure from Chicago of business, industry, and white residents, the County Board still has an automatic two-thirds Democratic (and essentially Chicago-elected and Daley-controlled) majority. What has evolved is an aura of "cooperation." Indeed, a benchmark of the board's overall integrity could be the degree of "cooperation" existing between the ten Democrats who call the shots in the unincorporated areas and the six Republicans who are elected to represent those areas. A lack of complaint on the part of the Republican commissioners regarding developments that require County Board approval might be taken to signify that the board is acting prudently in the public interest—when it authorizes, say, the building of a highway that is of special benefit to the Arlington Park race-track—or it might signify that someone got paid off to implement this impressive expenditure of county, state, and federal funds.

By statute, the County Board president holds an autonomous office; in fact, since the ten Democrats who dominate the board are dependent for slating upon the Democratic machine, the president is obligated to defer to the desires of the mayor of Chicago when the mayor is also the Democratic czar. The incumbent County Board president, George Dunne, was frequently spoken of in 1974 as a likely successor to Mayor Daley. Yet, so dependent is Dunne upon Daley's favor (as head of the party organization, Daley could easily have denied Dunne reelection) that it would have been unthinkable for Dunne to have challenged Daley in any way. Even when a Republican is Cook County Board president—and there have been two, William Erickson and Richard B. Ogilvie, since Cermak's time—a politically strong mayor like Daley can frustrate him with the two-thirds Democratic majority.

The first thing to note about Daley's Chicago is that since 1931 the Republicans have offered the Democrats only token resistance in the one-sided fight to control the city. True, there are diehard pockets of Republicans in the fifty wards of Chicago just as there are a few predominantly Democratic counties in the Republican downstate area, and just as there are signs of increasing Democratic strength in the reaches of Cook County as white Chicagoans flee the city, at least half a million whites having transplanted themselves to the burgeoning bedroom communities. True, the Republicans have tried to maintain organizations in each of the fifty wards of Chicago, going through the motions every four years of electing a ward committeeman, as the Democrats do. But the Republicans do not really count in Chicago. For example, they elect few aldermen—and, when they do, their man is frequently adopted by the Daley Democrats, casting his vote for whatever it is that Daley happens to want the City Council to approve. While the Republicans have Central Committees for both city and county, they are ineffective copies of the Democratic committees that Daley heads.

In no other city in the nation is Democratic party control so absolute as in Chicago, and in no other city is there so absolute a boss as Richard J. Daley. Not since 1931, when Czechoslovakian-born Anton J. Cermak defeated the outrageous incumbent mayor, William Hale Thompson, has the Republican party amounted to much in Chicago. The raucous Thompson was a gross and shameless character who had kept the Republicans in control of Chicago during two four-year terms as Mayor—elected in 1915 and reelected in 1919, declining to run against the Democratic reform candidate, William E. Dever, in 1923—and who had successfully returned to the political wars in 1927, easily defeating Dever's bid for a second term. The Republicans of Chicago had their last hurrah when Cermak clobbered Thompson by almost 200,000 votes in April of 1931, Chicago then being in such a state of shame and insolvency that Big Bill the Builder should have realized that he did not have a chance to remain in charge.

The only fierce rivalry to be detected among the politicians of Chicago is the constant struggle between the various ward organizations, some of them headed by committeemen who are disdainful, if fearful, of Richard Daley —but who nonetheless maneuver, sometimes in a vicious if not treacherous way, to win his favor. Likewise, though to a lesser degree, most of the thirty Cook County township committeemen—who make up, with the fifty Chicago ward bosses, the eighty-man Cook County Democratic Party Central Committee—are continually reaching for a higher rung on the Democratic ladder. But that is about the extent of political rivalry in Chicago, and even in the struggle for power by the township committeemen, it is the Chicago people who call the shots in party affairs, and Daley is Number One in Chicago.

There are three seats of political power in Chicago: mayor, finance chairman of the City Council, and chairman of the Democratic Central Committee; and a man must have possession of at least two to control the city. In all of Chicago's history, only two men have managed to maintain undisputed claim on the office of mayor and chairmanship of the party. Cermak was the first, and Richard J. Daley, who has either copied Cermak's style or independently hit upon the same methods of control, is the other; indeed, Daley's mastery has been more absolute than that of Cermak in the vital third area of controlling the City Council.

The frequent adulatory accounts of the remarkable efficiency with which Daley has put together his political Machine deny credit that is justly due to Cermak, for it was he who had the genius to gather the ethnic and racial loose ends of the Democratic party into a cohesive organization. It was Cermak, for example, who proselytized William Dawson, one of the two black aldermen then serving in the City Council, to change his party allegiance from the Republicans. Although the conversion was sealed by Edward J. Kelly when he succeeded Cermak as mayor, the credit for this crucial act goes to Cermak, who thereby assured Democratic control of Chicago for the next forty years. For example, a study of election returns of Daley's first five campaigns for that office offers convincing proof that Daley would not have made it the first time, nor in running against an apostate Democrat, Benjamin S. Adamowski, in 1963, had it not been for the heavy vote that Dawson produced for him in the South Side ghetto.

Remembering that through his close association with Cermak's Irish pal, McDonough, Daley got an intimate look at Tony Cermak's methods of dictatorial control of the party machinery, it is virtually certain that Daley followed Cermak's design, beginning with the first premise that you reward your friends. Moreover, the similarities of character between Cermak and Daley are striking.

The parallels are obvious if you compare Daley, say, to the personality analysis of Cermak by biographer Alex Gottfried in his extraordinary book, *Boss Cermak of Chicago*. Tony Cermak, Gottfried wrote, was a close-mouthed man with a few personal friends, who cooperated with his enemies when it was expedient, and who kept no diary and few records—operating out of the memory bank of his head. Cermak, according to his biographer, trusted no one, was reluctant to delegate responsibilities, permitted nothing to transpire that he did not know about, had tremendous energy, had no feeling for culture that was not backed by wealth, found satisfaction in the deference that persons of power and social prestige were eager to show him. Not for an instant was Cermak ever personally involved in scandals related to sex; he would have a drink or two occasionally but was essentially a sober man; he was suspicious if not fearful of any forces that even remotely threatened to topple him from power. Cermak was not known as a compassionate man. He was secretive about his own affairs while setting up lines of communication that brought word to him on every trivial thing that was going on in Chicago, keeping informed regarding all things being a vital ingredient of control. Cermak, last of all, was a strict party disciplinarian, demanding and harsh, who knew in his guts that total control was the basic requirement of survival as dictator of the Machine.

The similarities are incredible. Like Cermak, Daley is not comfortable in the presence of educated or cultured men. In fact, in all these areas Cermak and Daley could be one and the same. Needless to say, there were differences, too; they are not the same man. Daley is a devout Roman Catholic; Cermak had no religious affiliation or interest. Cermak, indifferent to public opinion, consorted with gamblers and had a working accommodation with members of what is called the crime syndicate. Familyman Daley, a daily communicant, probably would not have paid so high a price as was extorted from Cermak to gain and retain control of Chicago—although some of the worst of those who operated under the nose of Tony Cermak can even yet be detected on the fringes of Daley's organization. Cermak had to claw his way to the top, whereas Daley was boosted up the ladder by others one rung at a time. Cermak got to be boss because he fought his way to the point of control, dealing ruthlessly with his enemies. Daley got there by ingratiating himself with those above him and was chosen, ultimately, as party leader because of the misjudgment of those who selected him that he would be manageable. The decision to promote Daley was made largely by those who had known Tony Cermak, by wise heads who certainly did not want another domineering boss like Cermak and who did not dream that the man they selected in 1953 would prove to be a more dictatorial boss than the first one, who had died in 1933.

The second most powerful office in Chicago government is that of chairman of the City Council Finance Committee. Anything that moves, creeps, or crawls in that unique legislative chamber, the full council, is certain to come to the attention of the finance chairman. The office traditionally is held by the brightest, cleverest, most persuasive of the fifty Chicago aldermen, and getting oneself elected chairman, in the trading that goes on after each of the quadrennial city elections, is invariably the springboard to influence as well as affluence. Indeed, the rise to power in recent decades of such finance chairmen as Jacob M. Arvey, P. J. ("Parky") Cullerton, and Thomas E. Keane amply bears out this latter contention.

If the Chicago City Council were to function as the priority power of government, conforming to the strong council-weak mayor concept of the state constitution, the finance chairman would emerge as the decisive force in Chicago affairs. Indeed, when the tough and brilliant John Duffy was finance chairman, his practice was arbitrarily to inform the weak Mayor Martin Kennelly of what actions "we" would take at impending council meetings, what ordinances "we" intended to pass and which ones "we" would reject. "This is what we are going to do," Duffy would say—to which the acquiescent Kennelly would meekly reply, "Oh, are we? That will be fine," knowing full well that he did not dare challenge Duffy's planning.

When Daley was chosen to be mayor, council dealers such as Alderman Thomas E. Keane were confident that he likewise could be led around by the nose and were subsequently shocked to discover that the well-schooled Daley intended to have it the other way around. Indeed, Daley's consistent craftiness in upstaging the finance chairman, getting away with this because he kept a tight grip on the patronage that was vital to the survival of the ward bosses, is the hallmark of Daley's own survival. If the finance chairman is permitted to function as a free agent, compelling the other aldermen to seek his imprimatur, rather than the mayor's, on everything they want done, the chairman becomes—as John Duffy did under Kennelly, as Jacob M. Arvey did when Mayor Kelly left to Arvey a great deal of responsibility for making decisions—a more powerful and independent figure than Daley cared to have around him. Daley never for a moment has lost sight of the fact that finance chairmen, like incorrigible children, are quick to take advantage of every opportunity to get away with something, and jealous of his own interests, Daley believes in the principle of retaining control in his own hands. His fellow Democrats never cottoned to this practice of his, but there was precious little that they could do about it, other than obey his dictates; as Daley's erstwhile pal, Benjamin S. Adamowski, once said, "Daley is not loved—he is feared; and there's one hell of a lot of difference."

Ironically, there is some question of what Daley's future would have been if Jacob M. Arvey had not been a powerful finance chairman in Ed Kelly's day, Kelly recklessly delegating control of the City Council to Arvey. It was only *because* Kelly had allowed Arvey to sit on the edge of his throne that it was possible for Arvey to move in as party boss when Kelly was encouraged to move out. It is not madness to speculate that Richard J. Daley might not have amounted to very much if it had not been for Finance Chairman Arvey. There are no genuine ties of admiration or affection between the astute Jewish tactician and the unpolished younger man from Bridgeport, despite the intuitive sense that Arvey displayed in divining the fact, since Daley's ascendancy, that Daley was a man upon whom one *should* shower effusive praise if one wanted to stay in the game. Arvey has consistently praised Daley and has discreetly been careful never to say anything critical about him, despite the fact that—when he became boss—Daley bluntly let Arvey know that he, Daley, *was* boss and treated Arvey shamefully on at least one public occasion. Yet Daley owed his last and final rise to Jake Arvey.

Arvey knows what it is like to come from humble beginnings. He was punching doorbells on behalf of the presidential candidacy of Alfred E. Smith, back in 1928, doggedly working his precincts in a ward, the Twenty-fourth, where everyone knew what bar mitzvah meant, and few had the smallest notion of what the Sacrament of Confirmation was, and no one would have put any stock in it if he had. To his last day, Arvey will remember ruefully that, in 1928, his people would sooner have served pork pie to the rabbi on the Sabbath than cast their votes for a Roman Catholic (the quotient of religious tolerance in Jewish voters had increased enormously by 1960, when they eagerly pulled election machine levers for John F. Kennedy).

A Chicago precept has it that "A man ain't going no-

where without he has his Chinaman," a Chinaman being a
political patron. A pair of brothers, Moe and Ike Rosenberg, were young Jake Arvey's Chinamen, just as, later,
Arvey was Daley's. For some twenty years the Rosenbergs
were the political czars of the Twenty-fourth Ward, the
political custodians of a consortium that included professional gamblers, brothel keepers, crime syndicate assas-
sins, and payrollers. This extraordinary conglomerate was
held together by the Rosenbergs' ability to deliver massive
pluralities for organization candidates on election day; in
return, they had a free hand in the Twenty-fourth.

Chicago politics are a maze of interconnected tissue.
Thus it can be documented that one typical protégé of
the Rosenberg brothers was the syndicate's man in charge
of all West Side gambling, Julius Annixter—delightfully
called "Lovin' Putty"—while another was Jake Arvey,
without whom one may doubt that there would have been,
eventually, a mayor of Chicago named Richard J. Daley.

The chain is long. The Rosenbergs put in with Tony
Cermak when he busted up the Irish by gathering into his
camp all of the anti-Irish ethnic groups plus a few self-
serving Irish such as Big Joe McDonough and Daley.

The Twenty-fourth Ward was the immediate neighbor
of Cermak's Twenty-second, and the Rosenbergs had an
active interest in a propagandist organization, the United
Societies for Local Self-Government, which had been set
up in 1906 and was run by Tony Cermak to protect the
saloonkeepers, brewers, and distillers from growing public
insistence on enforcement of state and local closing hours.
When the United Societies grew into a political force in
Chicago, holding parades and electing candidates to public office, Cermak supplied campaign money that he had
covertly received from the breweries. When Cermak got
himself elected in 1922 president of the County Board,
making him "the mayor of Cook County," with great
authority in the matter of who would be permitted to
operate vice and gambling joints beyond the limits of Chicago, the Rosenbergs were very much in league with Tony,
raising money for his United Societies from their bootlegging and gambling friends in various parts of the city
and suburbs.

Out in Bridgeport, Richard Daley was only twenty at

the time and only vaguely familiar with Cermak's development of an invincible political machine on the foundation of his saloonkeepers' trade organization. However, Daley's sponsor, McDonough, knew what Cermak was up to, and Jake Arvey, Daley's ultimate mentor, also was acutely aware of how Cermak was cleverly fitting together the ethnic groups that had no leadership and what the implications of this move were. For his part, Arvey, who had joined Cermak with the Rosenbergs, was rewarded by being elected, in 1923, alderman of the Twenty-fourth Ward.

It cannot be said that Arvey was the worst of the rogues who prospered in the City Council during the remarkable ascendancy of Cermak, but in all honesty it can be said that he was a serious contender for the title. Jake Arvey was part of a new breed of Chicago alderman. For example, he was among the first of the aldermen to practice law, these attorney-alderman slowly replacing the bawdy-house, saloonkeeper, gambling-joint aldermen who had been gauche in their corruption. Arvey was one of many who suddenly recognized that in the new and more sophisticated era that was beginning, the practice of law was the politician's profession of choice. Daley himself was witness to the changes in City Council meetings and membership. For one thing, parliamentarian methods began to replace brutish behavior in council chambers as Arvey and the other attorney-aldermen began to rise.

Arvey, who had a brilliant mind, was admitted to the bar in 1916, when only twenty-one years of age. He would have been highly successful in the practice of law if he had avoided politics, but he juggled both interests with great skill, gaining such a reputation that all the younger men, including Daley, were openly in awe of the tough little man who was called Jake.

Arvey was conspicuously on the attack when the obscene-looking William Hale Thompson was mayor, helping to make life miserable for this deliberately uncouth man. By the time Tony Cermak seized control of the Democratic party, following the death of George Brennan in 1928, and successfully ousted Thompson in 1931, Arvey was well on his way to the plum post of finance chairman. Daley watched Jake at all times, ingratiating himself with the budding council leader at every opportunity, and, vain as all politicians are, Arvey gloried in Daley's admiration and was at pains to encourage the young man to keep at his books and get his law degree, promising Daley that great public offices were certain to be his reward. Like a Plato listening to Socrates, Daley was enthralled, and when, eventually, Arvey was elevated to finance chairman, Daley smugly confided in his Bridgeport pals that the future looked good because Jake was his "connection."

Daley needed all the help he could get. Cermak hardly knew that he existed, much less cared that Daley's ambition was one day to hold his job. During the brief five years that Cermak was absolute boss of the Democrats of Chicago, including the final two years when he was mayor, Daley—twenty-nine years of age when Cermak's reign began—could do little but sit at his desk in the back area of council chambers, help get out the vote in the Eleventh Ward on election days, and struggle on in his night school effort to get his cherished law degree. When Cermak indulged Daley with a brief smile, it was only because Daley was "Joe McDonough's kid."

Until his illness in the summer of 1974, it was only on the rarest occasions that Daley failed to preside at City Council sessions. He has always run the council with a firm hand, insisting that the members remain in their seats, cracking down on those who tried to interject contentious debate. In all this Daley learned from watching Cermak, who frequently informed the aldermen: "I want your co-operation, but if I cannot have it, I will go ahead anyway." Daley learned much more, too. Cermak's cabinet members, the heads of the various departments of city government, admired his sagacity but had little personal affection for him—and the same has often been said about Daley.

When Cermak got himself elected mayor, he inherited a finance chairman named John S. Clark, a George E. Brennan man, just as Daley inherited a Martin Kennelly man, P. J. Cullerton, in 1955. Cermark permitted Clark to keep his title, but he actually worked through Vice-Chairman Thomas E. Keane, eventually pushing Parky upstairs to the county assessor's job, which is exactly what happened to Clark, too. Cermak was, last of all, acknowledged to have been a decisive presiding officer—the best, it was agreed, that the Chicago City Council had ever had;

in this, also, Daley presents almost a photographic copy of Cermak's method.

In the public's blissful ignorance of how the Democratic party of Chicago works, the post of chairman is a designation without definition, although the Democrats would not long endure as a potent force without a strong one. By virtue of being elected by open vote of the fifty ward committeemen, the man chosen obviously has had to be acceptable to a majority of them, and this is true whether he has been elected chairman on his own merits or whether he is the designate of a super-boss like Cermak or the not-so-silent partner of an Ed Kelly. The chairman, in short, represents a special kind of power, and only bad leadership can jeopardize his status.

The chairman runs party headquarters, presides at central committee meetings, arbitrates disputes, and exerts considerable control—by reason of his prerogative to name a small group of committeemen to screen potential candidates—over who gets to run for office. The chairman is expected to maintain discipline, while respecting the partial independence of the individual committeemen. He has much to say about fund raising, has overall responsibility for leading the party to election victories and for imposing assessments on ward organizations by way of raising a war chest to win the elections.

The chairman has considerable authority in doling out patronage when elections are won, passing judgment on ward bosses who perform poorly, and providing special treatment for those who do exceptionally well.

The Democratic chairman of Chicago, in short, is a big cheese, and it is in this area, therefore, that you find a striking strategic difference between Cermak and Daley. Cermak was satisfied to let his political ally, Patrick A. Nash, head of a sewer construction company that received multimillion-dollar contracts from Chicago and Cook County, serve as party chairman. Wiser than Cermak, Daley planned from the beginning to retain the political office for himself—even though counseled by Jake Arvey, when he sought to grab party control, that the chairmanship would cripple his ambition to be mayor. In fact, it is not likely that Daley could have stayed on as mayor as long as he has had he not retained control of the party machinery and the patronage that keeps it oiled.

Daley's mayoral reign was, of course, far in the future in 1933. He was still, to the Democratic powers, simply a minion, if a minion who could stand some watching. But that all changed when, in mid-February 1933, Cermak reached to shake hands with President-elect Franklin D. Roosevelt at a waterfront rally in Miami, Florida, and was fatally wounded by a bullet that supposedly was intended for Roosevelt.

Pat Nash, the sewer man and chairman of the Chicago Machine, decided that his pal, Edward J. Kelly, tainted though he was by his involvement in multimillion-dollar scandals in the Chicago area's sewage disposal system, the Metropolitan Sanitary District, was rightful heir to the office of mayor. Thus, the house that Cermak had built— sheltering such rogues as Mathias P. ("Paddy") Bauler of the Forty-third Ward and Charles H. Weber of the Forty-fifth, two capricious men, who traveled with Cermak, shared the pleasure of his company, indulgence, and anti-Irish commitment, running handbooks, peddling booze, and delivering the Germanic vote—came tumbling down.

The gods who run the game must have smiled at the return of the scepter from Bohemian to Irish hands, especially, according to Alderman Bauler, since Mayor Cermak had no desire to pay his respects to the President-elect on that fateful night. That February, in fact, Cermak was holed up in Paddy Bauler's winter home, bought and paid for with Bauler's hard-won earnings in the bootlegging and horse book trades, and was not disposed to inconvenience himself for the man whose nomination he had tried vainly to block at the 1932 convention.

As Bauler, an uncouth character who was blessed with a photographic memory, reconstructed the situation years later: "Cermak said he didn't like the son of a bitch— this Roosevelt—and didn't want to go see the son of a bitch. I sez, 'Listen, for Cry sakes, you ain't got any money for the Chicago schoolteachers and this Roosevelt is the only one who can get it for you. You better get over there and kiss his ass or whatever you got to do. Only you better get the goddamn money for them teachers, or we ain't goin' to have a city that's worth runnin.' So he goes over and, Christ Almighty, next thing I hear on the radio is that Cermak's got shot."

Having held back the Illinois votes at the 1932 Democratic Convention in the Chicago Stadium until his belated support of Roosevelt's nomination was of no consequence, Cermak was on bad terms with FDR. Only by quickly making up for lost time had he succeeded, by December 1932, in reaching an accommodation of sorts with James A. Farley, Roosevelt's Machiavelli, on the matter of getting federal patronage for the Cermak faithful. In February, however, the deal had yet to be sealed by the Prince, and—as Bauler had said—the city of Chicago coffer was bare and Cermak had no choice but to seek emergency funding from Washington.

It was known that the President-elect was to interrupt a pre-inaugural cruise to attend a reception in his honor in Bayfront Park, Miami, on the night of February 15, 1933. Aware that Farley was already promising federal patronage to Cermak's enemies, Mayor Cermak's intention was to show his disdain by being off on riotous holiday in Havana, Cuba, with Bauler and Charlie Weber when Roosevelt arrived.

Cermak was shot as he approached the open car from which the President-elect had just made his talk. Immediately, he was hauled into the car, which raced for a nearby hospital. The nation shivered with pride when it read in the newspaper that, in this moment of agony, Cermak had whispered to Roosevelt, "I'm glad it was me instead of you." Actually, Cermak never said that; a Hearst political writer named John Dienhart, who doubled on the sly as Cermak's traveling companion, confidant, and public relations adviser, later admitted that he dreamed up the story. "Jesus," Dienhart said, "I couldn't very well have put out a story that Tony would have wanted it the other way around."

Cermak did not die immediately. He suffered a punctured lung, and the bullet lodged in a vertebra, but he still was transported by train to a hospital in Chicago. There his condition deteriorated rapidly, and nineteen days after he was shot, Pushcart Tony died, on March 6, 1933.

There is no record that Daley went to the wake. He probably did; thirty thousand persons took part in the funeral march, upward of twenty thousand were able to jam into the Chicago Stadium to hear prayers spoken over Cermak's mortal remains, fifty thousand crowded into the Bohemian National Cemetery as the first and only foreign-born mayor Chicago has ever had, or is likely to have, was placed in the grave. The temperature in Chicago was at zero on burial day. So were the hopes of the anti-Irish politicians who had climbed into Pushcart Tony's wagon.

Cermak was not even in the grave when the Irish ward bosses closed in to take possession of the political tabernacle that is the mayor's office on the fifth floor of Chicago's City Hall. Fate had delivered this citadel of power back into Irish hands, the only question being: Whose? Party Chairman Pat Nash, Cermak's alter ego at Democratic headquarters, was juggling ultimatums as if they were hot rivets—three competitive groups of the South Side Irish and at least two others from the West Side asserting that, with Cermak dead, *they* intended to take over. And since no détente existed between any of the Irish who had been cut out of things, the prospects were that in the ensuing fight for control they would tear to shreds the cable of party discipline that Cermak had cunningly crafted to keep in one piece a Democratic Machine to dominate Cook County politics. The only man who did not pester Pat Nash with telephone calls was Big Joe McDonough, the now-ostracized pal of Cermak— the man on whose coattails Richard Daley had hoped to be dragged into an office of importance.

As the various Irish ward bosses worked out their individual strategies, exchanging nothing more than grim nods of greeting, Big Joe McDonough, believing that all was lost and that there was not one damned thing he could do about it, hied himself to Paddy Bauler's speakeasy and got roaring drunk—turning over a big heating stove in the center of the place (Paddy said) when he thought he had been insulted, struggled to his feet to take a swing at the fellow, missed, and all three hundred pounds of him put a body block on the stove. ("Goddamn near set the whole place on fire," Paddy said.)

Young Richard Daley—thirty-one now, still chained to his menial tasks in the rear of council chambers—spent the night at his home, with his parents, his De Paul University law books spread out on the kitchen table, and brooded.

With Cermak dead and his Eleventh Ward benefactor out of favor with everyone who had a chance of running things, Daley felt desolate, with ample reason to believe that the future now held nothing for him.

CHAPTER 4

Up for Grabs

"Those who reach the top, particularly in the political world, have to develop a certain tough realism as far as friendships and loyalties are concerned."

—*Richard M. Nixon*, Six Crises

One of the incongruities of Chicago's history is that in every listing of those who have served as mayor of the city, the name of the man who was chosen to succeed Anton J. Cermak is missing. There were three logical candidates: John S. Clark, the finance chairman, alderman for the rather affluent West Side Irish Thirtieth Ward and nominally the leader of the City Council; County Commissioner Dan Ryan, handsome young son and, he claimed, logical successor of a deceased president of the County Board who had done profitable favors for road builders who contributed generously to individual Democrats and their party (Ryan was of course aware that he was precluded from consideration by reason of the Municipalities Act, which specified that the aldermen were obligated to choose a member of the council, yet he was confident that a solution to this legalistic problem could somehow be found); and incisive, independently wealthy Alderman John Duffy of the Nineteenth Ward, which is located in the upper-crust Far South Side section that is called Beverly.

Yet faced with these Irish aspirants for Cermak's office—each of whom represented constituencies where the idea seemed to be that ownership of well-trimmed lawns and real lace curtains made one more acceptable in the sight of God—party chairman Pat Nash rejected all three. Surprisingly, Nash opted for an inconsequential fellow named Francis Corr, alderman of the Seventeenth Ward, located in the middle-South area beyond Bridgeport and populated by a mixture of blue collar-white collar working class citizens who exhibited no inclination to take control of anything other than their own lives.

Alderman Corr was probably the most surprised member of the City Council when Nash called him in to advise him that he was to be the next mayor of Chicago. But if so, he could hardly have been surprised when Nash informed him quite frankly that his was to be a temporary honor, conceived in the womb of expediency. Mayor Corr was elected as acting mayor on March 14, 1933, eight days after Cermak died, and presided until April 13, when Edward J. Kelly, Chief engineer of the Metropolitan Sanitary District, was elected by the Democratically controlled City Council to take Cermak's place.

Corr was in office a month simply because it took that long for Nash's men in Springfield to work out the deals whereby the legislature passed a special bill setting aside the state Municipalities Act, which said an interim mayor must be elected from the membership of the City Council.

Corr's final act was to sign the ordinance electing Kelly. Thereafter, Pat Nash quickly made him a judge of the circuit court, where he served out his life, perplexing counsel, who must have wondered, frequently, how such a dolt as this got on the bench, although in the Chicago scheme of things Judge Corr certainly was not unique in his lack of qualifications for juridical service.

Even Ed Kelly's enemies, and he had compiled a considerable number of them in his many years of recommending acceptance and rejection of bids on multimillion-dollar Sanitary District contracts, had to concede that he was an imposing figure—a tall, beefy man, with a severe and jowly look. Five-foot-nine Daley, for one, must have been envious. Since he has been able to control such matters, Daley has been careful to avoid, as far as possible, appointing aides who are taller than he is, and even the police bodyguards who surround Daley are of moderate size.

John Duffy, Dan Ryan, and John S. Clark remained grimly in disapproval of Pat Nash and Ed Kelly, even though the Kelly-Nash partnership embarked on a policy of letting bygones be bygones. The Nash technique was expected—as County Commission Ryan remarked, "Why shouldn't they want to deal with us, when they've got everything by the ass?"—and largely successful. To a considerable degree Kelly and Nash brought peace to the embroiled Democratic Machine. Their tactics were hardly masterpieces of subtlety, healing the wounds of the anti-Cermak factions by cutting their brooding enemies in on a share of the spoils—contracts, patronage and the like. There is, perhaps, nothing more crass than an appeal to greed, but, likewise, in politics there is no more effective a palliative. The Chicago word for power is *clout* and the unique gift of Chicago politicians whose priority interest is maintaining themselves in power is that they have a sixth sense in knowing when and how to share it. It is not always necessary that you *"do* something" for the Machine to get the clout working for you; the Machine is sometimes even more solicitous toward those who refrain from doing it damage when in a position to do so.

Politically Mayor Kelly was an astute man, but in the fashion of Cermak and Daley he was deplorably inarticulate—inventing words and phrases that were meaningless, getting lost in a verbal stew of double negatives, mixed tenses that seemingly are translatable only by fellow politicians and a select few media people who have come to understand after long years of listening to it the meaning of Chicago political jabberwocky. If the good nuns who instructed the Kellys and the Daleys obviously spent much time teaching them penmanship—almost without exception their signatures are impressively legible—this concentration on instruction in the Palmer Method, alas, worked to the detriment of syntax and diction. Conversely, politicians have a universal talent in arithmetic, their only known weakness in this area surfacing occasionally in federal income tax evasion charges. In the dominion of practical politics—and that, by the way, is the only kind of politics there is—Chicago's Mayor Kelly rated marks almost as high as Cermak and Daley.

Having restored some order in the party chaos that he inherited from Cermak, giving refuge in his inner circle to Paddy Bauler and Charlie Weber, both of whom had been politically orphaned by Cermak's death, Mayor

Kelly's first stride toward local acclaim was made by securing a federal grant that enabled him to provide Chicago schoolteachers with the first paychecks they had received in more than half a year. Thereafter, federal subsidies in other forms—public aid money, public works money, and the like—flowed into Chicago; President Roosevelt delighted in doing business with Kelly, now that Cermak was gone. Quietly sitting at his desk in the back area of City Council chambers, Richard Daley observed that a good connection in Washington was a prerequisite of municipal solvency. This was a lesson that he never forgot.

Kelly likewise set Daley the example of dominating his equals with but a minimal display of being domineering. Kelly was a venal man—and there is precious little evidence that Daley is—but each followed a policy of tolerance toward the dubious manipulations of the greedy Democratic wolves through whom they operated. Neither Kelly nor Daley could be accused of projecting themselves as superior to those who did their bidding; neither man ever made an issue of flaunting his power—it is enough to exercise it.

Like Cermak, Kelly and Daley found nothing untoward in public disclosure that their cronies had taken bribes for passage of ordinances that were not in the public interest. Even the federal indictment of prominent Democrats for malfeasance made no particular impression on Cermak, Kelly, or Daley—the indictments being regarded merely as misfortunes that were more or less to be expected in the political game. Only revelations of scandalous sexual involvements of their underlings would light the fires of outrage in all three mayors. Of all Ten Commandments, the one dealing with the coveting of another man's wife was the most mortal of sins—and God knows with what personal grief a man like Richard Daley took the news that even U.S. presidents engaged in such diversions on their brief stopovers in the best Chicago hotels.

One of the first things Ed Kelly did, as mayor, was get the message across that prudence was the greatest of political virtues. He wanted his people to be ever aware that there was a line in the jungle of graft and corruption beyond which a sensible man dared not go. He knew it well, from experience. Prior to his becoming mayor Kelly had been shocked to discover that the income tax returns of public servants were as eligible for audit as those of such gangsters as Al Capone. The federal government had forced him to admit that, during the 1920s, when he was but the modestly paid engineer of the Metropolitan Sanitary District, he had a mysterious personal income of $724,368—although his cumulative reported earnings for that decade barely reached $151,000. An unexplained part of this disclosure—although the explanation appeared to be that a solicitous President Roosevelt protected Kelly from indictment by the Justice Department—was the government's willingness to let him off the hook for a mere $105,000 in back taxes and penalties. (Pat Nash, the Democrats' county chairman, simultaneously got nipped for $175,000).

Apart from that, Kelly did little with Chicago, except let things run away from him. Repeal of the National Prohibition Act, coinciding with the start of Ed Kelly's fourteen-year reign as mayor, relieved the pressure of quantitative gangland murdering that had earned for Chicago its international reputation as the city of violence. The warring gangsters were quick to see that an era had ended; there were no longer any questions of territoriality to settle, by death or otherwise. Yet, having become accustomed to a big-money life-style, and in conformity to the old rule that idle hands are the devil's workshop, organized crime shifted its attention to the horse book business, and a continuing glow of bloodshed, during Kelly's years as mayor, came of that.

It was in Chicago, in Ed Kelly's time, that the alumni of the Al Capone era, largely through the wizardry of Jack ("Greasy Thumb") Guzik, a sad little guy with one kidney and a calculator in his head, brought to its finest flowering the nationwide racing wire. This was the system over which, on wires leased from American Telephone and Telegraph, running descriptions of all races at all tracks were transmitted almost instantly to betting parlors in all sections of the United States.

If there is any single thing that can be held responsible for the development of the unique American phenomenon that is called a national crime syndicate, it was not booze but the ingenious method employed by the Capone gang to ensure their control of the information that was the life-blood of bookmakers throughout the nation. The profits generated by the Chicago race wire proved to be the catalyst of syndicate crime. The basic conclusion of the U.S. Senate Crime Investigating Committee headed by the late Senator Estes Kefauver was that the interstate transmission of racetrack results was the heart of the national crime problem; the evidence turned up in committee hearings clearly showed that instantaneous transmission of information vital to illicit bookmaking was the nerve system of organized gambling, the foundation stone of syndicate crime.

The Chicago race wire was the nation's bookmakers' only available source of instantaneous information concerning *all* the betting opportunities currently existing at *all* the tracks, and, indeed, the cash flow of the bookie joints was significantly greater than that of the tracks. The total pari-mutuel betting at the tracks runs into the hundreds of millions of dollars, and it is beyond question that the take in the nationwide network of bookie joints ran into the billions.

The Capone gang fed its wire into its own horse parlors and those of its politically connected friends in the Chicago area and wholesaled its information to bookmakers everywhere, with trusted crime syndicate people in various parts of the nation serving as middlemen. The profits everywhere were far in excess of the sum needed to cover the necessary operating expense of corrupting politicians, the courts, and police departments

In Ed Kelly's day as mayor of Chicago, 1933-1947, an educated guess is that the mob was laying out locally something like $20,000,000 a year for "protection." But the payoff was not exclusively a franchise fee for the unharassed operation of horse books and gambling joints such as those that flourished in suburban Cicero, on Dempster Street north of Chicago, or in such places as the Chez Paree on the city's Near North Side, which was one of but a few of the truly big-time night clubs to be found in the nation. Part of the graft encouraged official eyewinking at other activities such as whoremongering, the numbers (the lucrative black ghetto rip-off known colloquially in Chicago as policy), syndicate-controlled slot machine operations, and other such illegal pleasures.

Corruption, in short, ran deep in Kelly's period, and inevitably, if gradually, citizen ire began to build. One can cast into any part of the foul waters of Ed Kelly's fourteen years and catch a hook on a dead fish that stunk up his reputation and that of Chicago. The National Education Association made a study of the Chicago Board of Education and was appalled by the ineptitude and corruption of Kelly's school system. Taxes were high; the city was broke; police captains had orange crates of cash in the basements of their palatial homes; the rector of fashionable Fourth Presbyterian Church complained to Kelly that he was getting propositioned by prostitutes when he went out of an evening on North Michigan Avenue for a breath of air.

By 1946, Chicago was in one hell of a shape and out of control. The streets were dirty; payrollers and police were shirking their work; the board of education was so indifferent to public opinion that contracts for sporting goods, footballs, and the like were casually let to a well-connected Loop furniture store. Yet, even more serious, Kelly was unable to address himself to the need for shaping things up. He was out of the city for extended periods of time—nursing a case of colitis in Palm Springs, California—and he had no one back home to keep the Chicago Democrats in line.

Pat Nash, Kelly's partner, had died in 1943, and Kelly had taken over chairmanship of the Democratic party, thus exposing himself further to criticism. Nash had been a tougher, wiser man than Kelly, with more guts, but even he had been having trouble fending off the Kelly-Nash political enemies. For example, when, in a burst of patriotism that served a secondary purpose of disconnecting himself from a deteriorating situation, Jake Arvey, the finance chairman of the City Council and a strong Nash-Kelly man, had resigned in 1941 to go off to war with the Thirty-third Division, Illinois National Guard, in which he held the rank of captain, smart, tough John Duffy, leader of the Kelly-Nash opposition, moved into the finance chairmanship vacated by Arvey. Nash could only acquiesce, and the chain of power stretching back to Tony Cermak's coup was broken.

With Nash gone, Kelly was at the mercy of the Duffy people and the citizens. Moreover, Duffy had a substantial power base, not only in the City Council but in the Democrats' Central Committee as well, by the time that bemedaled Lieutenant-Colonel Arvey returned from military service in the autumn of 1945. With Kelly spending more and more time in the California sun and quite incapable of controlling affairs in Chicago, Arvey, the logical Kelly-Nash successor, clearly had his work cut out for him.

At least Arvey was decisive. He immediately and gladly —he later protested he took the job as a service to the Democratic party—accepted chairmanship of the Democratic organization, which Kelly arbitrarily bestowed upon him—making a point in his announcement to the party's committeemen of identifying the new leader as *Jack,* not Jake. Then he set about taking control. Unfortunately, his first major step was a disaster: the 1946 ticket.

Arvey disclaimed responsibility for the ticket as soon as it failed, pointing out that he had been hospitalized and claiming that it was Kelly's ticket; but it was nonetheless his—as Federal Judge Abraham Lincoln Marovitz, a West Side boy who had served in the state senate with Dick Daley, becoming Daley's bosom buddy, made clear. Marovitz, who had resigned from the senate to enter the Marine Corps—asserting years later that his farewell address was centered on a prediction that one day Daley would be elected mayor of Chicago—says that he discussed with Arvey, in the Philippines, the possibility of Daley's being slated for sheriff in 1946. Marovitz claims that Arvey liked the idea and promised to do something about it. Arvey's story was that Kelly wanted to give Daley the chance to run for an important office as a reward for the good work Daley had performed for Kelly in the state senate. Whatever version is true, one wonders if either Arvey or Kelly saw Daley as a future mayor, since traditionally getting elected sheriff of Cook County was regarded by politicians as a long step toward oblivion. In any event, the defeat didn't hurt Daley's career and might have saved it.

Fortunately, Duffy was not ready to act, seeing the 1947 mayoral election as the opportunity, not the election of 1946. Thus whatever responsibility Arvey might have had for Daley's being slated for sheriff, Finance Chairman Duffy and his crowd of anti-Kelly committeemen went along with the idea, and with Arvey's becoming county chairman. Duffy, who had had his sights firmly set on a takeover of the Democratic Machine, knew that Ed Kelly was finished and thought that Arvey, therefore, would not remain long in control.

Duffy was right in the first idea, but not in the second. Yet his mistake was understandable. He had considerable backing, for a start.

Even more important than Duffy, but standing behind him, was Thomas Nash, Democratic ward committeeman of the stylish Nineteenth Ward and the real power in opposition to Kelly. Nash, a nephew of Pat Nash, the late party chairman, was a partner with a brilliant criminal defense attorney named Michael Ahern—the Nash-Ahern law firm having given a job, briefly, to one Richard J. Daley when he graduated, finally, from law school. Tom Nash and Mike Ahern were regarded as the most prestigious defense attorneys in Cook County (some say that they cut Daley on the judgment that, as a lawyer, Daley would never make it), and they didn't think that Daley was ever going to amount to much politically.

Lined up with Duffy and Tom Nash, who were referred to by the Jake Arvey people as "The Irish turkey of Beverly," was Committeeman James McDermott of the Fourteenth Ward, who had got himself elected alderman in the early 1930s; County Commissioner Dan Ryan, still bitter at Nash's passing him over in 1933, who took pleasure in sipping away his evenings in the posh Camellia House of the Drake Hotel, politely expressing disdain for Democratic bosses of lesser breeding; and such potent West Side bosses as Johnny Touhy, who ran the Twenty-seventh Ward, in which the Chicago Stadium is located, and Albert H. Horan, committeeman of the Twenty-ninth, which borders to the west of the Twenty-seventh; and others, too, who thought they might be better off under Duffy than under Kelly or his assigns.

Of course, the Kelly-Arvey combine also had its supporters, particularly in the cluster of wards in control of the Poles, the Italians, and Cermak's Bohemians, not overlooking the Jews and the Germanic enclaves where Paddy Bauler and Charlie Weber ruled. Demographically—and this is the point that most students of the Chicago Machine seem to miss—the Democrats of Chicago must be viewed as a mosaic, comprised of ethnic bits and intra-ethnic fragments, rather than a uniformly photographic body of one piece. And the Democratic Machine of Chicago manages to hold together only insofar as those in charge can work out a reasonably equitable spread of the clout; in Chicago, a fair distribution of the spoils is essential if disparate groups are to be cohesive.

It was a time, then, of great flux and no single dominance, and Daley grasped immediately that there was a great opportunity beckoning him. Daley's problem as the battle shaped up in December 1946 for the overthrow of Ed Kelly was that he did not have a vote in the Democratic Central Committee. Moreover, since he had just lost his fight to be elected sheriff, he lacked the leverage that the patronage of the sheriff's office would have given him. His salvation lay in the fact that no one downtown would have time to worry about such a comparatively unimportant ward politician as Daley, and typically, when decisive action was called for, Daley was ready—having escaped the equally bad choices of standing with Kelly in the showdown or deserting him, thereby giving the anti-Kelly forces reason to mistrust him either way. With Kelly out, he was free to make a move of his own.

In every practical way, Daley was boss of the Eleventh Ward. The precinct captains were loyal to him, dependent upon him, rather than on Alderman Hugh ("Babe") Connelly, but Connelly had the vital credentials as the elected ward committeeman. Therefore, Daley had to make his moves quietly. With the confidential assent of Chairman Arvey, in January 1947 Daley summoned his precinct captains to a meeting in Eleventh Ward headquarters. Connelly, as usual, did not bother to attend, and in a move to match any putsch, Daley had his men vote Connelly out as their committeeman and replace Babe with himself. A delegation then proceeded to Connelly's saloon to break the news that he was no longer the committeeman and that while he would be permitted to serve out the remaining month of his term as alderman, Daley had picked a Pole named Stanley Nowakowski to run as the ward organization candidate in February.

Next morning, Daley strode into party headquarters on the third floor of the Morrison Hotel, where the First National Bank now stands, to take his place in the inner circle. At age forty-five, Dick Daley was showing his betters that he meant to amount to something. Arvey welcomed him like a long lost son. The anti-Kelly, anti-Arvey men merely accepted him, John Duffy scowling. As Dan Ryan said, "Daley figured to be a pain in the ass, having so much ambition, and 'in' with Kelly, and it was sort of unusual for a committeeman to move in without getting elected, but it wasn't worth arguing about." One reason Ryan was not inclined to argue about it was that Daley's boyhood friend, State Senator William J. Lynch —elected to the legislature in 1946 when Daley ran for sheriff, and Daley's law partner—had come upon Commissioner Ryan in court on a minor building code violation and, discovering Ryan to be without counsel, had gratuitously represented the commissioner, smoothing out the problem with an expertise that turned out to be the basis of a good relationship between them. Which is the way things very often turn out in Chicago, one small favor leading to the granting of bigger ones.

Committeeman Daley was not home free yet, however. Well aware of Duffy's plot to scuttle Kelly, and sensing that Jake Arvey was programmed to be booted out of the party chairmanship, Daley found himself cruelly torn. His loyalty was to Arvey, who appeared finished and therefore would not be able to help Daley become mayor. Yet, having himself just usurped the Eleventh Ward committeemanship, he could not flee from Arvey. On the other hand, it was at least partially with the consent of Dan Ryan and John Duffy that Daley had retained his comptroller's job in the county treasurer's office; an ambitious man could not afford to tie himself to a loser; and Daley now had family responsibilities. In 1939 he had built a seven-room, face-brick bungalow at 3536 South Lowe, on the block where he had been born, becoming the fanciest resident in Bridgeport. By 1947, most of his seven children had been born, and the responsibility of raising them weighed heavily upon him. Yet here he was, age forty-five, faced with the bad choice of standing with the Duffy-Ryan forces, who were scornful of him, or the tattered Kelly-Arvey team. What Daley did was the smartest thing: He did nothing and made himself as inconspicuous as possible.

Arvey, for his part, had the decency to stand with

Kelly when the inner circle at the Morrison decreed that Big Ed was finished, and it was Arvey who took upon himself the unpleasant task of informing Kelly of the Machine's decision to dump him. "I told him," Arvey said, "that I would stay at his side if he wanted to make a fight of it. But I thought at the time and I told him so— although I think I was wrong, now that I look back on it —that we'd go down in a primary fight, that Kelly couldn't win."

Arvey himself was far from finished. Appointing himself mouthpiece for the jackals who snapped at Kelly's heels was perhaps his most astute ploy, saving himself from a showdown with the anti-Kelly faction. With Kelly winding up his fourteen mayoral years in an atmosphere of near-disgrace, Duffy hesitated to mount a coup. Rather than force a confrontation with Chairman Arvey, Duffy opted to give him sufficient rope to hang himself—placing upon Arvey the obligation to come up with a mayoral candidate in 1947 who could be controlled and candidates for senator and governor in 1948 who figured to have no chance of defeating the Republican incumbents, C. Wayland Brooks and Dwight Green. Then, after Arvey fell on his face in November 1948, would be the time to put the heat on Arvey—or so John Duffy is said to have planned.

In December 1946, Arvey surprised Chicago with the announcement that the silver-haired Martin Kennelly, a moving-van executive whose chief claims to fame were that he had been productive in raising money for the American Red Cross, and that, from the very beginning, he had been articulately anti-Kelly, had been chosen to run for mayor by the Democratic machine. When Kennelly smothered his Republican opponent three months later by almost 300,000 votes, even the anti-Arvey bosses were forced to concede that Jake had worked magic. Arvey, in short, had nicely squared the circle.

Kennelly was made for Chicago politicians. Outwardly a white knight, he was, to say the least, naive. For example, when—after the election—Mayor Kennelly was asked by a newspaper reporter what thoughts he had about dealing with the crime syndicate, he innocently replied: "Crime syndicate? I don't know anything about any crime syndicate."

Even Ed Kelly must have smiled at that although it was just about all over for him. Politically finished, he contracted a mysterious physical ailment that seemed to evade diagnosis. In desperation, he purchased a golden spike that was supposed to have extraordinary curative powers and carried this thing in his pocket surreptitiously. But whatever wonders the golden spike performed for the fellows who talked him into buying one, it didn't do much for Ed Kelly. Kelly dropped dead on October 20, 1950, at age seventy-four, while leaving the office of a doctor who had just assured him he was in fine physical shape.

Ed Kelly went so fast that he didn't have a chance to tell his doctor that you simply cannot trust anyone. But Widow Kelly expressed this idea when Big Ed's will was probated and announced to total in assets a "paltry" $686,799. Widow Kelly indignantly charged that something funny was going on. One million dollars, she said, was missing.

Kelly was soon all but forgotten. Chicago seemed to be getting along nicely in the first few years of Kennelly's reign. Chairman Arvey remained in power, although he still stood on shaky ground as far as the John Duffy crowd was concerned and Duffy and his friends appeared to be slowly tightening their grip on Democratic party affairs. Richard J. Daley, having strengthened his hold on the Eleventh Ward, accepted whatever patronage and personal advantages came his way. Mostly, Daley bided his time—waiting for the Duffy people to make their move to take over the Machine, hoping all the while that somehow Arvey and his friends would outmaneuver the Duffy crowd.

Arvey did wonders to bolster his cause. Having elected the respectable Martin Kennelly, he startled everyone again by slating Paul H. Douglas for the senate and Adlai E. Stevenson for governor. With neither candidate given a chance, and both of them being dragged to victory by President Harry Truman's last-minute surge in November 1948, Arvey was ecstatic and Duffy's crowd viewed him with awe.

Daley had continued to hold what the politicians call "good jobs," meaning that he was earning enough to support his family in an honorable way, and clinging against all reasonableness—with nothing spectacular on the political horizon—to the dream that one day he would be the biggest man in all of Chicago. All he had to buoy him were the words of encouragement from old timers who were affiliated with Arvey, and the unwavering assurance of his pals, Billy Lynch and Abe Marovitz, that he was going to make it eventually. Daley did not know when the showdown would come, when Duffy would make his move. Daley knew only that the showdown would take place behind a guarded door at Democratic headquarters and that his political future hung on the question of which faction had the biggest clout—the majority votes to exert—and that his future would be dim indeed if the Duffy crowd, not liking him, had sufficient votes to seize control of the Democratic Machine.

In fact, the showdown came sooner than Daley had reason to expect, and, as frequently had been the case with Daley, the decisive vote was cast by the ultimate clout of human affairs, the Messenger of Death.

CHAPTER 5

Power Play

> *"Therefore, be it resolved that the New Bridge of the Congress Expressway, extending over the South Branch of the Chicago River, be dedicated and be hereafter known as the Clarence P. Wagner Memorial Bridge."*
> —Journal of Proceedings, *Chicago City Council, July 23, 1953*

Though Chicago remembers little of a Fourteenth Ward alderman named Clarence P. Wagner, Wagner was the man who fronted for John Duffy in the classic 1953 battle for control of the Democratic Machine. Moreover, had Wagner lived, it is almost certain that the political atmosphere of the last twenty years, not only in Chicago but in a vaster area, would have been far different from what it has been.

This is not to say that had Wagner lived Richard J. Daley would not have become mayor, although preventing this was Duffy's objective. But it is nonetheless true that had Wagner lived, Daley's reign would have been plagued by Duffy-generated contention.

Wagner was the protégé not of John Duffy but of an imposing, tough Irishman named James J. McDermott—a close crony of Duffy. Standing tall, with the rugged build of a professional football player, McDermott, a member of the Nash-Ahern law firm, took charge of the Fourteenth Ward in 1932, when he got elected Democratic committeeman. In 1933, he became alderman, too, lining up with Duffy in opposition to the Kelly-Nash Machine. Side by side with Duffy in all things, McDermott next got himself elected, in 1942, to the three-member Cook County Board of Tax Appeals, resigning as alderman. He had been urged to step down as ward committeeman also, an active role in politics being considered incompatible with the making of judgments in real estate tax bills, but had declined to do so.

McDermott also maintained effective control of the alderman of the Fourteenth, since Clarence Wagner, a lawyer and friend, was chosen by the Fourteenth Ward organization as its new alderman. The decision in such matters is always reserved by tradition to members of each ward, the committeeman, precinct captains, payrollers, and the like. Even in the Richard Daley years, apart from sending up a warning when a potential candidate for alderman or committeeman was discovered by headquarters to have been charged in the distant past with incest or sodomy or something, the policy of allowing each ward organization to make its own decisions has been inviolate.

Committeeman McDermott did not get off scot-free with his selection of Wagner, however. The Fourteenth Ward was patriotically Irish-American, principally, and it didn't sit too well that Wagner, whose old man had been a German, should be given control of the ward at a time when the United States was at war with Hitler and many local boys were already in uniform and some were already dead. World wars are of no great consequence, however, in the political affairs of Chicago, and the loquacious Wagner—referred to by intimates as "Gravels" by reason of the quality of his voice—confidentially reassured anyone who brought up the point that he was mostly Irish and as loyal an American as anyone in sight. For sure, his loyalty to McDermott and Duffy in their feud with the Kelly-Nash group was at all times beyond question. In fact, you do not survive in Chicago politics if, having locked yourself in with one faction or another, you do not fight to the last with your friends.

This quality of loyalty is apparent in even a cursory examination of who has held the clout in Chicago. Much more difficult to determine is the foggy question of who begat whom in the continual fight for control. For example, Daley is a descendant of the Jake Arvey set, and Arvey was the offspring of Ed Kelly, and Kelly would never have got to be mayor if he had not put in with Pat

Nash, whose connections traced back to Tony Cermak. Simultaneously, though, the men who were determined to block Daley—John Duffy and Jim McDermott—were the political progeny of Tom Nash, the criminal lawyer, and Tom Nash rose to power with the help of Pat Nash, his wealthy cousin. It is ironic only to outsiders that Tom Nash wound up in conflict with the latter-day Pat Nash forces. Political blood is far thicker than the real stuff. Tom Nash, of course, designated his alderman, Duffy— Nash was Democratic committeeman of the Nineteenth Ward—to be commander-in-chief of the anti-Arvey and anti-Daley forces simply because heading a law firm that had represented such conspicuous sinners as Al Capone as it had, Tom Nash had no delusions as to what his public image as a candidate for mayor would have been. All Nash wanted was to call the shot on who was to succeed Martin Kennelly. Hence, the men who were out front for Tom Nash were Duffy and Jim McDermott.

Tom Nash, through the confidential information that comes to so notable a law firm as Nash-Ahern, had excellent intelligence on where all the bodies were buried— and while it has always appeared that it was John Duffy who insisted that Ed Kelly was finished—until Arvey grabbed the initiative—actually it was Tom Nash who called the play. Duffy was out front for Tom, just as Clarence Wagner—even though he had become committeeman of Jim McDermott's Fourteenth—was out front for Jim. That's how it is frequently in the City of Clout; the fellow you see is not neccessarily the guy with the gun in his hand.

Clarence Wagner, a bright and audacious lawyer, with a sardonic sense of humor and a taste for strong drink, moved up to committeeman of the Fourteenth when McDermott resigned to get elected to the superior court— good form dictating, even in Cook County, that a ward boss cannot simultaneously preside as an important judge. To take the chronology one important step further, and to clarify the formidable barriers that confronted the Arvey-Daley scheme to place Daley in charge of Democratic affairs in Chicago, including his eventual succession to the office of mayor, Alderman Wagner—with Tom Nash, John Duffy, and the "non-political" Judge McDermott behind him—was elected chairman of the City Council Finance Committee in 1950 when the then finance chairman, Alderman Duffy, resigned to run for president of the Cook County Board. As the 1950 election loomed, the Nash-Duffy-McDermott-Wagner oligarchy looked to be on its way to taking charge of government in Chicago and Cook County as well.

The battle line between Arvey and Duffy would have been more sharply defined if Arvey had projected himself as the next Democratic organization choice for mayor; Duffy, who didn't consider himself as a desirable candidate for the office, would have exploded if Arvey had had the temerity to do that. Miscalculating, perhaps, the role of importance he would play in governing the city—not suspecting at this time, apparently, that Daley would insist upon holding tightly to the reins of power—Arvey opted to back Daley because Daley was the most promising man he had available, being clean, restrained, and non-contentious. If Arvey had ambitions to be mayor, he bridled them; a realist, he knew that his roots in the old Twenty-fourth Ward would be pulled up for public inspection and that his close relationship with the discredited Kelly would seriously handicap his chances. Finally, as a full partner in a highly profitable law firm, Arvey was satisfied to make a king rather than be one.

Duffy and his followers continued to watch Arvey carefully, however. Victory over the slippery Arvey had seemed so sure in the past and yet had proved so elusive that Duffy and his friends were counting no chickens. Moreover, as dexterous a politician as Chicago has ever seen, Arvey had shown he knew how to fight. After glomming onto Kennelly in 1946–1947 and reaping the credit for Kennelly's 1947 mayoral election, in 1948 he had made yet another daring move, amazing the opposition bosses in his party by selecting two highly respected eggheads as candidates for high office as Democratic candidates, maverick Paul H. Douglas for U.S. senator and the politically unknown Adlai E. Stevenson for governor, *and* getting them elected. Douglas, the Fifth Ward alderman, was remembered for his evangelistic opposition to Mayor Kelly, and few regular Democrats had anything but scorn for him. In fact, few could have forgotten the glee that met Douglas's announcement during World War II that, even though he was fifty-one years of age, the U.S. Marines had accepted him for combat duty as a private. Alderman Bauler had shouted, "Good riddance to bad rubbish!" As for Stevenson, the party bosses had no idea who in hell he was; many could not pronounce his first name and never learned.

In 1948 the Democratic bosses felt no Democrat on a state ticket—let alone Douglas and Stevenson—had a prayer. Douglas was paired against the *Chicago Tribune*'s darling of conservatism, C. Wayland Brooks, who was seeking a third term. Stevenson was slated against Dwight Green, a two-time governor whose only liabilities—and they were severely discounted by the professionals—were that he had a personal problem staying sober and a public problem of having bribed scores of country-paper editors into giving him good notices with handouts of state money. Certain that defeat was awaiting the top of the ticket, the Democratic bosses grudgingly admired the political moxie of Chairman Arvey—picking so propitious a time to give their party a touch of class.

Brooks and Green were so confident of winning reelection that both consented to the recording of victory statements for NBC News, Chicago, one day in advance of the election—the agreement being that the statements would be used when the ballot-counting confirmed their expectation of easy victories. Both were running with Thomas E. Dewey of New York, the odds-on Republican party candidate for president, and except for last-minute signs of a turnabout in the public opinion polls, hardly anyone gave Truman a chance of winning. The *Chicago Tribune*, which had its first-edition banner line proclaiming that Dewey had beaten Truman in type before the polls had closed, had the bad judgment to go to press with it at an early hour even though the first returns to be tabulated gave strong indications that, surprisingly, the results might show the opposite to be true.

An NBC reporter, shuttling between the Paul Douglas headquarters and the Adlai Stevenson headquarters, found Douglas jubilant at the upset in the making. Douglas, who had stayed on the firing line, munching sandwiches and devouring election returns as they clicked in on the City News Bureau wire, was ecstatic and shouted at the reporter, "You didn't think I could win, did you!" The reporter replied: "Nobody thought you could win."

Half an hour later, at the other side of downtown Chicago, the reporter held an elevator so that Stevenson, his wife Ellen Borden Stevenson, and one of his sons could enter. The reporter asked the candidate if he thought the early trend would hold up. Trend? Stevenson did not know about the early trend. He had been out of touch for a couple of hours, he said, having dinner with his family. "Is it going well?" he asked politely.

Democratic party bosses, gathered in their headquarters on the third floor of the old Morrison Hotel, thought the whole election incredible.

Arvey had certainly pulled this one out of the fire, and, for his part, he intended to make the most of his success.

Governor Stevenson "owed" something to Arvey, as the politicians say. Early in the campaign, Arvey had grabbed Mike Howlett out of his job as head of personnel at the Chicago Park District and told him to see if he could straighten Adlai out. Stevenson was a hard-working candidate, but he pointedly kept a distance between himself and the reporters who were assigned to cover him—with the result that he was not getting a good press. Complaints also had come to Arvey from county chairmen outside of Cook County that this man "Ad-lie" was a hard fellow to know. Even at stopovers in small-town restaurants, Stevenson was acting as if he were now off duty. Then, too, contrary to custom, he never picked up someone else's check. When he picked up his own, he seemed to think that a dime was a big tip for the waitress. Howlett's assignment was to humanize the guy, if he could. And, specifically, Arvey told Howlett: "For God's sake, don't let him pay a check! *You* pay the checks, all of them."

There was no rapport between Stevenson and Howlett. Adlai regarded his extroverted babysitter with obvious dislike, cringing at the raucous laughter that frequently erupted from the politically worldly Mike. Howlett publicly referred to his fragile charge as "The Governor" and privately deplored Stevenson's lack of even a rudimentary knowledge of what politics is all about. At times of policy decision-making, Howlett would tell the candidate, "Arvey wants it done this way; Arvey says you should go after Green for trying to buy off the downstate newspapers." Stevenson would purse his lips and frown, clearly distressed by the idea that Howlett would be telling *him* what the gut issues were and how to go about his campaign. There are few politicians in either party that the garrulous Howlett ever disliked, no matter what their faults might be, yet he disliked Adlai Stevenson quite as much, but not so obviously, as he was disliked by Stevenson.

One can only wonder what Stevenson's reaction would be in 1975 with Howlett's occupying the politically important office of Illinois Secretary of State and being regarded by the professionals in both parties as the likely heir to Richard J. Daley. Having made many friends and few enemies, and having avoided involvement in ward politics or entanglements in factional disputes—loyal to Daley, but not beholden to him—Mike Howlett has come to be regarded by many persons in and out of government as the most honest and most able of the public officeholders in Illinois.

The turn of events in 1974, with such influential Daley administration people as Alderman Thomas E. Keane, his floor leader in City Council, Alderman Paul T. Wigoda, Keane's right-hand man, and Earl Bush, Daley's longtime press secretary, convicted in federal courts on such grave charges as mail fraud, malfeasance, and income tax evasion, the seventy-two-year-old mayor seemed anxious to improve his relationship with Howlett. Unlike the haughty Adlai Stevenson who had glibly fronted for the Daley Machine, hardly aware that the bosses frequently sneered, "He is not one of us," Howlett had working credentials as a professional Democrat—but he, also, was not "one of them," remaining aloof from participation in the big money deals that were commonplace. Though Howlett is suspect by such hard-liners as Alderman Vito Marzullo and other grubby ward bosses of that ilk—if only because they cannot pin anything on Mike—Daley, convalescing from serious arterial surgery and mortified by federal grand jury indictments and convictions that were being returned in wholesale numbers against his people, seemed to edge over toward Howlett.

In 1948 Howlett was a constant reminder that Stevenson owed his victory to Arvey. And since the golden rule of politics is that you promptly reward those who made victory possible, Arvey apprised the Governor-elect of what his political debts were. Specifically, he suggested to

Stevenson that he should find a place in his administration for Mike Howlett. Yes, indeed, the new governor replied haughtily; Arvey could tell Howlett that he could be chief clerk in any department of the executive branch. Howlett, who knew more about politics than Adlai would ever know, laughed and took an appointment with the Truman administration, through patronage available to Senator-elect Douglas, as regional director of the Federal Office of Price Stabilization—in which position he unearthed irrefutable evidence that horse meat was being sold in enormous quantities as beef hamburger throughout the state of Illinois. Governor Stevenson scoffed at this report when he received it confidentially from Howlett but said he would investigate immediately. After three weeks the governor righteously informed Howlett that his Department of Agriculture had made a thorough investigation and determined that there was not the slightest bit of truth in the allegation. Howlett sighed. "Governor," he replied, "your people in the Department of Agriculture—they're the ones who're allowing it to happen." Then he and his assistant director of the regional office of OPS, Hyman B. Raskin, lowered the boom.

Chairman Arvey had more success with a second nominee for important office in the Stevenson administration. He told the new governor that the post of state revenue director was an office that had to be entrusted to safe hands, someone who could simultaneously run the office and provide liaison between the upper-crust governor and the crusty legislators with whom the Stevenson administration had to do business. The man suggested by Arvey was a fine family man of great integrity and promise—in the prime of life, his late forties—chief deputy comptroller of Cook County, former Democratic leader of the state senate, a man who had delivered a monumental plurality in his ward for the Truman-Douglas-Stevenson ticket: Richard J. Daley.

As it happened, Stevenson became so enamored of his state revenue director that he inscribed a framed picture of Daley, Sis, and the seven children with a bold pen: "To Dick Daley, God love him!" The autographed photograph hung conspicuously on the wall behind Daley's desk in the State of Illinois Building, diagonally across the street from Chicago's City Hall—but not for long. The new state revenue director took office with Governor Stevenson in January 1949. Daley remained long enough to restructure the operating procedures of the revenue department, winning editorial nods of approval from the Chicago newspapers, but then, to the chagrin of Governor Stevenson, in March 1950, he packed up and was gone, back on the track of getting elected mayor.

The reason for Daley's departure was that an old rogue named Michael J. Flynn, clerk of Cook County, a valuable patronage office, had been called to his eternal accounting —the black flag dropping in Daley's favor once again. Clerk Flynn was fittingly buried with a requiem mass and all, his political associates having persuaded a parish priest that Christian charity dictated that Mike be permitted a deathbed repentance—the rationale being that Flynn had long since suffered atrophy of his personal plumbing and was beyond the reach of carnal temptation and that he now was entitled to be married in the Church to the woman he had been living with. Richard J. Daley attended all the services, naturally, wearing the somber face that politicians reserve for these occasions, though inwardly he was elated. He already had word from the Democrats who controlled the Cook County Board that he had been designated to serve out Mike Flynn's term, an important advancement for the state revenue director.

The clerk's office shares with the Chicago Board of Election Commissioners responsibility for the holding of elections, keeps the vital statistics of births and other personal matters, issues marriage licenses, and attends to various other records. In the political scheme Clerk of Cook County is considered to be an important office, and it was the first of its kind that the forty-eight-year-old Daley had ever held, giving him prestige, patronage, and better pay than he had ever had.

The year 1950 proved to be a very good year for Richard J. Daley, bad as it turned out to be for Jake Arvey and, contrary to John Duffy's expectations, most other Chicago-based Democrats. This was the year that Senator Kefauver brought his Senate Committee to Investigate Organized Crime in Interstate Commerce to town and inadvertently torpedoed his fellow Democrats. Kefauver, who plainly intended to gain national prominence with his committee, as Senator Truman had done with his investigation of military expenditures in the early years of World War II, certainly had not come to Chicago to stir up animosity toward himself; in point of fact, the senator invited Mayor Kennelly and the feisty state's attorney of Cook County, John S. Boyle, to testify in executive session. However, also in executive session the Kefauver committee took unsolicited testimony from Captain Daniel Gilbert, otherwise known as the Richest Cop in the World and the man slated by Arvey to be the Democratic candidate for sheriff of Cook County in the November 7 election. Gilbert's reputation was unsavory, to give him the best of it, and even the most indifferent of the Democratic party bosses in Chicago were astounded that Arvey would gamble on such a candidate. In Springfield, apprised of Gilbert's background, Governor Stevenson blanched. In Washington, Senator Douglas thundered that the selection of Gilbert for sheriff was an insult and that no decent person could campaign for the man.

"Obviously," Arvey said later, "I blundered; I had made a mistake. Actually, I thought that a police captain with Dan Gilbert's wide experience would have made a fine sheriff—worlds better than the man who defeated him. But, of course, I knew in advance—when he insisted on going over to Kefauver to testify, voluntarily, and I pleaded with him not to go—that there was going to be trouble."

Discreetly, Senator Kefauver decided to keep secret Gilbert's modest estimate that, among other assets, he held negotiable securities worth, perhaps, $360,000, that he had reported taxable income of $45,000 in his latest IRS return, and that he had been a gambler in stocks, bonds, grains, baseball, fights, political elections—"I have been a gambler at heart all my life," the Democratic candidate for sheriff admitted cheerfully. Rudolph Halley, chief counsel of the senate committee, is quoted in the official transcript of these proceedings as posing a question to the witness: "This gambling you do—that is not *legal* gambling, is it?" To which Gilbert replied, with a choice of words that indicates he had never considered this aspect of the matter: "Well, no. No, it is not legal. No."

It was known that Gilbert had testified before the senate committee. Not a word leaked, however, as to what he had said. However, a legendary Chicago reporter, Ray Brennan, passing himself off as staff member of the Kefauver committee, found the commercial printer who had the contract to set the Chicago testimony in type and told the printer he had come over to get the proof sheets. The printer hastily compiled a set.

The *Chicago Sun-Times* rocked the nation with a copyrighted report on November 2, 1950—under Brennan's byline—of Captain Gilbert's extraordinary apologia for his affluence. Page upon page of his hitherto-secret testimony laid bare the insensitive philosophy of a Democratic candidate for chief law enforcement officer in the Democratic party's national center of power. Even the cynical professionals in Cook County shook their heads in wonderment at a candidate for sheriff who would naively testify to a U.S. Senate investigating committee that he, personally, saw nothing objectionable about gambling. This from a man who aspired to uphold the law in the place where organized gambling had fathered syndicate crime? The voters of Cook County were appalled.

Five days later—November 7—outraged citizens trooped to the polls and soundly trounced Gilbert, giving his relatively unknown Republican opponent a plurality of 370,000 votes. It is an irony of time and circumstance that the victor in this contest, John E. Babb, proved to be a terrible sheriff. Finding himself immediately at odds with the top-drawer Chicago Crime Commission, which had unequivocally endorsed him, Sheriff Babb pulled up his roots and left the Chicago area when he finished, in quasi-disgrace, his four years of suspiciously lenient law enforcement.

There were, however, more far-reaching consequences of the November 7, 1950, election. Among those Democrats who were carried to defeat with Gilbert was Scott W. Lucas, Democratic majority leader of the U.S. Senate. The president's right-hand man was brought down, the anti-Gilbert vote in Cook County providing the difference, by a little-known ex-Congressman from Pekin, Illinois, who, one week earlier, was regarded as having not the slimmest chance to win: Everett McKinley Dirksen.

Dan Gilbert took his loss casually; he went to work immediately after the election as chief of security for the Arlington-Washington racetracks of Benjamin Lindheimer, a one-time bookmaking partner of Greasy Thumb Guzik, the crime syndicate's wizard of odds.

Jake Arvey, hailed as a magician two short years back, had finally made the wrong move. He immediately became a political pariah. He knew he was through as boss of the Chicago Democrats and, pleading exhaustion, left immediately for Palm Springs, California, to get away from the cold eyes of John Duffy and others who also had taken a lacing because of Arvey's mistake in slating Gilbert.

In fact, the only Democrat to come out of the November 1950 election "looking good," as they say, was Richard J. Daley. Convoyed by the personal endorsements of Senator Douglas and Governor Stevenson, Daley had campaigned for the retention of Mike Flynn's seat as county clerk with a special advantage. It likewise helped Daley that he was running against a bulbous-nosed Republican named Nicholas J. Bohling. A rumor had circulated that the Republicans had made a deal to "trim" Bohling—to sell him short—in return for the Democrats' doing likewise to John Duffy. There is no proof that Daley's victory was negotiated in advance; the fact is that Bohling, not a bad sort, was known only as alderman of the Seventh Ward. Whatever it was that made it possible for Clerk Daley to swim successfully against the anti-Democratic tide, he beat Bohling by 147,000 votes and thus became very much a man to be reckoned with.

John Duffy was clobbered by a Republican named William Erickson, thanks to Arvey's gaffe in slating Gilbert for sheriff, in his bid to be elected president of the Cook County Board. As a candidate for head of the board, Duffy had been required by statute to run simultaneously for reelection as a member of it and had been reelected almost automatically to one of the ten commissionerships that the Democrats firmly control, but that was small consolation. Four years earlier, Duffy had relinquished his seat as alderman of the posh Nineteenth Ward, and the finance committee chairmanship, to run for higher office, and he was bitter when Jake Arvey tried to explain his error in judgment. Duffy was a professional, however, and he followed the rule that professionals do not get mad—they get "even." So with Arvey forced to surrender control of the Democratic Machine in Chicago, Duffy, having lost any claim to leadership, was damned well going to have a say in deciding who was to sit in the driver's seat. Having relinquished his clout in City Council to run for a place on the county board, and having lost stature by reason of his failure to win the presidency, Duffy was in no position to seek the party chairmanship for himself —but he was still a political figure of consequence.

The fight for control was exclusively a battle between the emerging Bridgeport crowd of the Eleventh Ward and the tough Irish troika of the Fourteenth: Duffy, whose roots lay in the Fourteenth; Judge McDermott, who had been alderman of the Fourteenth; and Wagner, who was only half-Irish—the worst half of him, his enemies maintained—but who was alderman of the Fourteenth, ruler of Mayor Kennelly's City Council as finance chairman, and Democratic committeeman for the Fourteenth as well.

A few of the influential Democrats in the inner circle cast their fortunes with Daley's Eleventh Ward or Duffy's Fourteenth: Parky Cullerton of the Thirty-eighth put in with Wagner; Thomas E. Keane of the Thirty-first put in with Daley. Most, however, were circumspect and remained out of the fight, waiting to see who won. And there was, moreover, an impasse; neither the Duffys nor the Daleys had quite enough votes to take charge. What was needed, both sides knew, was a caretaker chairman of the Central Committee who could hold things together through the 1952 presidential year and then step aside.

The caretaker was not hard to find. The interim Central Committee chairman, chosen to succeed Jake Arvey after a lifetime of exposure to patronage, was Joseph L. Gill, sixty-six, committeeman of the Forty-fourth Ward, in the upper Lincoln Park section of the city, and, as clerk of the municipal court, the dispenser of vast patronage. He was also a go-along, low-keyed man, politically well schooled, and he enjoyed the necessary credential of being unencumbered by further political aspirations.

In his new role Gill made a quite presentable Illinois delegation chairman—National Committeeman Arvey seated next to him, County Clerk Daley seated next to Arvey—as Adlai Stevenson was awarded the mission-impossible assignment of running for president against General Dwight D. Eisenhower at the 1952 national convention, which was held in Chicago's International Amphitheatre. The whole affair was another Arvey goof, more grist to the Duffy mill because of Arvey's failure, despite a public effort, to persuade Eisenhower to be the Democratic candidate. Arvey knew that Stevenson didn't have a chance; Gill knew this; so did Daley and all the others. The only one who didn't seem to realize that the cause was hopeless was Stevenson; as Stephen A. Mitchell, who ran Adlai's campaign, remarked when Stevenson was soundly beaten that November, "The sad part of it is that the fellow had actually convinced himself that he could win."

The Chicago Democrats realistically faced the prospect that they would lose the state, with Adlai at the top of their ticket. They did. They hoped, mainly, to retain control of the Cook County state's attorney's office—and they did. Otherwise, they concentrated on the "family" fight that carried over into the next year for the control of the Chicago Machine.

Joe Gill's role, when he gaveled the Cook County Democratic Committee to order, at an electrified meeting in the Morrison Hotel headquarters on July 8, 1953, was to tender his resignation. The Arvey script then called for Dick Daley to be elected as his successor. But the John Duffy-Judge McDermott bloc had other ideas, and somehow they prevented a vote in a long, drawn-out, closed-door meeting.

A reporter, waiting in Clerk Daley's private office to interview the new Democratic chairman, was startled when Daley came into the office in a state of shock, his eyes moist. The reporter said: "They didn't give it to you?" Daley shook his head; he was crushed.

"Well," the reporter said, "If *you're* not the chairman, who is?"

"Nobody," Daley replied. "Joe Gill is still 'Acting.'"

"What the hell happened?"

"Clarence [Wagner] stopped it. Gill calls for a motion to nominate me and Clarence gets up and says, 'Now, wait a minute. Let's not be hasty.' And there was a big argument and we didn't get to vote."

"Duffy's plan?"

Daley nodded. "He wants it for McDermott."

"McDermott can't be chairman; he's a judge."

"He'll quit as judge. Clarence will quit as committeeman of the Fourteenth and Jim will take that. Then he can be chairman."

"And Duffy will run the show," the reporter said.

Daley nodded, and now there were tears in his eyes. "That's their plan."

The only vote that carried at the meeting was on Wagner's motion to adjourn for two weeks. The City Council finance chairman having done his job—it was up to Duffy and McDermott now to line up enough committeemen to stop Daley—he took the wheel of the limousine that the city provides for its council leader and, with his friend and neighbor State Senator Donald O'Brien—now a circuit court judge—at his side, two of their sons in the back seat, sped off on a fishing trip to Canada. A reckless driver, with bad vision, Wagner was clipping along at a good speed two mornings later when he missed a curve in the highway near International Falls, Minnesota. He was killed when the Cadillac went shooting off the road. Black flag.

Mayor Kennelly wept. John Duffy and Judge McDermott sighed. County Clerk Daley, Joe Gill, Jake Arvey—everybody—paid their respects to the widow when Clarence was laid out in the living room of his luxurious Fourteenth Ward home. The house was stifling with the fragrance of floral pieces, which were stacked against walls haphazardly in every room, and the body odor of the seemingly endless line of the Democratic party's little people, who journeyed from all parts of the city on orders of their ward bosses, in testament of the gospel that—with the Democrats—it was all for one and one for all when a big man is dead.

A hundred policemen were summoned to the scene to keep traffic moving in the neighborhood, to keep space open in front of Wagner's house for the cars of dignitaries. A few stood inside the house, directing the line of human traffic through the front door, into the living room, past the casket. Everyone kept moving toward the kitchen and out the back door—the "mourners" having only an instant to glance at the corpse as they paraded glumly past it. Notables got special treatment, of course, a police captain escorting to the front of the line any important personage.

The political ambitions of Judge McDermott died

when Clarence Wagner died; Jim McDermott knew that the Daley people would give him the treatment now. McDermott had one good round in the pistol, though, and he blasted his enemies with it before Wagner was placed in the ground. "They" had had the sheer guts to come demanding something from McDermott before Wagner had been borne from his living room to his requiem mass in Visitation Church, on nearby Garfield Boulevard. And, in return, McDermott pulled the trigger, hitting Wagner's erstwhile colleagues where it hurt—in their wallets.

Judge McDermott, who had been friend and counselor of Clarence P. Wagner and was stipulated in the alderman's will as executor of his estate, had been on brief holiday at his summer home in Long Beach, Indiana, when the news reached him that Wagner had been killed in the auto accident at International Falls. As gently as he could, he broke the news to Nora Wagner, Clarence's wife, and then drove to Chicago, a 90-minute trip from the Indiana dunes, to see what had to be done.

McDermott gave first priority to the matter of getting into Wagner's safe deposit boxes: one at the American National Bank in the heart of downtown Chicago and the other in the Colonial Savings and Loan Association, in his home neighborhood. Quite how the judge gained access to the boxes has never been made clear; safe deposit boxes are supposed to be sealed at first word of the owner's death, to keep inviolate for inheritance tax purposes an accounting of what they contain. Perhaps McDermott's name was on the boxes and he had his own keys; perhaps the judge was extended the professional courtesy of having the locks pulled. In any event, Jim McDermott wasted no time getting into the boxes, and immediately after it was rumored at City Hall that McDermott had been "bowled over" by the great amounts of cash he found therein—as much as $400,000.

However much it was, before the day was gone Judge McDermott had a caller—Alderman Harry Sain of the West Side's Twenty-seventh Ward, chairman of the City Council rules committee. Alderman Sain was afflicted with fractured syntax, as were many others, but he came right to the point with McDermott: "Jim," he said, "there was an envelope Clarence was holding for us and I come over here to get it."

Envelope?

"There was an envelope with a hundred grand and it's our money and the boys want I should get it."

Was Sain's name on the envelope? Did he have a letter from Clarence, a document of any kind that would identify this envelope—if there *was* such an envelope—as being held for the boys?

Obviously, Alderman Sain had no documentation. "You know I ain't got no letter," he is reported to have said.

To which Judge McDermott is reported to have replied, softly: "Well, in that case, I think the money—if there was any money—belongs to Nora and Clarence's children."

Presumably, if there had been any money in Wagner's safe deposit boxes, it went to Nora and the children. Tax records of the state of Illinois show that McDermott closed out Wagner's estate in probate court on November 5, 1954, with payment of only $4,044 in inheritance taxes. But, of course, in the tax settlements of dead politicians, certain courtesies are customarily extended in this area, also.

In any case, Alderman Sain and various others had no difficulty in looking sad as they attended the funeral rites of Clarence Wagner. Even Mayor Kennelly, who had heard the story of the envelope, looked perplexed, as if pondering the fate of Clarence's soul, as he openly wept.

Mayor Kennelly wept again, next day—July 13—at a special City Council meeting that had been called to memorialize Clarence Wagner, the desk of his dead floor leader draped in black cloth, as is the custom when an alderman passes on. Harry Sain and his pals murmured "Aye" on the resolution to perpetuate Clarence's name on the new Congress Street bridge.

On July 21, the date that had been fixed at the insistence of Wagner for the showdown of the Duffy-Daley forces, Richard J. Daley was routinely elected chairman of the Cook County Democrats—Duffy softly voting "Aye."

Daley was by this time not a stranger to Democratic party headquarters. Throughout the period that Joe Gill was acting chairman, Daley was almost always at his side —standing respectfully alongside the seated Gill during press interviews, for example, quick to chuckle when Joe scored a point with reporters who frequently joshed with him. From Gill Daley learned the mechanics of running the Machine; he became quite aware of the power that a chairman could exercise in the area of deciding who should be chosen, say, to run for mayor. Gill, who was well up in years—about twenty years senior to Daley— had no ambitions for himself and had run the organization with a paternalistic hand; Daley did not intend to be so indulgent, and he knew very well who he wanted for mayor—himself. The Duffy crowd likewise understood Daley's intentions. Other important committeemen, the ones who had hesitated to take sides, knew that the death of Clarence Wagner had destroyed any dreams of power that Duffy might have had. The best that Duffy could hope for now was that Daley would bury the hatchet and let him pursue his own career, which is precisely what Daley did.

"I don't think Duffy and McDermott could have stopped Daley," Paddy Bauler said much later. "They didn't have the votes. *I* would have went with 'em and Charlie Weber and some more of the guys. Only, Gill and Arvey and those fellows had the guns. Things would have been different, though, if Wagner didn't get kilt; he'd have been on Daley's ass all the way."

Alderman Bauler, and Charlie Weber also, had a begrudging, posthumous admiration for Clarence P. Wagner. One evening in Bauler's saloon at 403 West North Avenue, as he and Weber reminisced with a reporter, Bauler said: "Should I tell you how it was with Clarence as finance chairman? You could trust the guy. Only . . . we had this pot, see? And certain things that we got together on and voted for went into the pot, cuttin' it up at the end of the year—the guys who were in, that is. So Clarence has this envelope and then he gets kilt and that son of a bitch McDermott sits there pretty as pie and won't give back our money."

"How much money, Paddy?"

"Oh, hell, I don't remember."

"Go ahead and tell him, Paddy," Charlie Weber broke in, adding: "It was a hundred grand."

"Where did it come from?"

"I don't know," Weber said. "It was one of them franchise renewals, the phone company or the gas people or somebody. They wanted one of them exceptions to the ordinance or some bullshit like that; so they pay and we give them what they want."

"Listen," Bauler said, "you think we should do things for them people for nothin'? They got to have somethin' done—raise the cab fare or get a city parkin' lot lease or somethin' like that—holy Cry, you don't think they expect to get it for nothin', do you? What's fair is fair, you know."

Which is probably as good an explanation as any as to why there is no plaque in memory of the late Clarence P. Wagner on "his bridge," the multimillion-dollar span that carries upward of one hundred thousand vehicles per day in and out of the heart of the city where his archenemy, Richard J. Daley, has ruled since almost the moment of Wagner's death twenty-two years ago.

CHAPTER 6

Nomination

> *"His fellow citizens accepted him, because he was best fitted to be their leader. They might have preferred someone else, but there was no one else."*
> —*Hendrik Willem van Loon,* The Arts

Just as Pericles' fastidious eloquence and single-mindedness of rule disturbed the people of ancient Athens, many natives of mid-twentieth-century Chicago were disquieted by the ungrammatical preachments and arrogant authority of the man that the city was destined to follow: Richard J. Daley. There, of course, the resemblance ends. Apart from endless suspicion of their words and deeds, which both had to endure, the Greek and the Irishman were very different one from the other. Yet each rose to power because there really was no one else, each was essentially his own man, and whereas each was frequently accused of catering to the rabble, each ruled his domain with a take-it-or-leave-it disdain for the establishment's opinion.

If one had to put the pin in the one circumstance that led to the selection of Richard J. Daley for political pre-eminence, one might find the spot to place it in the February 29, 1956, *Chicago Crime Commission Report on Chicago Crime for 1955*. The most succinct paragraph in this document said:

> Throughout most of Chicago's history, the Civil Service Commission has been enmeshed in partisan politics. Thousands of city employees were given

temporary appointments and kept in this status, year after year, in order to keep them loyal partisan political workers.

If there is a fundamental explanation of what it was that made mild Mayor Martin H. Kennelly anathema to the Democrats who put him in office, it was the meticulous mayor's conviction that Chicago could not be a decent city until its army of payrollers was delivered from subjection to the Democratic Machine. This was heresy of an untenable kind, insofar as the bosses were concerned. They had accepted Kennelly in the belief that his head would be forever in the clouds, that he would take his pleasure in cutting ribbons at dedication ceremonies, that he would be *manageable*. They had not dreamed that this otherwise docile bachelor, a self-made millionaire in the van and storage business, would prove to be intractable in the *one* vital area that could lead to the destruction of the Democratic Machine.

It was not that the bosses wanted a reprise of the good old days of a wide-open town; those days were gone— and they knew it. If a politician was to make any money now, it had to be in the nonviolent fields of building-code variations, real estate tax reductions, the writings of big-premium casualty policies. The big graft now was in the providing of favors for those who were rich or wanted to be. Yet it was basic policy that the bosses had to maintain themselves in power and that doing so depended upon precinct captains who would kick back a portion of their city wages as a condition of employment and who would work their territories with apostolic fervor to turn out the vote on election days. And here was the amiable Kennelly, ripping out the foundation upon which the system rested. In the circumstance, the Democratic leaders of Chicago believed they had no choice but to get rid of Kennelly before he toppled them from power. And whatever "greatness" attaches to Daley's subsequent long reign, it was from the bitter soil of the Civil Service affair that it sprang.

By no means was Mayor Kennelly completely successful in his efforts to place all the nonexecutive, nonelected city workers under the umbrella of Civil Service. He succeeded, however, in maneuvering some 12,000 "jobs" out of ward bosses' control. An alderman or committeeman who had, say, 285 jobs to hand out during Kelly's or Cermak's time found himself with a mere handful by the time that the organization was able to rid itself of the man Alderman Bauler scornfully referred to as "Fartin' Martin." The collection of "dues" at the ward organization level—ranging from two to five percent of the paycheck, the figure depending upon the ward boss's greed—dwindled. Telephone calls poured in from angry citizens to the ward boss, because the man who worked the "presint" was no longer interested in repairing sidewalks, removing trees, or getting grandpa into Cook County Hospital—now that he was under Civil Service and damned well didn't have to "stay political" if he didn't care to.

The Civil Service move was the extent of Kennelly's "reforming" He didn't blink an eye at the petty graft that was passing through his City Council. He presided over a house of gross, raucous connivers who had a price tag on every driveway permit needed, every canopy that a place of business wanted to erect to shelter its customers from the rain, every no-parking sign that somebody wanted, and the mayor did nothing about it. In Kennelly's time, the then-owners of the Ambassador East Hotel, on North State Parkway, came hat in hand to Alderman Bauler, complaining that traffic congestion at the intersection one block to the south of the hotel was choking them to death. Couldn't Bauler get some no-parking zones established there, and policemen to keep the traffic moving? "It ain't in my ward," Bauler coldly replied. "That's the Forty-second and I'm the Forty-third."

Yes, the Ambassador Hotel people were aware of that. But couldn't Alderman Bauler . . .

"It'll cost you," Bauler said. "Twenty-five big ones."

"Twenty-five thousand dollars!" was the reaction.

Bauler was surprised. "What do you think—that you're a charity case? Lookit, I got to cut it with Dorsey Crowe on account of it's his ward and maybe some other guys to get it to pass."

When Bauler's personal physician intervened in behalf of the hotel people, Bauler reluctantly agreed to take care of the problem as a public service, but he felt dismal and frequently thereafter ragged his doctor for talking him into going "soft" on the Ambassador East.

Bauler was no exception. Almost all of the aldermen of Kennelly's time had something going for themselves—a law office, a piece of a real estate firm, an insurance agency. With the black aldermen, it was a steady payoff from the policy wheels. All but one of them—Reverend Archibald Carey of the Third Ward—were subservient to a short-tempered, one-legged black congressman named William Levi Dawson. Their game was Congressman Dawson's game: the policy racket, especially the most lucrative Erie-Buffalo wheel. It was only when things turned sour for Dawson, a one-time Republican who had been converted by Ed Kelly and who discovered that the pastures were indeed greener on the Democratic side, that he turned on Kennelly, initiating the beginning of the end for the mayor.

Back of the Yards, syndicate-owned pinball machines were part of the decor of neighborhood taverns; federal agents testifying before Chief Judge John P. Barnes of the Northern District of Illinois stated that each machine was geared to return a net of $1,200 per week. When the U.S. Court of Appeals upheld Judge Barnes's opinion that pinball machines were gambling devices subject to heavy federal taxation, three truckloads of them had been hastily hauled out of taverns in Alderman Clarence P. Wagner's Fourteenth Ward—presumably at no small loss in payoff money to Mayor Kennelly's council leader.

In many illicit ways, City Council members lived a privileged life under Mayor Kennelly. Inventive rip-offs are characteristic of Chicago's aldermen at any time. During the bootlegging and horse book reigns of Thompson, Cermak, and Kelly, Chicago's aldermen pocketed greater sums of money than they found available during Kennelly's eight years. Never, however, had Chicago's aldermen enjoyed such *freedom* as during the golden age of mayoral permissiveness that Kennelly provided. And one of the very best parts of this grafting was that, unlike in the Thompson, Cermak, Kelly eras, the politicians did not have to send a share of their take downtown.

In the circumstances, had Civil Service not become an issue, few Chicago politicians would have found fault with Kennelly. During the first few years of Kennelly's first term, everyone prospered. Things started to go bad as a result of the Kefauver hearings. In the first three years of

Kennelly's mayoralty, the syndicate—Dawson standing mutely aside—moved in on the policy operations, murdering, kidnapping, intimidating, and sending the black policy kings scurrying for safety. When the senate crime committee held hearings in Chicago that summer, 1950, a substantial part of the inquiry centered on the question of how it was that the crime syndicate was able to capture the policy racket that flourished in Dawson's ghetto.

Apart from hearing inconclusive evidence that various policy operators had been murdered or otherwise eliminated, the committee never seemed able to grasp how the racket had changed hands so smoothly. There was, however, rather convincing evidence of the *reason* for the syndicate efforts in the federal income tax returns of the syndicate's three key people in policy. Read into the record was the admission of one Sam Pardy that in 1947 he received a fee of $1,500 from the non-syndicate operators of the Erie-Buffalo wheel and that his earnings were $305,000 in 1948—after the mob had taken over. In 1949 the IRS returns of two other key syndicate figures, Peter Tremont and Pat Manno, showed that each had pocketed $135,000 from the Erie-Buffalo wheel.

There was yet another clue to the profits that accrued from policy. Thumbing through other income tax returns, senate crime committee staff members discovered that in 1949 the Erie-Buffalo wheel had dispersed the sum of $278,000 to two syndicate chiefs, Tony Accardo and Jack Guzik. The payment was listed as fees for "special services," not otherwise defined, and was reported in the Accardo and Guzik income tax returns simply as "miscellaneous income." Remarking on this to Eugene Bernstein, the syndicate accountant, Senator Kefauver said: "Mr. Bernstein, as an attorney and tax expert who is required to affix his signature to these returns, didn't you question your clients for more specific information as to the source of this money?"

To which Bernstein, visibly quaking, replied: "Senator, with these clients—you don't ask any questions."

These figures indicate what many a sharp operator was able to make running policy wheels, and few were smarter than Congressman Dawson. Thus, one can easily understand his rage when, the Kefauver Committee having hardly left town, Mayor Kennelly, mortified by the disclosures of who was running the policy racket, ordered a crackdown on the multimillion-dollar rip-off of ghetto blacks, especially since, elsewhere in the city, corruption flourished as usual.

By the end of 1950 Dawson had had enough. He served notice on the Democratic bosses that the reslating of Kennelly for mayor was unacceptable. Although it was not until four years later, at reslating time, that the bosses picked up the knife and frigidly cut down the mildest man Chicago ever entrusted to run the city, Dawson's opening salvo did not go unheard because, as even Kennelly knew, Dawson's political clout was considerable. When a heavy plurality was needed in Chicago in 1948, for Harry Truman, for example, it was Dawson who turned out votes in sufficient numbers to carry the day. No man can interfere with impunity in a political life-support system that is indispensable, least of all in Chicago. And the Democratic leaders were not about to let Dawson be totally alienated.

Yet for all Dawson's protests, the chute for Kennelly was greased not so much by Kennelly's continued crackdown on the numbers racket that flourished in Dawson's district but, as we have noted, by his stubborn insistence upon dismantling the patronage machinery on which the Chicago Democrats depended.

The propaganda line adopted by the Morrison Hotel crowd led by Chairman Daley to justify the December 1954 dumping of Kennelly was the ficticious claim that Kennelly had no vision and that his conservative policies were a deterrent to the economic growth of Chicago. The argument was in confiict with federal statistics, which showed that Chicago had experienced an industrial expansion of $2.5 billion between 1940 and 1950, much of it occurring in the Kennelly years, and that the annual manufacturing productivity rate was running at a lusty $15 billion by 1950. In fact, it was his frontal attack on Civil Service that destroyed him.

Throughout the Kelly years, control of the Civil Service Commission of Chicago had been vested in James S. Osborne, its secretary. Upon becoming mayor Kennelly immediately neutralized Osborne, persuading a trusted friend, Stephen E. Hurley, to be chairman of the commission. Hurley was an attorney of good reputation, past president of the Chicago Bar Association, and in every way eminently qualified to reform the city's employment practices. A realist, he probably understood that he would be subjected to pressure and abuse when he firmly established the new principle that no longer could, say, a police lieutenant buy or wheedle his way into a captaincy, no longer could ward bosses dangle the bait of ward superintendencies under the noses of precinct captains who consistently delivered a big vote, no longer were foremanships of city forestry crews or assignments to street-repair crews or garbage-hauling jobs or any kind of city employment, white collar or menial, at the disposal of the ward bosses who needed an inventory of patronage to maintain the loyalty of the people who turned out the vote.

So Hurley was ready for trouble. But rarely, if ever, in Chicago's history has a man performing an imperative public service been subjected to the abuse that Stephen Hurley received in the City Council. Particularly when the next year's corporate budget was up for discussion and debate, unconscionable insults were tossed at Mayor Kennelly and his Civil Service chairman.

In his remarkably naive way, Kennelly sat there and took it. A strong man would have smashed down hard at the first display of this insolence (Daley would have turned purple with anger and flattened them), and there are many weapons available to the chief executive of a city for the disciplining of recalcitrant council-members. City Hall can aggravate the constituents of rebellious aldermen by ordering disruptive street repairs in his ward, by ripping up sidewalks and parkways in overly prolonged street lighting projects, by harassing the business people of the man's ward with fire prevention inspections and building inspections, by rudely ignoring complaints of bad housekeeping from the ward office, or simply by stopping the collection of garbage—which is what Ed Kelly once did to a South Side alderman who got overly petulant. Instead, Kennelly did nothing to contain the viciousness of the attack that his City Council members launched at Chairman Hurley and himself.

The news media adequately reported the basis of the trouble in Kennelly's paradise, yet, inexplicably, even the better-informed citizens did not seem to appreciate the power struggle that was being waged. One reason, perhaps, was that the aldermanic cat-calling did not reach crescendo pitch until Kennelly was one year into his second term, when yet another gangland-style murder raised the frightening question of whether the mayor was capable of dealing with violence within the city. Then even his defenders in the City Council turned on him.

The murder victim, Charlie Gross, was almost immediately revealed to be a man despised by all who knew him, even his wife—a man who had given syndicate-connected people ample motivation to assassinate him. But he also was the Republican committeeman of the Thirty-first Ward, or so it appeared. In fact, his Republican credentials were spurious; he was a lackey of Thirty-first Ward Democratic Alderman Thomas E. Keane, the man who was to be one of the architects of the Richard Daley takeover. So closely allied to Keane was Gross, Keane customarily drove his flunky to City Hall each morning; so mysteriously intertwined were their dealings, Keane was patently in a state of terror after his man was blown apart by double-O shotgun pellets near a busy intersection in the modestly prosperous Thirty-first Ward. In a condition of near-panic, in fact, Keane pleaded with Mayor Kennelly for a police bodyguard—which, incidentally, he retained for more than twenty years, even after he was convicted by a federal jury on October 9, 1974, on seventeen counts of mail fraud and one count of conspiracy, all in connection with secret, conflict-of-interest land deals he had contrived to get approved by the City Council he controlled.

There was nothing unique, really, about the February 1952 murder of Gross. However, because of its political implications his assassination was viewed by the so-called better element of Chicago as appalling. The Don Quixotes of commerce and industry shook with rage and put together a windmill organization that they called the Citizens of Greater Chicago, furiously proclaiming that savagery in the streets would no longer be tolerated. The protestations were of such magnitude that the Democratic bosses quivered and, in an uncharacteristic lapse into good judgment, voted for the creation of a City Council Emergency Crime Committee.

The committee was dominated by anti-administration

aldermen, and although every effort was made by council leader Clarence Wagner to compromise its effectiveness, the committee's clumsy investigations flooded the news media for more than a year with bizarre revelations of how police and politics were living together in sin.

A melancholy Philadelphia cop who needed money, Robert Butzler, was secretly imported by the anti-administration crime committee members to do their undercover work. Most of his disclosures were dredged up in Alderman Paddy Bauler's Forty-third Ward, but apart from his disclosure that crime syndicate bosses—Tony Accardo, Paul ("The Waiter") Ricca, Sam ("Mooney") Giancana, Murray ("The Camel") Humphreys, Bauler's partner and pal Bill Gold, Ross Prio, et al—were meeting clandestinely in an old brick building on North Wells Street, most of what Butzler uncovered was, as Bauler declared to the committee, "pure bullshit."

Probably the investigation would have gone no further had not somebody turned in the payoff book of police Captain Redmond P. Gibbons, chief of the uniformed men of Mayor Kennelly's police department and former commander of the Hudson Avenue district, which was located in the heart of Bauler's ward. The entries in Gibbons's little red book dovetailed with the joints that Investigator Butzler had covered in his reports; the evidence clearly suggested that the captain had been paid off to leave these places alone. There was panic among other Chicago policemen when it was demanded that Gibbons bare his financial soul and, further, explain how he happened to have the private telephone numbers of syndicate hoodlums. Excitement was at a high pitch, and the pressure was on in Democratic ranks to get rid of Mayor Kennelly. Acting Chairman Joe Gill, Dick Daley at his side, didn't make a move to help him.

Kennelly, meanwhile, occupied himself with looking as busy as possible, as a cover for doing next to nothing about the disclosures that the criminal element was buying clout directly from district commanders. Fortunately for him, many Chicagoans gave him the benefit of the doubt for his lack of interest in the effort to squeeze an incriminating confession from Gibbons. After all, they said, Kennelly had rid Chicago of the plague of open gambling that had characterized Mayor Kelly's reign.

"Martin *is* trying," members of the elite Chicago Club reassured each other. Simultaneously, and ironically, by keeping a distance between himself and the somewhat hysterical headline-grabbing of the City Council crime investigators, Kennelly came to be regarded by Chicago policemen as "an alright guy."

However, whatever face-saving was involved came too late; political enthusiasm for Kennelly, despite his care not to antagonize those already embarrassed by the crime investigation, remained low. The word went out that the Democrats would deny Kennelly a third term in 1955. The heir apparent, as the insiders figured it, was County Clerk Richard J. Daley. The public knew little about him, but he now controlled much patronage. He wanted Kennelly's job. And, as most knowledgeable observers became aware, there was no other likely candidate on the Democratic party horizon.

Late in 1954, Daley had already served as chairman of the Central Committee for more than a year, during which time he had generally kept a discreet silence, seemingly satisfied simply to listen noncommittally to the ward bosses who profanely poured out their disapproval of Mayor Kennelly's destruction of the patronage system. Some of those who got Daley's ear in the privacy of his office in party headquarters at the Morrison bluntly told Daley it was his responsibility to "get rid of the bastard before he gets rid of us." Daley nodded and said nothing. The visitor invariably accepted silence as consent, which indeed it was. And, like all gossip, the word drifted down to the precinct level that, in 1955, Daley would be mayor and things would be different. They would be. But having promised nothing, Daley felt obligated to no one.

Anyhow, he had first, in the fall of 1954, to get a county ticket elected—himself included for another term as county clerk. With few exceptions, among them County Assessor and Forty-ninth Ward Committeeman Frank Keenan, who looked upon Daley with unconcealed disdain, Chairman Daley was pleased with most of the Democratic candidates he selected. Daley was not overjoyed that Commissioner Dan Ryan, his detractor, was running for president of the County Board and figured to win, the Republicans being out of favor in an off-year election, despite Eisenhower's occupying the White House, and it nettled Daley still further that craggy Commissioner John Duffy, who also held him in low esteem, was a cinch to become finance chairman of the Cook County Board, replacing Ryan. But otherwise Daley felt well pleased. The advancement of Ryan and Duffy would put great patronage in the hands of his enemies—but, as was the case with Keenan, Daley was prepared to accommodate himself to the intra-party opposition, since he was not yet strong enough to deal with it. His thinking was that Ryan and Duffy would be pliable, if they won, and time proved that his assessment was accurate.

The reslating of Keenan filled Daley with particular foreboding, because Keenan was an avowed admirer of Mayor Martin Kennelly, and Daley knew he'd have a fight on his hands with Keenan when he and his friends made their play to dump Kennelly. Indeed, Daley would have dumped Keenan from the ticket in 1954—if he'd been stronger. The assessor's job was too rich a plum to pass up if it could be snatched for a loyalist. The graft available to the assessor was enormous and tempting, the so-called decent element being eager to pay off in return for having their real estate taxes reduced. But Daley simply was not yet big enough to take on Frank Keenan. It would have been foolhardy to invite a showdown with the man who set real estate evaluations on some fifteen billion dollars' worth of property and consequently had the wealthy anxious to bend their knees to him, and Daley was far too shrewd to start a fight that he could not win. So, for the time being, Daley piously passed Keenan off on the public as another of his "blue ribbon" candidates.

Personally, in 1954, Daley's immediate problem was exposure. Even though he had been county clerk for almost five years and party chairman for more than one year, Daley was hardly known outside political and media circles. Many powerful local and state politicians are virtual unknowns to the public, and in 1954 Daley was one of these. Such people, especially the politically ambitious ones, hunger for recognition and are easily persuaded to chance doing reckless things to achieve it. County Clerk Daley was one of these, and he therefore leaped at a chance in October 1954 to appear on a local NBC television program, "City Desk," to state his case as a candidate for reelection. The program served his purpose; he did indeed become widely known, but the public was aghast at Daley's belligerent responses to questions about his secret ambitions to succeed Martin Kennelly as mayor —coming across on the tube as a gross, insufferable, ungrammatical clout.

Daley's Republican opponent, Alderman John J. Hoellen, an obese, voluble minority bloc member of City Council, who had a penchant for melodramatic outcries, had previously appeared on the program. This was to be Daley's equal opportunity period. Candidate Hoellen had been guilty of ambiguity, if not sheer inaccuracy, in many of the things he had said, and Daley came on hard, in the process making his private elocution teacher (the fact that he had such a teacher was, and is, a well-kept secret) Irving J. Lee, then head of the speech department at Northwestern University, despondent.

The program was conducted by William B. Ray, currently Chief, Complaints and Compliance Division, Federal Communications Commission. The panelist were John Dreiske, political editor, *Chicago Sun-Times*, Charles Cleveland, political editor, *Chicago Daily News*, and the author. One part of the program went like this:

> Cleveland: I'd like to start out with a question regarding your future. There has been a lot of speculation that you may run for mayor. In the event that Mayor Kennelly decided not to run next spring, what guarentee will we have that, if you're elected county clerk, you won't serve a few months and then run for mayor?
>
> Daley: Mr. Cleveland, before I answer that question, I'd like to go into some statements that were made two weeks ago on this very program. [Voice rising] The man that was on that program made a most reckless, unwarranted, vicious, and malicious statement that . . .

Whereupon Daley went sailing into a thunderous, denunciatory rebuttal of Candidate Hoellen's implication that Clerk Daley had manipulated election returns to benefit Democratic candidates in some 1,500 voting precincts under jurisdiction of his office, responsibility for the collecting of Cook County votes being shared by the clerk and the Chicago Board of Election Commissioners.

Daley: A man running for a public office to make such a statement without consulting the statue [*sic*] of Illinois and the laws of Illinois, gentlemen, it's ridiculous.

Daley talked on, ticking off his bill of particulars in a free-flowing recital, one sentence flooding into the next. Finally, apparently satisfied that he had cleared up the record insofar as Hoellen's previous remarks were concerned, Daley was momentarily pensive.

Daley: Mr. Ray, it points out to me a very serious problem in this new mechanism of television. And that is when statements can go out over the air wholly and totally inaccurate and untrue and can be verified by anyone who will reach for a statue [*sic*] of Illinois and tell the people the truth, I say that it's about time that we would start tellin' people on these various programs and we candidates the truth and I think when a man appears on a program like this and attempts to tell you four men or this large listenin' audience of the city of Chicago and the county of Cook bareface inaccurate, malicious, reckless, and unwarranted statements, then it's about time some steps be taken to correct it. Surely you wouldn't want to deprive me of the right to correct the good people of Chicago and Cook County and tell them the truth, that you know as well as I do is the truth, would you?

Moderator Ray assured his guest that he had been invited to appear on the program so that he could voice his views.

Cleveland: Let's consider this question then: In the event that Mayor Kennelly does not run, your name has been mentioned. What guarantee do the voters have that if they elect you as county clerk on November 2nd, you will serve out your term? That you won't serve only a few short months and then run for mayor of Chicago?

Daley: Well, Charlie, that question is highly problematically and loaded, as you know . . . you would think, then, that they should not elect me as county clerk. Is that your interpretation?

Cleveland: If you're going to run for mayor, a few months later, I think not.

Daley: I think I'm a candidate, Charlie, and you know it, for county clerk . . .

Cleveland: Will you serve out your four years as clerk, or will you . . .

Daley: The question you asked, Mr. Cleveland, had too many contingencies and too many possibilities for any intelligent man to answer it at the present time.

O'Connor: Then you will not say that you will not be a candidate for mayor next year?

Daley: I am not discussing the mayoralty of a candidate and I appeared on this program as a candidate for county clerk. . . . The mayoralty's another step . . .

Dreiske: I'd like to ask you, Mr. Daley: Your opponent, Mr. Hoellen, points out that, besides being county clerk, you are county chairman of the Democratic party. Do you feel you can serve all the citizens properly, without divided interest?

Daley: Mr. Dreiske, I would say to you, that's an attackt [*sic*] on my integrity and no one has ever attacked my integrity as long as I have been in public office.

Dreiske: He did.

Daley: Sure he did. Because of his remarks that he made in the early part, which I tried to refute and which you all agree was inaccurate and . . . The unwarranted and reckless attack on the county chairman is what? . . . I took the chairmanship of the party and you people know what I did, to try to do something with the Democratic party, to improve it, and I think we did when we come with the candidates we did here in 1954, some of the finest candidates ever presented to any public at any time, any place, anywhere . . .

So the program went. Daley had exposure, and he

managed to avoid committing himself on the subject of running for mayor. Chicago, for its part, had its first good look at the Democratic party chairman. He did not make a good impression, but on November 2, under the chairmanship of Richard J. Daley, the Democratic candidates who had been described as the finest anyone had ever seen were swept into office.

Taking a lesson from Daley's abysmally unproductive appearance on the panel show "City Desk," the Democrats reverted to the tried and true method of dumping their campaign money into the dependable wards and suburban areas, where the dollar buys a predictable return of votes. A bit of money was spent on newspaper advertising, as always, and the billboards of Cook County suddenly sprouted with 24-sheet slogans: "Elect Dan Ryan, A County Board President You Can Trust," "Re-elect Richard J. Daley, A Trusted County Clerk," and "Vote for County Assessor Frank Keenan, For Honesty In Government." Mostly, however, the campaign money wound up in the pockets of precinct captains, and, as usual, they got out the vote.

The winners included:

• County Assessor Frank Keenan, who subsequently was indicted, tried, found guilty, and served time in federal prison for not reporting substantial sums of graft he received from property owners whose taxes he set.

• County Judge Otto Kerner, Jr., who subsequently was indicted, tried, found guilty, and sentenced to prison—the only active federal judge in the nation's history ever to have these distinctions—for his involvement in a quarter-million-dollar racetrack bribery case.

• County Clerk Richard J. Daley, future mayor.

Kennelly looked on, fully aware of the implications. Ignored by the Machine during the 1954 campaigning—not invited to the Morrison Hotel luncheons for the 3,500 precinct captains, hardly ever asked to "speak for the ticket" at ward meetings—Martin Kennelly had sufficient notice of what his political fate was to be. Yet Kennelly gave early warning to the Democratic party bosses that he would not meekly be led to their guillotine. On December 1, 1954—with Chairman Daley, his potential nemesis, elected—he let them know that they would have to drag him, in full view of the voters, to the chopping block.

Hardly anyone was prepared for the news when Mayor Kennelly summoned reporters to his fifth-floor office in City Hall to make a statement that would shake the city.

"Eight years ago," Kennelly said, speaking softly, "I was asked by the Democratic party to run for election as mayor of Chicago. I conceived it to be the duty of the mayor to administer the affairs of the city for the benefit of all citizens. With this understanding, I was nominated by the Democratic party and duly elected. . . ." Having performed honorably for two terms, Kennelly went on, he would now seek a third.

When a reporter asked if the mayor had conveyed his announcement to the party bosses, Kennelly flashed a smile and replied that, no, he intended to put in a call to Chairman Daley when the reporters cleared out.

The *Chicago Daily News,* then a John S. Knight newspaper, found this to be a bit too much. In a December 2 editorial, entitled KENNELLY RUNS, the *Daily News* said:

> It is symbolic of the difficulties that have arisen between the mayor and the party machine that only after handing his announcement to the press did he telephone the news to Richard J. Daley, the Democratic county chairman. It is this aloofness which angers and alienates the ward committeemen.

The Knight newspaper, missing the point completely of why Kennelly was being dumped, guessed that Daley, "who undoubtedly could have the organization backing for himself, by merely asking," would not run. And it then compounded its error with a comment that it was better than even chance that the party would ride with Kennelly. The paper was wrong, as soon became evident, but Kennelly's unexpected announcement had knocked the Morrison Hotel time-frame out of focus.

Daley's plan had been to buy time by denying Kennelly reslating at as late a date as possible. The party bosses anticipated that dumping Kennelly would cause an uproar with the business community with whom Kennelly, for his anti-patronage and anti-corruption stances, was popular, but they also gauged that the prospective uproar would not evoke much of a popular response, at least partly because an effective opposition would not have time to form. That had been a rough plan, but here, three weeks in advance of confronting Kennelly and his influential friends with a fait accompli, was Kennelly putting the party on the defensive.

The turmoil was enormous—so much so that when phone calls came in to party headquarters from the likes of National Committeeman Jake Arvey, who was attending an important meeting of the Democratic National Committee in New Orleans, no one at the Morrison, particularly Daley, was interested in Arvey's reports of serious differences of opinion over the selection of a new national chairman. Indeed, the Morrison crowd was annoyed that Arvey, not so out of touch with things that he was unaware of the plot to scuttle Kennelly, would trouble headquarters in its time of crisis with such an unimportant question. As Arvey knew only too well, appealing for advice and counsel as to whether Illinois should prefer James Finnegan, president of the Philadelphia City Council, for chairman, or hold out for the election of Paul Butler of Indiana was rather like asking Winston Churchill to divert his attention, during the aerial battle to save Britain, to the distant problem of how best to invade Europe.

Yet even this minor distraction tells us something about Daley, for when Municipal Court Clerk Joe Gill, to whom Arvey finally turned in the effort to get through to the top Machine men, passed on to Daley the problem of whether Chicago should side with Butler, the Stevenson-Mitchell nominee, or Finnegan, the choice of Governor David Lawrence of Pennsylvania and the favorite of the New York, New Jersey, and Massachusetts Democrats, Daley, looking to the future, when the big city-big state bosses might well join forces to nominate presidential candidates, told Arvey to hold out for Finnegan. It was the first national clue that the "new man" in Illinois, Daley, knew something about how to play the game on a national scale.

Of course in December 1954 Daley was merely an applicant for membership in the inner circle of Democratic leaders who aspired to rule the nation by dictating to the party. Yet what he did was indicative of the man. A man of lesser personal ambition—or more sensitivity—than Daley possesses might have had a qualm, running contrary to the desires of Governor Stevenson, his old patron. Yet Daley operates in every area on the principle that *all* others are expendable. Even though a tough primary fight with Kennelly confronted him, or soon would, and even though the Republican mayoral candidate might give him a run, Daley exhibited utter confidence that he would win his battles in Chicago and that, therefore, deserting his patron on the question of installing Paul Butler of Indiana as national chairman was clearly in the future mayor's best interest.

Later Steve Mitchell reported that he tried to explain to Stevenson that politics is a cut-throat business. "I told Adlai that Daley was an ambitious fellow," he said. But Stevenson, who remained resentful at Daley's refusal to accept him, a defeated presidential candidate, as titular head of the party, was, as we have seen, somewhat of an innocent in the practicalities of politics. His naiveté, in fact, was never more evidenced than when, a few weeks after Daley had deserted him, Stevenson shocked his upper-crust friends by turning the other cheek in good Christian fashion and warmly endorsed Daley in preference to Martin Kennelly.

It never seemed to register with Stevenson that Daley had stepped on him in order to climb into a position of national influence or that Daley always considered his own good each time an issue presented itself. Thus in 1956 Daley was as enthusiastic as anyone else when Stevenson was again nominated to run against Eisenhower because he knew no one could defeat Eisenhower—even Stevenson himself was aware of how hopeless was his cause—but in 1960 went with Kennedy, in Daley's mind a winner against Richard M. Nixon, rather than with Stevenson, who thought himself both a winner and a man who had earned the right to run again.

Of course, this was all far in the future in December 1954. And that is the point. Daley always has his eye to the future—even when, as was the case that month, the political action was frantic.

First of all, on December 3, 1954, Congressman William L. Dawson got a reminder of why he hated Martin Kennelly when four of the Manno Brothers (Tom, Fred, Nick, and Sam), together with Sam Pardy, the crime syndicate's Erie-Buffalo wheel boss, pleaded guilty in the federal court of Judge Julius J. Hoffman to charges of income tax evasion (the grand jury indictment stipulating that the five defendants had failed to pay taxes on $2,152,043 of income from the sale of fake policy wheel tickets).

Also on December 3, Benjamin S. Adamowski opened his headquarters as an independent Democratic candidate for mayor. Adamowski, a born maverick who had been closely associated with Daley when both were in the Illinois Senate—the two of them and Abe Marovitz making up an inseparable triumvirate who were sober, virtuous, and got Chicago bills passed for Mayor Kelly—was corporation counsel of Chicago from 1947 to 1950, named to the job by Kennelly as the mayor's first appointee. Having quit in anger in 1950, charging that Kennelly was too subservient to the bosses, too bashful to stand up and fight, Adamowski was determined to make it as a "real" reform mayor, his respect and admiration for Dick Daley having long since vanished.

On December 14, 1954, Kennelly opened his reelection headquarters. It is a Chicago custom for business people to drop in and pay their respects to a favorite son when he opens his political headquarters, and many such dignitaries—including Chairman James B. Forgan of Chicago's First National Bank and most of the State Street merchants—personally conveyed their good wishes to Mayor Kennelly. A reporter for the *Chicago Daily News* asked Party Chairman Richard J. Daley if he planned to show up. Daley replied, "No, I have to take my kids to see Santa Claus." The *Chicago Tribune* reported: "Of the hundreds of Democratic party and public officials invited to the opening of Kennelly's headquarters, it was believed that most will not attend for fear of incurring the wrath of the Democratic Machine. Business and civic leaders will be present in force, however." The *Tribune,* at pains to let Chicago know where it stood in this business of Kennelly's getting the knife, stuck its own into Chairman Daley, picturing him—"good family man" propaganda being churned out by the Morrison notwithstanding—as the overly ambitious foil of evil men. If there is one thing that Daley could not then or ever abide, it is the implication that, basically, he is a ruthless fellow who will condone the illicit dealings of his cronies—so long as there is something in it for him. Daley's soft underbelly is his sensitivity toward criticism of his un-blemished personal reputation, and the *Tribune* kicked him right in the guts:

> The grafters and fixers, the policy racketeers and others who can't do business with Kennelly and his department heads are yearning for a city administration they can do business with. They will back anybody against Kennelly and, having done so, they will expect the man they backed to deal with them.
>
> Mr. Daley is no hoodlum, but if he runs he will be the candidate of the hoodlum element. He will also be the candidate of those who wish to load the city's offices once again with political payrollers and thus undo the great work of Mayor Kennelly in giving the City a real merit system of appointments and promotions. Mr. Daley will also be the candidate of those who want to see the city purchase of supplies and the contracts let in the good old-fashioned way, with a nice percentage for the politicians.

The *Tribune* pulled no punches. There were many who felt the same. But there were few Machine Democrats among Daley's opposition. There are fifty ward committeemen in the Democratic Central Committee of Chicago. Fifteen of them, referred to in the newspapers as "murderers' row," comprised the slate-making group that went through the motions in mid-December 1954 of listening to Martin Kennelly make a three-and-a-half-minute pitch for renomination. Chairman Daley, who was not a member of the committee, nevertheless attended the session, sitting apart from his slate-makers, head bowed, chin on his right fist, stolid as Rodin's *Thinker*, monitoring Kennelly's even-toned recitation. Not a member of Daley's committee got up to greet the mayor when he entered the sanctum sanctorum of party headquarters in the Morrison. Not a word of greeting was expressed. Puzzled, Kennelly stood before this unfriendly jury and read his prepared statement, beginning: "You are all familiar with my record as mayor since April of 1947. I am proud of my administration. Our many achievements reflect credit on the Democratic party." At the end of his reading,

Kennelly looked up and asked if there were any questions. Not a slate-marker moved.

Kennelly was wearing a sad smile when he came out of the closed-door room and went back to work in City Hall. This was December 15, 1954, and a day that he would remember. When Chairman Daley appeared, having allowed time for Kennelly to clear out, the reporters asked why he had been present. Daley said: "My office as chairman is next door to the room where the committee is meetin'; I pop in now and then." Asked if he were a candidate for mayor, Daley replied innocently: "That's up to the committee."

December 16: Alderman Robert E. Merriam, grinning like the Cheshire cat, opened his headquarters to seek the Republican party nomination. He was a registered Democrat, but—lacking any other attractive candidate—the Republican ward committeemen were delighted to embrace the youthful University of Chicago-area reformer who had forced creation of the City Council crime investigating committee.

December 18: Kennelly announced that Frank Keenan, Cook County assessor, would manage the "Greater Chicago Committee for the Re-Election of Mayor Kennelly." The Democrats grumbled over the word "greater"; this meant that Kennelly was counting on the financial backing of the well-heeled folks who resided in the affluent suburbs of Chicago. (In later years, in subsequent campaigns, Daley had a "greater" Chicago committee of his own and his committeemen did not grumble; on the contrary, they were delighted and Daley was proud to have acquired this support.) Keenan, a bald, pink-cheeked professional who had the big property owners by the throat with his tax-assessment powers, claimed that there were silent defectors on Daley's side. "A lot of the committeemen would like to be with Kennelly, if they had their own free choice," Keenan said.

December 20: Santa Claus visited Daley. The slate-makers submitted their recommendation to the fifty ward committeemen that Chairman Daley be the organization candidate for mayor. The proposition carried, 49 votes for Daley, 1 vote (Keenan's) for Kennelly. City Hall reporters went racing to Kennelly's fifth-floor office. "It wasn't much of a surprise, was it?" Kennelly said. Why had he been dumped? Kennelly said that he was now free to disclose that, six months previously, a Machine alderman whom he refused to identify had paid him a quasi-official call to tell him that he could have party support for a third term if he would drop Stephen Hurley as president of the Civil Service Commission. Kennelly said that he told the organization emissary that he would not deal on those terms. Kennelly added that the one other thing the Machine could not live with was his system of centralized city purchasing. "They would prefer," Kennelly said politely, "to let the independent departments make their own deals."

Speaking for the Daley side, Barnet Hodes—Jake Arvey's law partner—a tiny man with the visage of a bird that is simultaneously curious and indignant, declared that the slate-making committee, of which he was a member—representing the Fifth Ward—"resented newspaper stories that the decision to dump Kennelly was cut and dried."

Kennelly immediately replied that the decision was indeed cut and dried, "and the entire city knows it." Kennelly went on: "The 'draft' of Daley was phony. Integrity of local government is now the issue. The question is whether the people of Chicago will rule, or whether the city will be ruled by the willful, wanton inner-circle of political bosses at the Morrison Hotel."

Benjamin Adamowski, who had spurned an invitation to plead his case before the slate-makers—"If they don't know my record of public service, they are more ignorant than even I have believed"—had only one comment about the selection of Daley: "This is an arrogant display of machine politics; it is a mockery of the Democratic process."

Candidate Daley, placid as a plaster saint, said that he was honored to be the party's candidate. Daley said he hoped that the primary campaign would be free of "smears, fears, and false accusations." He thereupon growled that the reason Kennelly had been dumped was simply that "Kennelly has failed."

In what way had Kennelly failed? "In every way," Daley replied.

If this were so, why were the three major newspapers and an overwhelming number of the most substantial and best educated and informed people in Chicago standing with Kennelly? Looking grim and embarrassed, Candidate Daley made no response. He turned and marched into his private office at Democratic headquarters, closing the door behind him.

That night, in virtually every Democratic ward office in the city, the bosses called in their precinct captains. At every meeting, the message was the same: "We have won some and we have lost some and it hasn't made a hell of a lot of difference. *This* time, we are fightin' for our lives."

CHAPTER 7

Coronation

*"Like Moses in the wilderness, I feel like look-
ing up and saying, 'Lord, they would stone
me!'"*
——*Senator Everett McKinley Dirksen*

If ever a political prophet is to take hold of the citizens of
Chicago and lead them out of the Democratic Machine's
bondage, victory over what is construed to be the forces of
evil will have to explode on a cataclysmic election day
with an eruption of voters insistent upon a change of
control.

For almost half a century, the organization Democrats
have gone into every election with a predictable advantage
of more than one hundred thousand votes; this is the
seemingly impassable barrier that confronts any candidate
who has the temerity to run against the Machine. Indeed,
it was a sudden awakening to the untenable fact that,
historically, the Chicago Democrats have gone into every
election since the victory of Anton J. Cermak in 1931 with
a built-in advantage of no less than 103,000 votes that
made U.S. Attorney James R. Thompson, a popular,
successful, and ambitious federal prosecutor, decide in the
fall of 1974 that, appearances to the contrary notwithstanding, it would be useless for him to run against
Richard J. Daley, or any other organization candidate for
mayor, in 1975.

Potentially, the votes to upset the Machine are there;
practically, no candidate seems able to inspire the apathetic good-element folks to register and get to the polls
and strike the only kind of blow that counts. Thus Thomp-

son, above all a realist, recognized that the Daley Machine remained unassailable, despite his reputation for cutting down prominent Democrats with guilty findings on extortion, bribery, mail fraud, and income tax evasion charges.

In the early months of 1955, not one but three prophets who sought to lead the citizens of Chicago to the promised land were stoned at election time: Martin H. Kennelly, Benjamin S. Adamowski, and Robert E. Merriam. All three fell victim to the invincible organization Democrats in the most dramatic mayoral battle Chicago had ever seen. Two of these three—Kennelly, in the Democratic primary of February 1955, and Merriam, the Republican party candidate in the deciding election in April—were conceded to have a reasonably good chance of defeating the relatively unknown Daley, who was suspected in the good government circles of being nothing more than the clumsy figurehead behind whom evil bosses were plotting a reprise to the good old days of open gambling, patronage, and spoils. The explanation of Daley's double victory is that the Democratic Machine of Chicago is not only better organized than those who oppose it, it is also politically more skillful.

With the major newspapers of Chicago laying down a barrage that evil bosses were using Richard J. Daley, a respectable family man, as a front—hardly a day passed without praiseworthy mention of how Kennelly had served with honor, spending hundreds of millions for city improvements without a hint of scandal—Daley's campaign was constructed on a vague claim that "positive leadership" was what Chicago needed, his pitch being that *he* was the man who could provide it. Daley promised that, when elected, he *would not* sabotage the chaste Civil Service system that Kennelly so zealously guarded, he *would* keep the centralized city purchasing system whereby Kennelly had minimized kickbacks to city department heads, and that he *would* strive to maintain the nonpolitical administration of the massive public school system that Kennelly had liberated from City Hall's control. Indeed, Daley promised, he would expand the reforms that Kennelly had instituted. This campaign line was cunningly contrived to pacify anxieties that the moral tone that Kennelly had brought to city government would be lost if Daley were elected. On the positive side of the Daley campaign, there was only his amorphous claim that he could provide leadership that Chicago was lacking—the claim being at odds with Daley's implied approval of what Kennelly had achieved.

The 1955 primary fight between Daley and Kennelly—and no observer figured Adamowski to run better than a respectable third—proved to be the most expensive local election Chicago had ever seen. Each of the major candidates raised a war chest of $750,000; Kennelly's money came principally from business and industry, many of whose leaders hedged their bets with secret contributions to the Daley campaign. For the first time in Chicago's experience, both sides resorted to television, Kennelly spending far more than Daley. Kennelly, smooth and vocal, with an attractive rich-uncle television image, did much of his own talking on the political commercials that saturated Chicago stations. Daley, uncomfortable and bumbling in front of the cameras—neat, but not yet designated as one of the nation's best dressed men, this honor coming to him later from the high-price custom tailors who padded his shoulders and elegantly draped him—was mute in his commercials; the burden of telling the viewers what a great mayor Daley would be fell to a professional announcer, who sold the product convincingly as a new brand of miracle detergent, film clips of a cherubic Daley flashing by. The premise of the Daley commercials was that he could be saying all these wonderful things about himself if he cared to and were not so modest.

The need for money on both sides was great; commercials are expensive to make and, because they take a practical view about getting paid, unpaid campaign bills tending to be ignored, television stations insist upon prepayment before political commercials are aired. For Kennelly, County Assessor Frank Keenan really turned the screws. On one occasion, with a reporter in his office, one of his aides came in breathlessly with a suitcase and dumped an impressive pile of packaged tens and twenties on Keenan's desk. Kennelly's campaign manager looked at the money impassively; in an aside to the reporter, Keenan said, "This is from Henry Crown." Henry Crown, the head of a huge building supply company, Material Service, had more or less invented the system of delivering great loads of concrete to construction sites in big trucks, the ingredients mixing as the trucks rolled from the Material Service yards to the place where the concrete was needed. Vigilant civic groups occasionally complained that Crown's heavy trucks damaged city streets, and periodically an editorial appeared in the newspaper, coyly raising the question of whether the charge against a big advertiser might be true. Obviously, Colonel Henry Crown was vulnerable in the area of having to make general campaign contributions.

"How much is there?" Keenan asked his aide, pointing at the cash.

"Ten grand," the man replied.

"Ten grand? He thinks we're going to be satisfied with ten grand? Well, you put it back in your case and take it back to him and tell that sonofabitch that we are running an expensive campaign and that Frank Keenan isn't satisfied with a shitty ten grand. You tell that sonofabitch that I want twenty-five. Not a goddamn dollar less than twenty-five."

Daley's pressure was applied to the ward organizations. The ward leaders were called from the Morrison and told what the "assessment" was for Daley's campaign. "Jesus," Charlie Weber said, "them guys are really spendin' the money." In theory, some of the organization money was sent back to the wards prior to election day, to be parceled out to the precinct captains who needed it to buy up the vote. But the distribution of the "precinct money" is, at best, uneven in practice. "The niggers get it," Weber said. "Dawson and them fellas. We send it downtown, the assessment, and we don't ever see it again." Personally, Weber operated on the basis that, needing a vote to maintain one's influence in the party, it is best to remember the adage that heaven helps the ward boss who helps himself.

In his own old-fashioned way, Charlie Weber was a perfectionist. He kept his Democratic ward organization people loyal by keeping them on public payrolls, striving to keep residents of his Republican-inclined, anti-Irish ward contented by providing them with services that they could see—clean streets. efficient garbage collection, curbing and sidewalk repairs. If a precinct captain reported that one of his voters was in need of a new garbage can, the alderman himself was known to make the delivery in his Cadillac. Weber frequently complained that the trouble with his pal, Alderman Paddy Bauler of the Forty-third, was that "That sonofabitch Bauler won't do nothin' for nobody; he likes only to sit on his ass and drink the goddamn beer from Germany." Weber, on the contrary, was ever alert for an opportunity to do anything for anybody. When, for example, a housewife called the Forty-fifth Ward office to complain that there was a dead rat in the alley back of her house, Weber immediately got into his big car, drove to the spot with dispatch, ceremoniously kicked the dead rodent into a paper bag, and carted it away in his Cadillac—an act of charity, observed by many kitchen-window peepers, that was rewarded with compliments and general admiration of the dead-rat lady's neighbors.

In 1955, with advance notice that he could not carry the Forty-fifth for Daley, Weber poured out his money in an effort to salvage what he could. If the people in his ward couldn't be wheedled into voting for Daley, perhaps they could be influenced by a little beer and bratwurst money *not* to vote for Kennelly, voting instead for the third candidate, Adamowski. There is a rule in professional politics that if you cannot get a vote for your man, do what you can to prevent the vote from being cast for his major opponent. The rule is predicated on the equation that every vote that goes against you translates into two votes—the one you must pick up to neutralize it and the one you must get to top it. A ward boss is one vote ahead, he figures, if he can avoid having the vote cast against his man. This was Charlie Weber's ploy in 1955.

That was all party headquarters was asking of Weber and other such ward leaders. The Morrison Hotel people knew what the situation was. Daley wasn't going to win in wards such as the Forty-fifth; he was going to win in the ghetto wards and what Chicago refers to as the "river wards," the low-income wards. However, getting the ghetto vote and the river ward vote would not be sufficient; the anti-Machine vote had to be held down elsewhere.

Conversely, Frank Keenan, Kennelly's campaign manager, recognized that the mayor's chances for renomination were dependent upon a large turnout of registered voters and therefore exhausted Kennelly with a heavy schedule of personal appearances in the "nice" neighborhoods, where people are not much inclined to vote in primaries. One Keenan trick involved buying newspaper advertisements in the name of a nebulous organization called "Republicans for Kennelly" with the message: "Republicans, you can vote for Kennelly; just ask for a Democratic ballot."

Meanwhile, Daley was making an extraordinary number of appearances in the ghetto and river wards, repeatedly referring to Bill Dawson at all-black rallies as "The distinguished congressman." Over and over again, Daley cried, "I don't say that Bill Dawson is a boss; I say Bill Dawson is a leader of men." However galling news of this was to Daley's people in Bridgeport, Daley was ready to do what was necessary to get the black vote.

Daley's campaign was being run, of course, from his private office in Democratic headquarters at the Morrison. The phones were constantly ringing. Mary Mullen, Daley's private secretary, and Matt Danaher, his neighbor and aide—(administrative assistants known in Chicago as the "coat holders," this being one of their duties when their man is dropping in somewhere to make an appearance and plans to get right out again)—decided the priorities of the phone calls. Important ward bosses were put right through to Chairman Daley, unless an important businessman or union leader was already talking to Daley, in which case the ward bosses were kept waiting. Mary Mullen, who was sort of a mother superior in Daley's office, kept track of the appearances that the chairman had to make. After Daley and Danaher had squeezed in dinner in their homes on the 3500 block of South Lowe, Matt Danaher raced around with Daley to the various ward offices where he was booked to give an inspirational speech to the troops.

There are lookouts posted at every ward office at times like this, and space was kept open in front of each office for the candidate's car. The plan was always to have somebody of consequence up at a microphone, haranguing the precinct captains as a candidate of Daley's importance entered the hall. The precinct captains would know or sense that the Great One was now in their midst, but no heads would turn; the custom was for the ward boss to make the big announcement, having told whoever had been speaking to shut up and sit down: "The next Mayor of Chicago and a great guy—Dick Daley!"

Then, striding through the howling, applauding mob of payrollers—fingering the necktie that Abe Marovitz had delivered up the backstairs of his house at 3536 South Lowe ("Sis, for God's sakes," Abe had said to Daley's wife, handing her a box, "take those ties he is wearing and give them to the Salvation Army or somebody.")— grabbing hands that were stretched out to him—"How are ya?" and "How you doin'?"—acknowledging this one and that one, the computer in Daley's head clicking away bits of information on who was sober and who was a little drunk and who it was who owed him a favor. Finally, after another exaggerated introduction, Daley would be formally introduced: "Next mayor of Chicago. Our friend, great guy . . ."

And then would come the dismal speech about what a great ward this was, proud to be part of a great city, great victory if everybody worked hard . . . Candidate Daley said nothing, of course, about the payrollers who would be out on their ears if he didn't win, nothing about all the jobs that would be available when he did win—the precinct captains knew what they were cheering for.

Then there came the quick dash out of the place, the strident platitudes of the ward boss fading as the door closed and Daley and Danaher climbed into their car and headed for another ward meeting, where they would go through the same ludicrous routine once again.

It was sometimes midnight when finally Daley was free to turn toward home, soft in the head from all the monotonous cheering and empty praise that had engulfed him in smelly, smoky rooms crammed with precinct captains. The only consolation that Daley might have had was that Martin H. Kennelly had spent his night in the same fashion in the better-income wards, and that Benjamin S. Adamowski had done the same in the numerous Polish wards.

Money was no longer a personal worry of Daley in his campaign. Having got off the ground with a borrowed ninety thousand dollars—Daley, Billy Lynch, and a third man reportedly signed personal notes at the Continental Bank—contributions poured in from union people and real estate developers. The AFL trade unions negotiate highly favorable contracts for their members who work exclusively for the city; these union workers get regular private industry scale, with all fringe benefits, plus the benefits that accrue to city payrollers who are not in union-monopoly categories—holidays, easy work, and casual supervision being the principal fringe benefits that the non-union payrollers enjoy. The real estate developers, in need of a good relationship with City Hall in the purchase of sites that had been cleared by Urban Renewal bull-dozers, zoning changes, and construction permits, pru-dently snuggled up to Daley, giving him more money on the sly than they were giving to Kennelly out in the open—both camps aware that the developers were playing it both ways and neither camp complaining.

All that was business as usual. So, too, were the charges and countercharges made by either side. In this election it was the wide-open-town issue that became the focus of attention.

Prior to the February 22 primary, the Daley forces were accused of trying to buy votes. Some registered Democrats in the low-income areas reported that they had found envelopes containing dollar bills in their mail boxes, together with a message that said, "This is your lucky day. Stay lucky with Dick Daley." Kennelly hinted at the likelihood of vote fraud: "We are going to win this cam-paign but we're not going to stop worrying until all the votes are counted." Kennelly declared: "This election is a question of the people against the bosses."

Daley exploded: "The newspapers, big business and big influence—people sittin' in ivory towers, the 'holier than thou' people—are attemptin' to dictate to the people that they can't have a real Democratic primary."

On the eve of the primary, Cook County Judge Otto Kerner, Jr., predicted that something over 50 percent of the 1,930,097 persons registered to vote would turn out. The Kennelly forces cheered; one million would be a big vote and this big a vote indicated that Kennelly had an excellent chance to win. Unfortunately for Kennelly, Kerner's prediction proved to be 260,000 votes over the actual number cast. Kennelly lost the election to Daley by 100,000. The vote count showed: Daley, 364,839; Ken-nelly, 264,775; Adamowski, 112,072.

There was some grumbling among the better element that Kennelly would have won if Adamowski had stayed out of the race. Looking back on it now, however, the argument does not seem to wash. Adamowski's vote came principally from the four wards where the Polish-Americans resided, and lacking a man of their own to vote for, this ethnic group historically voted for Machine candidates. Daley would have gotten most of Adamowski's vote—as indeed he did when, six weeks later, he ran against Robert E. Merriam, the Republican convert.

More likely, Daley would have been beaten except for his breathtaking pluralities in the ghetto and river wards. In such wards, the best Kennelly could have expected, if he had had honest poll watchers in these precincts, was a more honest count than he probably got. If you reduce the February 1955 primary results to a table of statistics, ignoring the heavy vote that Bridgeport turned out for Daley in his Eleventh Ward and ignoring various other Machine wards where the voting was light but still heavily weighted for Daley, the evidence of how Daley managed to win by 100,000 is compelling (see Table 1).

In other words, whereas Daley defeated Kennelly by 100,064 votes, he picked up almost 99,000 votes of this total in eleven controlled wards. Two of his eleven wards functioned with the imprimatur of the crime syndicate, five did the bidding of Congressman Dawson, the political heirs of Jake Arvey held a death grip on the now-black Twenty-fourth, the racially indifferent Alderman-Committeeman Harry Sain was still czar of the now-black Twenty-seventh, Municipal Court Bailiff Albert Horan was still able to deliver a "good" vote in the Twenty-ninth, which was rapidly turning black, and Alderman Thomas E. Keane, one of the bosses who dug Kennelly's grave, was a second generation dictator of the Thirty-first, his father having ruled that roost when Tom was boning up on parliamentary procedure in the state senate.

Letting his eyes run over these figures on election night —Daley having carried twenty-seven wards, Kennelly nineteen, Adamowski four—Mayor Kennelly heaved a sigh and said, "They're unbeatable, just unbeatable, aren't they?" Kennelly ran almost even with Daley in the remainder of the city, despite fierce opposition from virtually all of the thirty-nine other ward committeemen. Yet even here Kennelly had additional—insurmountable—problems. For example, in some wards the Daley votes were counted

twice; his, not at all. Everywhere the decent element failed
him by refusing to go to the polls. The "good citizen"
vote he was counting upon was not cast.

Table 1*

Ward	Daley	Kennelly	Plurality	Control
1	13,275	1,961	11,314	Crime syndicate
2	13,257	1,663	11,594	Dawson
3	13,046	1,671	11,375	Dawson
4	11,444	4,890	6,554	Dawson
6	9,334	3,538	5,796	Dawson
20	11,918	1,675	10,243	Dawson
24	13,607	3,654	9,953	Machine/Arvey
27	12,773	1,720	11,053	Machine/Sain
28	8,061	2,802	7,259	Machine/Syndicate
29	11,178	4,001	7,177	Machine/Horan
31	9,126	2,585	6,541	Machine/Keane
	127,019	30,160	98,859	

*Over the years, control of the individual wards of Chicago trans-
fers from the hands of the Dawsons and the Arveys and the Sains
to new bosses who rise out of the pack by virtue of their ability to
get out the vote and do favors, death taking some like Dawson, Sain,
and Horan—joy of the battle burning out in others, Jake Arvey and
Paddy Bauler, for example. Many of the Chicago wards in which
the Democrats traditionally have been strong retain their old identi-
ties when organization people mention them—to this day referring
to the Twenty-fourth as "Arvey's old ward," to the Twenty-seventh
as "Sain's old ward" and so on. In the election result tables that
have been included in this book, in the interests of avoiding the
confusion that might result from an updating of those who have
succeeded to control of the Automatic Eleven, it seemed desirable
to attribute control to those who were running the wards when
Daley was first elected in the mid-fifties—even though these wards
have long since been taken over by men who fought or maneuvered
themselves into power. If an Irwin Horwitz manages to scratch his
way to the top in the Twenty-fourth, or State Senator Bernard
Neistein, who identifies with members of the crime syndicate, does
likewise in the Twenty-ninth, they rise to power through the cur-
rency of votes—and, like having plenty of money in one's pocket,
it matters little where you get it, so long as you have enough of it.
When, in 1975, the pressure would be on to get Daley a big vote,
Horwitz and Neistein and Edward Quigley—head of Daley's sewer
department and, since Alderman Sain's death several years ago,
head of the Twenty-seventh ward—could safely be counted upon to
deliver it. As Ben Adamowski had been forced to admit in his defeat at the hands of Daley in 1963, the machine always delivers
when it is under orders to do so.

Congressman William L. Dawson, gloating, was an early arrival at Democratic headquarters at the Morrison on election night. A smiling Daley greeted William A. Lee, president of the Chicago Federation of Labor and head of the Bakery Drivers Union (AFL), William McFetridge, international vice-president of the Flat Janitors Union (AFL), Stephen Bailey, president of the AFL Plumbers' Union, and Joseph Germano of the CIO Steel Workers. Robert Sargent Shriver, a Board of Education member, and his wife, Eunice, a daughter of former Ambassador Joseph P. Kennedy, were among those who stopped in at Daley's office.

When a goodly crowd of his admirers had gathered, the nominee-elect was escorted to a bank of microphones to deliver a statement that his victory over Kennelly was a great victory for the people. Daley concluded by saying, "I shall conduct myself in the spirit of the prayer of St. Francis of Assisi: 'Lord, make me an instrument of thy peace.'"

The *Daily News* reported: "The well-wishers broke into cheers and applause."

From the moment Daley's primary election was apparent, Democratic Alderman Robert E. Merriam, Republican candidate for mayor and evangelistic leader of the City Council's minority bloc, went on the attack: "The crime syndicate in your city is rich, rugged and powerful. The Democratic political Machine is wealthy, strong and deceptive. To make matters worse, the worst elements of the Democratic Machine and the worst elements of the Republican party are tied together in dirty politics."

Merriam's response to Daley's victory in the February 22 Democratic primary was a statement that set the issue on which the April 5 election would be fought: "My whole campaign will demonstrate that the Democrats have put the lie to any claims that they have the welfare of the people of Chicago at heart."

Stephen E. Hurley helped—and hurt—Merriam's cause by announcing, the morning after Kennelly's defeat, his resignation as president of the Chicago Civil Service Commission. Hurley thus put the mark of damnation on the Democrats, but the implication of his act was that the Morrison Hotel candidate, Daley, figured to win and, ergo, that the battle to preserve a merit system of employment was all but lost.

Mayor Kennelly, wet-eyed and brooding, had privately concluded that, somehow, Merriam's insistence on a City Council investigation of crime and politics had contributed to his defeat. Would Kennelly work for Merriam? "That's a very intelligent question," he said. "I have no comment." In fact, he sat out the April 5 election.

County Assessor Frank Keenan said he intended to be active in Merriam's campaign, and at age fifty-two, Richard J. Daley, at the threshold of the office of his dreams, had a sinking feeling when the news came through that Keenan, a tough professional who hated him, was going to fight him all the way. He had already seen, or thought he had, what a dirty fight Keenan could conduct.

Shocking a politician could be one of the more difficult-to-achieve pleasures of life, but Daley had been shocked during the primary when word got to him, through the manager's office at the Morrison, that some people had been caught in the act of tapping Daley's private line in Democratic headquarters. The culprits, the manager said, had claimed to be policemen, and the house detectives had let them go. The policemen, in citizens' dress, had claimed they were bugging the line of a New York thief, not identified, who was registered at the Morrison—only they had been caught trying to tie into Daley's line.

Daley soon determined that this botched job had been the work of Captain Joseph F. Morris, chief of the secretive "Scotland Yard" unit of Mayor Kennelly's police department, working, Daley believed, at Keenan's behest. In any case, a hint of things to come for all who crossed Daley in the future was seen in one of Daley's first acts upon taking office: he suggested to his police commissioner that the department could get along nicely without the services of Scotland Yard. The unit was folded as quickly as a dull book.

For Chicago's citizens, perhaps the most intriguing aspect of the 1955 mayoralty campaign occurred when a well-known neighborhood merchant, Morris B. Sachs, who had run with Kennelly in the primary as candidate for city clerk—and who had wept with Kennelly on the night of their defeat—was picked by Daley to run as *his* candidate for city treasurer, the third office under the mayor.

Daley needed a new candidate for treasurer because his own—a carefully selected Mr. Clean alderman who had been quietly faithful to the Democratic majority—came under fire following the primary on charges that he had a nasty habit of demanding payoffs from business people of his ward who were in need of building code variations. Morris B. Sachs, who had got into the dry goods business as an immigrant youth with a pack on his back—claiming, in later years, to have sold Dick Daley's mother her lad's first pair of long pants—had made a remarkable showing in the primary; he had been defeated by a mere 21,000 votes while his leader, Kennelly, was losing by 100,000. More than this, friendly old Morris B. was sort of beloved by Chicago folks, having for years been sponsor of a popular weekly radio show, featuring dubious talent in the performing arts, the Morris B. Sachs Amateur Hour. Daley figured that lovable old Morris would bring in his share of votes in the battle with Merriam, and he was right.

Frank Keenan was of another mind, considering Morris B.'s vote-getting power. When a reporter called Keenan for his reaction to this latest development, the county assessor snarled: "That traitorous little sonofabitch!" In a subsequent face-to-face encounter with Sachs, Keenan demanded to know how Sachs could have put in with the enemy. Embarrassed, Sachs replied: "I had to run: they insisted on it." To which Keenan retorted: "Horseshit! Nobody has to run for anything—ever. All you have to tell them is 'No!'" Even so, Keenan would have been the first to concede that pragmatic Daley had notably improved his chances by taking on Morris B.

Editorially, the three anti-Daley Chicago newspapers voiced warning of the many dreadful things that would ensue if the Morrison crowd got power. Personally, Colonel Robert R. McCormick, publisher of the *Chicago Tribune,* simply could not abide Daley, whom he held to be a dreadfully uncouth creature from Back of the Yards. However, the newspapers were eminently fair in giving equal coverage to Daley and Merriam—if anything, the advantage fell to Daley. Mostly the papers were repelled more by the evil Machine that was foisting Daley upon the city than by the man. Even an antagonistic press finds it unseemly to be vicious toward a church-going candidate, father of seven children, who is untouched by scandal and whose only fault appears to be his injudicious surrender to a consuming political ambition. The anti-Daley newspapers could not bring themselves to the point of attacking him personally.

Compounding the problem of lambasting Daley was the matter of having to support a Republican party candidate who was a turncoat Democrat. Robert Merriam was too bright-eyed and a touch too zealous for the newspapers' taste, but they felt that he had to be endorsed on the grounds that he was the symbol of resistance to the dark Democratic plot to plunge sweet Chicago into its old abyss of crime, corruption, and commercialized copulation.

It was all very confusing. Too, the outcome, though with hindsight it was never in doubt, was not being counted on by the Democratic ward committeemen. In a desperate final blast, Candidate Merriam cried that the Democrats were spending money like water. "The Democrats," he declared, "are dumping $750,000 into the wards to buy this election." Ready to buy it or not, the Democrats were digging deep to win it. As in the fight with Kennelly, the Democratic leaders were determined to deliver at least half of the fifty Chicago wards for Daley—and put the pressure on to get out the best possible vote for Daley in the wards that they figured to lose.

When it was all over, Daley had prevailed in 29 of the 50 wards. It was something short of a mandate, but at least he had won. Alderman Charles H. Weber's Forty-fifth was one of the wards that was lost. Weber grimly had called the shot on that. Speaking to a reporter in his office the day prior to the election, Weber said: "I could tell you we're gonna win, only we ain't; it'll be Merriam by five thousand in this ward and there ain't anythin' we can do about it"—though he gave it a try.

The winning of elections in Chicago has not been reduced to a formula. Each committeeman has his own method of getting out the vote. The thing that is common to all is the little people who push the doorbells to "sell the ticket" in advance of an election. All have jobs of some sort with the city, and they have to protect these jobs by making a respectable showing.

In ghetto and river wards it is common practice for the captain to stay in contact with his voters; frequently he must dip into his own pocket for a couple of singles or a fiver to keep his folks in line. It works. By the time that the decent-element "watchers" go on station at the break of dawn on election day, most of the voters in such precincts have been soaked in what the ghetto women call "the whiskey money." In Alderman Paddy Bauler's Forty-third, the practice was to station a couple of trusted aides, their pockets bulging with silver dollars, outside his saloon. The ceremony of passing a few cartwheels to the potential voter consisted of the potential voter's expressing a few extravagant compliments about Alderman Bauler, followed by a promise of voting a straight ticket, followed by a polite warning from the aide that the alderman would be counting on it, followed by a brief shaking of hands by way of passing the money. In the Skid Row wards, centering on West Madison and North Clark, the vote was not bought until a few minutes before the wino was to go staggering in to cast it. Indeed, in some Skid Row precincts, where the captain simply did not trust his charges, the bottle money was paid out *after* the down-and-outer had been inside and had signed a card attesting that he was a registered voter whose name was so-and-so and who lived at such-and-such an address. Then it mattered not at all that some of these good citizens stumbled out without bothering to vote; the precinct people would do that for him, later. "There is all kinda ways," Charlie Weber once explained. "Every guy's got to do it his own way, only you better get it done, by God, or them guys downtown will crucify you."

Results were what counted, winning. And therefore Kennelly's outrage during a personal inspection of voting procedures in the river wards on primary election day at the careless fashion in which anyone wandering into the polling places was given a ballot, the precinct election judges not making the slightest effort to determine whether the stranger was eligible to vote. Kennelly's vehement protest simply drew an insolent response from a precinct "judge" who had operated in the same fashion *for* Kennelly in two previous elections: "Mayor, will you get your ass out of here and stop interferin' with our election?"

Nothing so gross as this occurred in Weber's Forty-fifth, which inclined to the Republican side. There Democratic workers had to wean voters away with the tender loving care that some Chicagoans now bestow on their house plants—constant attention laced on election eve with enough of the "green" to ensure they will blossom. In 1955, it cost Weber some ten to fifteen thousand dollars to keep down Merriam's plurality. It was money well spent, Weber thought. As he said, "All I got to do is do better than I told 'em I was going to do; everybody's got to check in with downtown, you know, and let 'em know what your count is gonna be and so I tell 'em I can't do no better than hold Merriam down to a plurality of eight thousand or maybe seventy-five hundred. Now what I'm gonna do—hell, I'll tell you right now what the count is gonna be: I won't lose to Merriam by more than forty-five hundred—less than that. So they'll be happy downtown when I call in our ward and they'll say, 'That sonofabitch, Charlie Weber, he really tries,' and then I'm all right when Daley is the mayor. That's all there is to it. See?"

On April 5, 1955, Charlie Weber got value for his money. With 29,053 votes cast in the Forty-fifth, Merriam limped out of a ward that he figured to win by a substantial margin with an advantage over Daley of only 3,869—and downtown presumably cheered when Weber called in his results. The people, and Charlie Weber's money, had spoken.

Citywide, Daley defeated Merriam 708,222 to 581,255 —a plurality of 126,967. There was an uncommonly heavy vote cast: 67 percent of the 1,930,097 Chicagoans who were eligible to vote did so—contrasting to the 44 percent turnout in the February 22 primaries. Considering the eleven big Machine wards only, this picture emerges (see Table 2).

In addition to the eleven charted wards, Daley carried eighteen others while losing twenty-one to Merriam. Considering that Daley went out of his own Eleventh Ward with a plurality of 15,010 votes—giving him a locked-in plurarity of 140,000—Merriam ran remarkably well in the moderate and higher-income areas of the city to lose by only 127,000 citywide.

The same people who visited Richard J. Daley on the night that he defeated Martin Kennelly—the union people, the R. Sargent Shrivers—were back to fawn over him when he defeated Merriam. The only new face in the crowd was Morris B. Sachs's. Morris B. was not weeping now. He had been elected city treasurer, and he was jubilant—thrusting himself upon people to say: "I was only a penniless orphan boy from Lithuania and I started

Table 2

Ward	Daley	Merriam	Plurality	Control
1	18,233	2,304	15,929	Crime syndicate
2	17,856	4,439	13,417	Dawson
3	17,045	5,247	11,798	Dawson
4	16,085	8,057	8,028	Dawson
6	14,518	8,799	5,719	Dawson
20	16,406	6,005	10,401	Dawson
24	18,329	1,658	16,671	Machine/Arvey
27	15,576	2,153	13,423	Machine/Sain
28	10,934	2,440	8,494	Machine/Syndicate
29	17,277	4,732	12,545	Machine/Horan
31	15,531	6,777	8,754	Machine/Keane
	177,790	52,611	125,179	

selling with a pack on my back . . ." Most of those who heard that much of his story turned away. To give the former orphan boy from Lithuania his due, the final vote count would indicate that he should have run for mayor: Sachs got 27,000 more votes than Daley.

Martin Kennelly, who had class, bent a little on election night and sent Daley a telegram: "My best wishes for a very successful administration."

The *Chicago Tribune* faced the fact of Daley's election: "We congratulate Richard J. Daley. . . . We hope, for his sake, as well as Chicago's, that he will do nothing in the coming four years to sully his good name."

The *Chicago Daily News* said: "Some of the finest, high-principled men in the Democratic party worked for Daley in the election. So did some of the most notorious rascals in politics anywhere. Both kinds helped to deliver the votes to the winner. Daley knows which is which. We pray he has the strength to govern himself and the city accordingly. He can destroy his fine personal reputation and ruin the city if he pays off some 'political obligations' in the coin the claimants will demand."

Mayor-elect Daley's first words were that his goal was to "make this a better and more beautiful place to live."

Mrs. Richard J. Daley was asked if, now that her husband had made it, the Daleys would be selling the bungalow at 3536 South Lowe and moving into a nicer neighborhood. "We wouldn't dream of moving," Mrs. Daley replied. "We love Bridgeport."

No tears were wasted on Robert Merriam, the bright young gladiator whose career had just died. To the victors now, clearly, belonged the spoils—although the ward bosses who had provided the victory immediately began having doubts as to what they would gain from it.

When Mayor-elect Daley had made his election-night phone calls to each of the ward bosses who had done well, including Bauler who had "carried" and Weber who had made an extremely good showing, there had been no insistent invitation to the Webers and the Baulers to hustle downtown and take part in the jubilation, no promises that they would get a fair share of the pie, no sign from Daley that he would be at pains, as Tony Cermak and Ed Kelly had always been, to reassure his pals that they could now ask for anything within reason and get it.

With Cermak and Kelly, the bosses who brought in the vote would have some say in how city government in Chicago was going to operate; "everyone" knew that. During the 1955 campaign, ward bosses had exchanged knowing glances when they heard Daley decry allegations that the Martin Kennelly pattern of good government would disintegrate if Daley were to be elected. "Everyone" knew he had to say that. When the time came, "everyone" knew, Daley would come through according to pattern. Thus it was with intense misgivings that Daley's failure immediately to call in the bosses was viewed. Had the bosses miscalculated their candidate's intention?

Alderman Thomas E. Keane, for one, was concerned. Son of a long-time Thirty-first Ward alderman whose seat he now occupied, Tom was a bright, smooth-talking attorney who had served in the state senate with Daley—where he had treated his future leader with the same arrogance that he characteristically adopted toward anyone he privately regards as inferior to himself. Interested mainly in well-heeled clients in search of the special help and counsel that he could provide through his excellent political connections, spinning off law business to aldermen who needed it as much as he might need their votes in special situations, Keane gloried in being cocky and scornful. Even on the day he knew he was to be sentenced to prison as penalty for hoodwinking his fellow aldermen —hoist by his own petard some twenty years after Richard Daley had come to power, having carelessly resorted to use of the U.S. mails in carrying out some land-grab schemes—Keane had brazenly swaggered into court to hear the bad news. Daley had disliked him at first sight, having got a look at young Tom in the days when his old man was serving in City Council with the Baulers, the Duffys, and the Sains; Daley probably envied Keane his self-assurance and feared him, if indeed he trusted him.

Tom Keane attached himself to Daley when the power fight was on in 1953 and had helped plan the coup to scuttle Mayor Kennelly. Openly cruel toward politicians who scrounged for petty graft, interested only in big league deals where the quasi-legitimate money was to be made, Keane had set his sights on serving as Mayor Daley's barn boss of City Council. When, with Daley elected, it appeared that Daley had no plan to replace the plodding, more gentle Parky Cullerton as finance chairman, Keane was disappointed and dismayed; what had Parky done for Daley, he asked his cronies, that Daley should keep him as head of the council?

During the campaign Keane had worn the look of a fat cat that was about to take charge of a mynah bird—all the while doing his bit for Daley. Indeed, in the bitter campaign with Merriam, Keane had struck the dirtiest blow of all for Daley when he sanctimoniously professed to be scandalized that Merriam had married a divorcée and that the children he was raising were not his own but another man's. It was reported by those close to Daley that he was sorely distressed that Keane would violate the political code and make an issue of his opponent's private life, but if, in fact, Daley was upset by the reference, he did not publicly denounce it. Yet having paid his dues in full, Keane was not at once rewarded. Daley remained silent. The omens for the bosses were not good.

Indeed, immediately following the election of Daley, the ward bosses got a feeling that the man that they had picked for mayor was somehow slipping away from them;

the labor union people, particularly William McFetridge of the Flat Janitors—whose members did the housekeeping and much of the engineering in the major buildings in Chicago—seemed to have maneuvered themselves uncomfortably close to the mayor-elect. It was going to take several years for Daley to win the approval of the upper crust, but the ward bosses grimly scanned the newspaper reports of those who had dropped in on Daley at the Morrison on election night to extend their compliments. Even in Tony Cermak's time, the understanding was that the organization was superior to the man; this was certainly true during the fourteen years that Ed Kelly was mayor and the eight years thereafter that Kennelly had served. It now appeared, at least the ward bosses had made an immediate gut judgment, that under Daley it was going to be the other way around.

Alderman Charles H. Weber, a realist who had seen the violent destruction of many men and many well-laid plans, merely grinned when asked on election night if Daley was going to be a patsy for the bosses. "Let me tell ya," Charlie Weber replied, "this Daley—he's gonna be one tough sonofabitch."

Another old crook, Alderman Paddy Bauler—Weber's pal—who is remembered for his election night declaration that "Chicago ain't ready for reform!"—said something else, more telling and prophetic: "Keane and them fellas —Jake Arvey, Joe Gill—they think they are gonna run things. Well, you listen now to what I am sayin': they're gonna run nothin'. They ain't found it out yet, but Daley's the dog with the big nuts, now that we got him elected. You wait and see; that's how it is going to be."

CHAPTER 8

Taking Charge

"Find the corrupt officials and then prosecute them and send them to prison!"
—*U.S. Attorney General John N. Mitchell, Republican Governor's Conference, Hot Springs, Arkansas, December 13, 1969*

A full complement of Chicago aldermen, about a third of the fifty as new to the game as Mayor Richard J. Daley was to his, got up and applauded as he marched into City Council chambers to preside for the first time. He quickly got the meeting started, bringing on a preacher to beg Providence for guidance and enlightenment of all assembled, cuing the city clerk to start his drone of the roll call and the introduction of ordinances. Business was immediately to be attended to. Daley had already made a speech, on the night of April 20, when he had been inaugurated as Chicago's thirty-ninth mayor (the tenth man to serve since four-year terms became the rule in 1907, two-year terms pertaining before that, and one-year terms originally), letting the membership know that, in his own way, he intended to run things.

Mayor Martin H. Kennelly had sat through eight years on the little platform in front of the aldermen, tolerant and serene. Privately, he had suffered the boorish behavior of his councilmen—wandering around the floor at will, talking loudly to each other about personal matters, some of them sometimes dozing, or chomping on food, or reading the *Daily Racing Form*. Daley's first act as mayor was to pass the word that he wasn't going to have any of this. And whereas the Chicago City Council might be "the cunningest body of legislative bastards to be found in all of the western world"—which was the considered opinion of a former member, U.S. Senator Paul H. Douglas—its deportment improved markedly when Richard Daley came to power. He gave immediate attention to that.

Getting the City Council to terminate its adventure in crime investigating was another item of priority on Daley's agenda. Alderman Parky Cullerton, a squat go-along man of placid countenance who had succeeded to the finance chairmanship when Alderman Clarence P. Wagner had so unfortunately been killed, in 1953, had arrived at the meeting with a death certificate for the council crime committee that would have delighted Clarence: an ordinance, prepared in Daley's office, transferring responsibility for the investigation of wrongdoing on the part of city employees to His Honor the Mayor. The ordinance which provided the mayor with an appropriation of some $200,000—these funds to be expended as he pleased—ruled that the mayor would hire the investigators, that the investigators would report solely to the mayor, and that the mayor could use his own judgment as to whether the fruit of these investigations were to be made public. In short, crime investigating was at an end. With Alderman Robert Merriam of the Fifth now gone from the council, even the once-frightening minority bloc aldermen purred "aye," docile as heavily tranquilized cats, when the roll was called.

In any case, Daley began his service as mayor with a promise he has never kept. On Wednesday, April 6, 1955, the morning after his election, Daley volunteered that he would soon resign as county chairman of the Democratic organization to "devote all my time to the mayor's office." The wisest heads in Chicago politics said that they would believe this when they saw it happen. Jake Arvey had tried to dissuade Daley from seeking the chairmanship, in the belief that getting it would cripple Daley's chances to be mayor. Daley had wisely rejected this well-intended counsel, his guts telling him that he would never be mayor, at least not the dictatorial kind he desired to be, if he did not first seize the power to arrange it. And having become chairman, Daley was not about to renounce such power to someone else.

Arvey's advice had been well intentioned, however. Democratic headquarters was widely regarded as the center of political evil in Chicago and the man who heads up the Machine could reasonably be a target of public opprobrium. Acting Chairman Joseph L. Gill, who had been chosen to hold things together when Jake Arvey had been chased out, had provided a cushion of respectability for Chairman Daley to sit on, however, and he was in favor of Daley's succeeding him. Mr. Gill—everyone called him that—had survived and prospered, largely through an insurance brokerage business, for more than half a century in public office. He played the game of providing for his friends, and yet he had won the respect of such diverse business and social figures as William Wrigley, Jr., the chewing gum magnate, Oscar F. Mayer, the meat packer, and Jane Addams, founder of Hull House, the nation's first settlement center. Mr. Gill's sole blemish, in the eyes of his nonpolitical admirers, was that he chaired the slate-making committee that put the knife in Martin H. Kennelly. But Daley was no Gill. And it was probably because his political nerve endings told him that Daley was lacking in the go-along gentleness of Joe Gill and a belief that the aggressive Daley would damage himself in the office of chairman that Jake Arvey was against the idea of Daley's contriving to get the job. Daley, however, saw many advantages and no problem in serving as both party boss and mayor—although not even Tony Cermak had had the audacity to chance it—and having got a good grip on both hats in 1955, it would have been highly uncharacteristic of Daley to have let one go.

Daley's first move when he succeeded Gill as chairman in late 1953 had been to set the wheels in motion to get himself elected mayor in 1955. Having got himself elected, Daley's first step as mayor involved soliciting the advice of informed people regarding possible replacements for Kennelly's cabinet. He made inquiry of conditions in the police department. He reached out to La Salle Street in search of information on the status of Chicago's financial health. In every private conversation of this nature, Daley would gently present his question and then sit back, upright in his chair, hands folded over his belly and listen. When he had heard enough, he would pop up from his chair, grab his informant by the hand, pat him on the back with a gentle shove toward the door, and say, "Thanks a lot, pal." Some of the best informed people in the city left his office in a quandary as to whether they had helped the man, offended him, or merely left him in a state of confusion.

In most instances, Daley's final decision was to stick with Kennelly's people—Kennelly's chief of police, his commissioner of aviation, his commissioner of public works. The new mayor's decision to keep the old team, if the Kennelly people would now be loyal to him, was based on Daley's assumption that Kennelly had probably put together the best staff he could find: an ironic admission given Daley's campaign rhetoric.

Daley was forced to make one immediate appointment, however, and replacing Stephen E. Hurley, the organization's worst enemy, who had resigned as president of the Civil Service Commission, could only meet with the disapproval of Chicago's better element. With one strike against him already, Daley went for broke, choosing William A. Lee, head of the Bakery Drivers' Union and of the AFL unions in Chicago. It was patently a political payoff. The Chicago Crime Commission branded Lee's appointment as a "danger signal" and declared that it was incongruous and "wrong in principle" to place the merit system of Chicago, so carefully nurtured by Stephen Hurley, in a union leader's hands. At year's end, the crime commission said, "Throughout the administrations of former Mayors William Hale Thompson and Edward J. Kelly, civil service in Chicago was politically controlled and dominated." The crime commission concluded that, under Richard J. Daley, politics would again be the rule.

In the years that followed, the Greatest Mayor Chicago Has Ever Had proved to be decidedly weak in the area of Civil Service. Control of city jobs—patronage—had been the issue in the decision to dump Kennelly, and Daley never for a moment forgot this. Also, in his scheme to be a mayor who truly ran things, he *had* to have an army of patronage workers. The uninitiated might think that, so many jobs having been locked into Civil Service by Hurley, Daley had an impossible task of recruitment. Not so. As Daley quickly proved, it was relatively easy to circumvent the job security system set up by the

Kennelly administration; without disturbing the Civil Service ratings so precious to Kennelly, and so aggravating to the ward bosses, Daley resorted to making temporary appointments of deserving precinct workers to better paying jobs. So long as those holding the temporary assignments behaved themselves and brought in the vote on election day, they had all the job security they needed. As death and retirement took their toll of ward superintendents and top-flight clerks at City Hall and in other coveted areas of the payroll, Daley's supply of positions to be filled on a "temporary" basis increased—his Civil Service Commission exhibiting a remarkable lack of interest in holding examinations to fill the vacancies. Martin Kennelly, back in his North Clark Street office of the storage and moving van building that he owned, occasionally made a mild public protest at what Daley was cleverly doing to the Civil Service system, but few of his fellow citizens seemed to mind that Daley had supplied an effective cure for the political anemia his ward bosses had suffered during the Kennelly years.

Unlike Big Bill Thompson or Ed Kelly, Daley did not delegate the handling of patronage to someone else; he handled it himself. Democratic aldermen and committeemen, a few of whom were to be seen almost every morning in Daley's outer office, waiting like penitents to be ushered into his presence, came out of his office slightly dazed. Invariaby, in asking for a few city jobs "for the ward," the petitioner would get an immediate recital by Daley of how much patronage the man already had received, what kind of jobs he had been given to dole out, what the wages were and what kind of a vote the recipients of these jobs were producing.

"For God's sake," Alderman Joseph Burke of the Fourteenth was heard to murmur, coming out of Daley's office, "you'd wonder how he could run the city, keeping all the shit about how many jobs you've got in his head."

Actually there was nothing magical about Daley's having such data on the tip of his mind. His man, Matt Danaher, a Bridgeport neighbor who served Daley as his confidential aide, was always seated at an inconspicuous desk in the outer office, the patronage files within reach. Prior to ushering an alderman or political boss into the mayor, Danaher would come in with an up-to-date report on how many jobs the man's ward had already received. When the man who wanted to ask for something came in, Daley was prepared.

In contrast to Martin Kennelly, who had been a leisurely mayor, never appearing to be in haste, Richard Daley seemed a man of inexhaustible energy. Getting to be mayor had provided Daley with his big chance and if, privately, he harbored a fear that someone might try to take the office away from him, he clearly was determined to go to any limits to avoid flubbing his opportunity.

The establishment, unaccustomed to having as mayor a man who likewise was the city's political boss, was wary of him, and the new mayor was quite aware of their distrust. Consequently, he was self-effacing in his contacts with civic business backers. When, for example, he braced himself to make an uninvited appearance at the Tavern Club, the Michigan Avenue watering place of Chicago's business chiefs, he went alone and quietly took a seat close to the elevator. For some minutes, the chief executive of Chicago sat there, hardly drawing a glance from the members who heartily greeted each other. Finally, an officer of the club—Jules Herbuveaux, general manager of the NBC Chicago operation—beckoned to the maitre d' and, pointing to Daley, asked why someone was not taking care of him. The maitre d' replied that he had asked Daley if he were waiting for someone and that Daley had simply said no. Herbuveaux said the mayor had obviously dropped in for lunch. "He's not a member of the club," the maitre d' explained. Herbuveaux exploded: "Not a member of the club? Listen, you dumb bastard, that's the mayor of Chicago. Give him a table." They did even better than that: They gave him an honorary membership, which he still uses, strutting into the place on frequent occasions as if he owned the club.

His modesty was less in evidence when he was on his home ground. Thus he grandly cut ribbons on projects that the Kennelly administration had begun, carefully avoiding mentioning Kennelly's name—except, of course, when the former mayor was sitting with the dignitaries, at which times Daley would acknowledge him as "Martin." Daley's style might seem strange—smiles were stifled when Mayor Daley promised Chicago's citizens that they were going to have government "better than you never had it before," or when, at the dedication of a new U.S. Customs House at Midway Airport, Daley declared that this was but another sign that Chicago was the most "hospitial" city in the world—yet he was showing that he could get things done. For example, faced with a jurisdictional crisis that he had inherited from Kennelly—the problem of Chicago's not being contiguous with its new international airport, O'Hare, many miles northwest of the city limits, the city lacking therefore in jurisdiction over access to the site, Daley ingeniously prevailed upon the various towns and villages located in between Chicago and O'Hare to deed to the city their bits of the expressway that led to and from the airport. As Daley said, if they didn't, they'd have to take responsibility for policing and maintaining this long strip of highway. The deeds were drawn up.

The town and village representatives, well-educated people for the most part, had stifled their smiles when Daley said he would have the corporation counsel's "staff" draw up the implementing legislations. Frequently during the bargaining, the bedroom community representatives were startled that Daley consistently referred to O'Hare as "O'Hara" airport. Until you get accustomed to it, Daley's speech is disconcerting—when, for example, in defending Chicago's reputation against what he held to be grossly exaggerated network television reports of disorders at the 1968 convention, Daley snarled, "Never did I see a more disorderly convention in the history of my many years in the Democratic party," it took some instant translating to determine what he was complaining about. Or, when he said, "The family is the very essence around this entire country," his listener was left to figure out whether Daley considered that to be good or bad. But if it is accurate to report that he never has mastered the pronunciation of the word *precinct*—the word coming out of Daley as "preesint"—he has proved second to no one in milking one for every vote that is in it.

Slowly, steadily, deserving Bridgeport neighbors and relatives infiltrated the Daley administration: Matt Danaher, who lived down the street from Daley; a new fire commissioner, a new corporation counsel: Mrs. Daley's relatives. Of the 20,000 to 30,000 payroll jobs in the city of Chicago, Bridgeport residents were soon believed to hold about 10 percent. If faithful Bridgeport people do not work for the city, they work for the courts, the Metropolitan Sanitary District, the Democratically controlled Cook County Board, the Board of Election Commissioners, the office of the Cook County sheriff, the Chicago Transit Authority, or somewhere else. The career of State Senator William J. Lynch is typical. When Marjorie Lindheimer Everett was in need of an attorney for her Arlington Park-Washington Park racetrack enterprise, Daley's boyhood chum got the job; when the CTA had need of a general counsel, Lynch likewise got that; and when, in time, there was a vacancy on the U.S. District Court of Northern Illinois, Lynch got that, too.

Slowly and steadily the business and industry crowd warmed up to Daley. They were first of all pleased when Chicago did not relapse into a slough of vice and conspicuous corruption. The real estate interests were delighted to find that Daley was not only agreeable toward their plans of building high-rent apartment complexes on dilapidated sites; he enthusiastically made the land available to them through the scorched-earth use of urban renewal bulldozers. Such entrepreneurs as Arthur Rubloff and Arthur Wirtz became fast friends of the mayor, aiding his campaigns and dancing at his weddings.

The *Chicago Tribune* was impressed with Daley's early effort to demonstrate that he, too, wanted a decent city. The *Tribune* came into Daley's debt when he used his influence to force passage in the legislature of a massive memorial to the newspaper's late publisher, Colonel Robert McCormick: McCormick Place. The first McCormick Place (later destroyed by fire) was a beige-colored block of a building, reminding some of a Pharaoh's tomb. If Colonel McCormick would have been appalled that such a thing would be built with public funds, the state buying up $20,000,000 of the bonds when the financial community declined to touch them (the debt was to be serviced by a share of the state's cut of the horse-player bets at the racetracks), well, McCormick Place was what the folks then running the *Tribune* wanted and this was what Daley made it possible for them to get, making it possible for the paper to support him for reelection in 1959. When the world's largest retail operation, Sears, Roebuck and Company, became frightened over the encroachment by blacks on its mother house on the West

Side in the mid-1960s, Daley did his best to get Sears some federal Model Cities money to set its administrative offices apart, in a sort of white island, from the new neighbors.

If the University of Chicago in Hyde Park was disenchanted, as were others, by Daley's indifference to Daniel Burnham's historic pleading for preservation of the lakefront, the university, through its political-sociological subsidiary—the Southeast Chicago Commission—found City Hall to be quite cooperative in defending its area against the illegal conversion of Hyde Park's oncefashionable apartment houses into tenement flats. Responding to the whip of the Southeast Chicago Commission, the police department provided the university area with protection.

The appointment by Daley of various commissions and committees to deal with problems is his hallmark: wellknown people were gradually recruited to serve on these bodies, and most were flattered to be invited, even though control seemed always to be vested in William McFetridge of the Flat Janitors' Union, a hard and clever fellow who was not at all affronted to be referred to as "Daley's House Man."

There is no city in the nation where the affinity between labor and government is closer than in Chicago. Daley is Labor's man. From his first campaigns in 1955, the unions gave gobs of money to his election funds, the political action sections of both the AFL and CIO whipping up votes for him. In return, Daley has taken care of Labor— appointing union chiefs to sensitive positions in his administration, as witness his appointment of William Lee of the Teamsters Union to chairmanship of the Civil Service Commission, his selection of William McFetridge of the Flat Janitors' Union to be president of the Chicago Park District, and the honors he has continually bestowed in other areas upon those who control the unionized working stiffs of Chicago.

Of them all, having more guile and a bit more class than most, McFetridge became Daley's favorite. When McFetridge conceived the idea of investing millions of dollars of his union's money in construction of two cylindrical apartment buildings, Marina City, on the blighted north edge of the Chicago River at State Street, it was through Daley that McFetridge arranged federal financing to make the project possible. When, in turn, Daley was in need of someone he could trust to provide subtle control of a supposedly independent commission or committee that he had appointed, McFetridge invariably popped up as a member—reporting privately to Daley, but representing Labor's interests as well. There was hardly a single body of planning or development during all the Daley years—the Mayor's ill-conceived idea of putting a billion-dollar airport in Lake Michigan, the reconstruction of McCormick Place after the original one was gutted by fire in 1967, the selection of Orlando W. Wilson to reorganize the Chicago police department in the wake of a scandal in 1960—that did not include McFetridge. Better-known Chicagoans, big men in business and finance and persons of social status, sought membership on these various commissions and committees, but the ubiquitous McFetridge was always in control, navigating these groups into the channels that Daley wanted them to travel. Even in the matter of Daley's gaining a reputation as the great arbitrator of labor strikes, the mayor paternally interjecting himself into deadlocks with the comment, "The mayor's office is always open for the parties to meet and discuss their differences," it was McFetridge who supplied the formula of settling the disputes by giving the union people pretty much what they were demanding. Every prince, in short, needs his Machiavelli—and McFetridge was Daley's.

Alliances aside, from the very beginning of his long reign as mayor, Daley has charted his own course. Painstakingly, sheltered behind Labor's wall, Daley planted his sprouts in the heretofore forbidden soil of the establishment and, in time, the birds were chirping songs of praise in these trees. At the exclusive Chicago Club, where the most influential men have lunch, it began to be remarked that Daley was proving to be not a bad sort; none of the members went so far as to say he'd like to marry one, but, as mayors go, this was not too bad a one to be in bed with.

Gaining the confidence of the business and financial community was a slow process, accelerated only by the need to get Daley's cooperation in furtherance of their private affairs. In his early years as mayor, Daley looked to be unsure of himself as he greeted those of celebrated or even royal status who found it either amusing or expedient to drop by to pay their respects. In those early days, Daley would rush off like a bridegroom to place himself with those he considered to be his betters. He stood at the foot of Congress Street on the lakefront in 1959, for example, visibly nervous as Queen Elizabeth and Prince Philip stepped off their royal barge. Slowly, though, his self-confidence soared, and while it still is his custom to race fifteen miles from his office to stand at the base of a ramp at O'Hare International airport to welcome a Lyndon Johnson or a Richard Nixon or a Gerald Ford or whoever happens to be occupying the White House, when Henry Kissinger, presidential emissary to China and Russia, visited Chicago in 1973, Daley did not go to greet him—it was Kissinger who went to see Daley.

Daley's improving regard for himself seems to be based on his conclusion that if he is not more important than anyone, he is more important than most. It is with smug little grins that the Democratic Machine people who work in Chicago's City Hall observe that the mayor is sort of like the pope when it comes to making distinguished visitors comfortable. When astronauts who had been to the moon were summoned to Chicago to be paraded and dined and to receive from His Honor the Mayor silver medals of honorary citizenship, the City Hall workers accepted all this with a shrug that said, "The Mayor is being pretty good to those guys."

In his elegant fifth-floor-office digs, where Daley sits with the self-confidence of a Benito Mussolini in his $500 House of Duro suits, it goes without saying that the visitor must mind his manners, no matter how exalted he may think himself to be. If, say, his City Council leader, Alderman Keane—before his conviction—came in to seek remission of late penalties that confronted a New York construction firm, Keane's law client, for falling behind schedule on the building of Chicago's $100,000,000 water filtration plant, or for being woefully tardy in completing its multimillion-dollar contracts at O'Hare airport, it was understood that Keane was approaching the throne as a supplicant and not as a man of political power who is demanding something.

Alderman Keane often figured in matters of importance

that were resolved by decision of the mayor. For example, together with a wheeler-dealer named Bernard Feinberg, Keane had an interest in privately acquiring title to parcels of real estate in a two-block long site at the western edge of the downtown area. It was on this site that Sears, Roebuck proposed to build a 110-story, 1,450-foot headquarters building, the tallest structure on earth and, with over four million square feet of floor space, the largest commercial building in the world. Feinberg was the front man for the real estate deal, and Keane was his clout, having the ability to get the necessary permits through the City Council. Yet there was a hitch in the Sears plan: the two-block strip was bisected by Quincy Street, which dead-ended at the Chicago River. Sears's problem was to buy title from the city of this one block of a downtown thoroughfare—and even in Chicago, arranging that can get a little sticky, this being particularly true in the Sears case by virtue of the possibility that Union Station, which stood across the river from Quincy Street, might eventually be torn down, in which case a bridge might be built at Quincy to carry traffic in and out of the glutted downtown area.

Gordon M. Metcalf, board chairman of Sears, Roebuck, was granted an audience with His Honor the Mayor to inform him of the great plan and to initiate negotiations for the purchase of 21,271 square feet of Quincy. Naturally, Metcalf hastened to assure Daley, Sears was prepared to offer the city a fair price for a takeover that would forever foreclose the possibility that Quincy could once again be an honest-to-God street, with a bridge over the river, easing traffic congestion. Also, Metcalf argued, Sears would create a vast number of jobs in the construction of its black monument, the cost of the thing bottoming out at closer to $250,000,000 than the $100,000,000 Sears had planned to spend on it, and locating the world's tallest building in Chicago was undeniably a vote of confidence in the future of the city.

Sitting there in his elegant leather chair, Daley pondered the proposition as an ecclesiastic might weigh a new interpretation of dogmatic theology. Holding his chin in the soft palm of his left hand, as he always does when there is a decision to make, rubbing his nose with his index finger, fondling his wattles, Daley looked deliberative as the board chairman of the world's largest store talked on. Metcalf unveiled for Daley a miniature conception of the proposed world's tallest building, talking all the while about the merits of this unique piece of merchandise. Finally, Daley said, "I don't think we'll have any problem. I think it will be a great thing for the city—havin' the biggest buildin' in the world. You go ahead with the plannin'; we'll help you."

The ordinance was drawn by Corporation Counsel Raymond F. Simon, a Bridgeport boy, and sailed right through the City Council Committee on Streets and Alleys —the deal downgraded by Chairman Harry L. Sain of the Twenty-seventh as simply "the alley them Sears-Roebucks want from the city." Without the imprimatur of His Honor the Mayor, this deal would have been dumped into the Rules Committee, the bottomless pit into which all anti-administration measures in Chicago City Council are cast. Presented to the full council as a mighty architectural prize, giving Chicago—with the John Hancock Center built and the Standard Oil Building already under construction—three of the five tallest structures on earth, there was no dissent when the ordinance was presented for vote. Bernard Feinberg, Keane's partner in real estate, was said to have been seated in the gallery of council chambers on this historic day; if so, he must have smiled at the successful completion of a very big deal.

You could drop the matter of how Chicago provided space for the world's tallest building right there, but there are other interesting disclosures to be made of how such deals as this have been worked out during Daley's twenty-year reign. The Daley administration gave Sears a list price of $130 per square foot, but as happens not uncommonly, there was a substantial but hidden discount. The U.S. District Attorney's office, which secured all of the documentation in connection with other real estate ventures of Feinberg and Keane, pondered the evidence in the suspicion that there was something kinky about the sale of one block of Quincy Street to Sears, Roebuck—and never did figure out where the discount was. Warren Skoning, vice president in real estate for Sears, might have thrown the federal people off their game with a remark that: "This certainly isn't any bargain basement deal." Yet, the facts are that it certainly was. The price of $130 per square foot was about $40 over the sale price of much less valuable streets and alleys, but in selling the block of Quincy Street to Sears at a price of $2,767,000, the city agreed to absorb the $1,122,000 cost of relocating the water and sewer lines beneath the street—and this cut the cost per square foot from $130 to $77, which was indeed a bargain basement price.

Gray cat aldermen such as Harry Sain were sorely aggrieved that they had to forego an opportunity to put the squeeze on Sears, Roebuck. With the Sears people petitioning for purchase of a city block of street on the grounds that they could not erect the tallest building in the world if they didn't get it, the merchandising firm was vulnerable to a shakedown. There was no way, however, in which leverage could be applied to Sears—not with Board Chairman Metcalf having gone directly to Mayor Daley, Chicago's ultimate clout.

Making deals at City Hall is part of the way of life in Chicago. Appealing to the good offices of the mayor, however, is rather like a prominent person's accepting total immunity from prosecution in return for testifying for the government in a criminal matter. There is no need to seek Daley's help if your proposition is unassailable, any more than there is need for a man who is not implicated in a criminal matter to accept total immunity in return for his damaging testimony against others. Families and business firms of integrity, jealous of their good reputations, eschew seeking special consideration from City Hall—preferring to pay the going price for what they want, rather than incur the risk of bringing suspicion upon themselves. When, after Sears had made its deal, for example, the Joseph P. Kennedy Foundation wanted to get title to a chunk of real estate that had lain fallow for a hundred years, the Kennedy people did not seek special favor from His Honor the Mayor; they simply put the matter in the hands of a prestigious, old-line legal firm, Wilson & McIlvaine, which "J.P." had personally selected years before to handle his real estate, and went through all the normal channels.

There is not a crumb of evidence in possession of the federal people who carefully scrutinized the details of the Sears deal that Mayor Daley received anything more than a letter of thanks from Chairman Metcalf. Of course, His

Honor the Mayor might possibly have accepted delivery at his home on South Lowe of some token of Sears, Roebuck's esteem. The demised chairman of Radio Corporation of America, General David Sarnoff (you get a clue as to what motivates Daley when you know that he boasted to members of his inner circle of his friendly relationship with Sarnoff; all his life, Daley has striven to attain status with the high and the mighty) once sent Daley with his compliments the most elaborate of RCA color television sets, for example. It is usually enough though, for Daley, the Godfather of Chicago, to know that when he has a favor of his own to ask of Sears at some time in the future, he will probably get a ready hearing. Already one can be sure that Sears executives have individually contributed to such causes as the Bi-Partisan Citizens Committee for the Re-Election of Mayor Daley—an amorphous adoration society that surfaces every four years in full-page newspaper advertisements that list columns and columns of influential people who are happy to declare their allegiance to The Greatest Mayor Chicago Ever Had.

As Lincoln Steffens found, big business in Chicago constantly rubs shoulders with Chicago politicians, and Daley in his career as mayor has seen acceptance by the business community as a useful means to increasing his political power. But however much he rubs shoulders with the business, industry, and society folks, Daley has never for an instant forgotten that it was politics, benchmarked in his 1955 victories over Kennelly and Merriam, that brought him into contact with those who rule the nonpolitical areas of influence in Chicago, and that politics, in whatever arena it is played, is the name of every game in town.

Thus, as Daley played out the 1955 calendar year as mayor and headed into his first real test as Democratic boss in the presidential year of 1956, "real" politics is what took up his interest. In the first place, the deck was stacked against Daley. First of all, the Republicans had the incumbent Dwight D. Eisenhower, a so-so politician but an invincible vote getter, at the head of their ticket, while all the Democrats had was a retreaded Adlai E. Stevenson, who had been flattened by the general in 1952. Second, the Republicans had an incumbent and a popular governor, William G. Stratton, who had the additional advantage of being well fixed with campaign money by reason of the $431,000,000 toll road he had launched (some of the contractor profits spilling over into the state GOP coffers). Third, the Republicans had a trusted, dashing downstater, Orville Hodge, the most popular candidate for state office that the Republicans had ever had, running for another term as auditor. A fourth barb in Daley's crown of thorns was the arrogant announcement of his erstwhile friend and now bitter detractor, Benjamin S. Adamowski, that he would run as the Republican party candidate for state's attorney of Cook County. In sum, Daley's prospects in 1956 were dismal.

The Republican state secretary of state was a man named Charles F. Carpentier, and James A. Ronan, the Democrats' state chairman, had a hunch that Michael J. Howlett, well known and well liked downstate, might have a chance to take Carpentier. Ronan, a personal friend of Howlett, argued that Howlett should have an opportunity in what figured to be a losing year to show what kind of a following he had. Daley and his cronies wouldn't hear of it. Howlett was not then, nor was he ever to be, "a Daley man," and while, as we have seen, Daley warmed to Howlett, it has been on Howlett's terms. In 1956 the most Daley would allow was that Howlett could run against the "unbeatable" Hodge.

It was a typical Daley move. He does not do away with those he dislikes; he puts them into impossible situations. In Howlett's case, there was even a personal animus. Daley was uncomfortable in Howlett's presence because, physically, Howlett towered over him. Daley always has preferred to be the center of attention, and he has surrounded himself with subordinates of modest girth and height. There is no question, in short, that Howlett's assignment was intended to be a one-way ticket to political oblivion. (It has likewise proven to be the peg on which the numerous political scandals of the past two decades can be hung.)

The most conspicuous thing about Orville Hodge was his Cadillac limousine, with its official license plate, "4," which was always parked at the fire plug on Walton Place at the Drake hotel. It was not altogether a secret that Orv, a hail-fellow-well-met man, was shacked up on a steady basis with a young woman who masqueraded as an interior decorator. Hodge, a flashy, hard-drinking man who spent money as if he thought he would catch a contagious disease if he hung onto it, was widely rumored to be a man of wealth; certainly, he grandly declined to accept more than token campaign contributions from any of the Republican party organizations in the 102 counties of Illinois. Too, there was not the slightest sign that he ever put the arm on contractors or business people. Most news people, many of whom accepted gifts from Orville, regarded him as a "great guy"; at every fund-raising dinner that he attended, bottles of liquor would magically appear on the press tables, "Compliments State Auditor Hodge." A special kind of magic attended him when he was a candidate for office; the Republicans in Illinois never had a vote-getter to rival him. By 1956, it was generally conceded that Hodge could push Governor Stratton out of office and take the job for himself—and that the only reason he did not do so was that, well, he was "just too nice a guy."

After looking him over carefully, with an expert's eye for the brush strokes, Mike Howlett confided to a reporter: "Hodge is a thief." Proving that, however, was something else—yet Howlett, on his own at first, and later with the reluctant help of only the *Chicago Daily News,* finally came up with evidence that resulted in conviction for embezzlement of Hodge, his administrative aide, and the head of a minor Chicago bank at which Hodge converted stacks of state vouchers into bundles of cash.

Having caught so large a fish as this, one might think that Michael J. Howlett would have been hailed by Daley and the other Democrats as a party hero. Something approximating the opposite of that was his reward. Whatever differences there might be among politicians of opposing affiliation, they are rather like rival saloonkeepers who share an apprehension when the waitresses in one place are unexpectedly arrested on charges of solicitation; there is a bit of there-but-for-the-grace-of-God-go-I when a politician is nailed to the wall for corruption. Inexplicably, a pair of downstate Democrats of power—Paul Powell and Joseph E. Knight—put their spiritual arms around the imprisoned Orville Hodge. Powell and Knight eventually became famous in their own ways. Powell's notoriety was posthumous, resulting from the finding of $800,000 in shoeboxes in a closet of his suite in a Springfield hotel. Knight was indicted with former Governor Kerner in the racetrack stock case but became fatally ill and escaped trial.

In Chicago, meanwhile, news of the Hodge scandal competed with the Democratic National Convention for space on the front pages. Daley benefited from the dull proceedings when the nomination of Adlai E. Stevenson for a second and hopeless shot at the presidency, no one else wanting it, brought a flicker of national attention to the mayor of Chicago, chairman of the Illinois delegation. With the pro forma roll call over, Daley turned to National Committeeman Jacob M. Arvey, at his side, and crisply ordered: "Go get him." Obediently, but with a look of wonderment at being so brusquely treated by a man he had helped to attain power, Arvey walked off to the nearby Stock Yards Inn, where the candidate was waiting, and escorted Stevenson into the International Amphitheatre.

There was one seat vacant in the Illinois delegation. Cook County Treasurer Herbert C. Paschen, Daley's candidate for governor, had abruptly departed. In the wash of Howlett's discovery that the fashionable Orville Hodge wore dirty underwear, reporters had gone poking into all corners of prominent politicians' financial affairs, and it was determined that Paschen, as did many other office holders, had maintained what is called a "flower fund" in his office. A flower fund, which can range, say, from $10,000 to $25,000, is the source of money to provide floral pieces at wakes and weddings and to finance other obligations that fall upon the office or its personnel. Paschen's gaffe was that he had borrowed several thousand dollars from the fund to help pay for a trip to Europe; there was a record of his loan, and the files contained an IOU.

In the climate that had been created by the Hodge affair, Paschen's naiveté had so infuriated Richard J. Daley, who above all detests mistakes, that he had arbitrarily dumped Paschen. When word of this had leaked to the press, reporters hit the floor of the convention hall to ask Daley for confirmation. With Paschen seated only three chairs away, utterly unaware that he was being sacked as Daley's candidate for governor, Daley said, yes, it was true. The Democrats would be running someone else.

This was the third week of August 1956. It was only one month since Orville Hodge, beaten to the wall by waves of incriminating evidence, had conceded that virtually every charge that had been brought against him was true. It was only one week since candidate Paschen had declared righteously: "The ouster of Orville Hodge will not end the need for a special legislative session to investigate state government generally." It was no surprise, therefore, that Paschen was stunned by the turn of events. When reporters confronted him, immediately after talking to Daley, and asked him to comment, "It can't be true," he said. Assured that Daley said it was true, Paschen got up and walked to where Daley sat and said, his tone of voice indicating he could not believe that he had been betrayed: "Dick, what the hell is there to this thing the reporters are saying?"

Calmly, looking straight ahead, Daley replied: "What did you expect?"

There is a saying in Chicago that when an organization man is obliterated nobody hits like Richard J. Daley. There is a lot of truth in that.

Stevenson's name had been placed in nomination by a 38-year-old senator from Massachusetts, John F. Kennedy. Daley had briefly been in this young man's company and liked his manner and looks. Perhaps Senator Kennedy's personal dream came through to Daley when, in asking the delegates to nominate Stevenson, the young man had said: "I ask you, therefore, to think beyond the balloting of tonight and tomorrow—to think beyond even the election in November. . . ." Whatever "thinking beyond" Senator Kennedy had instilled in Daley, when the fight began for the vice-presidential nomination, Daley swung most of the sixty-four Illinois votes behind Kennedy. The downstate delegates—notably Scott Lucas, the defrocked majority leader of the U.S. Senate; Speaker of the Illinois House Paul Powell; and Joseph E. Knight, a wheeler-dealer who, like Powell, always seemed to have a cushy deal of some kind in the works—were for Harry Truman's man, Senator Stuart Symington of Missouri. In any case, Lucas, Powell, and Knight instinctively disliked young Kennedy and bluntly told Daley that they would not vote for him— their opposition extending, in fact, into the convention of 1960, when the downstaters resisted Daley's entreaties to make the Illinois vote for Jack Kennedy unanimous. In 1956, there was another bit of frustration for Daley in the vice-presidential fight: Senator Paul H. Douglas, who had, as an ex-officio delegate, one-half of a vote, insisted upon casting it for his colleague, Tennessee Senator Estes Kefauver, a man who was anathema to the Democrats of Chicago after his crime investigating committee had destroyed them in 1950.

"In the most dramatic convention balloting in the memory of living men," wrote Walter Trohan, chief of the *Chicago Tribune*'s staff, in the next morning's paper, "Estes Kefauver of Tennessee late yesterday won the Democrats' vice-presidential nomination." In the first of two roll calls, Kennedy was within nine votes of being nominated. Then, unexpectedly, some of his delegates defected. On the second ballot, it was Kefauver 775½, Kennedy 589, with a few scattered votes for favorite sons. Senator Kennedy smiled and asked the convention to make the Kefauver vote unanimous. Crestfallen, unaware that he had barely avoided a political calamity, Mayor Daley had his automatic response when reporters talked to him. "The contest for vice-president shows the vigor and vitality of the Democratic party."

Only later, when Joseph P. Kennedy came home from Paris, where he grimly had been keeping an eye on what was happening at the convention in Chicago, was Daley told how close he had come to jeopardizing young Jack's political future—J.P. raising quite a bit of hell with Daley over the stupidity of entangling Jack in the rope of the millstone that was tied to Stevenson's neck. On the testimony of a Merchants and Manufacturers Club captain, a Guatemalan who, alone, was entrusted to serve lunch to Daley and J.P. in a private office of Kennedy's Merchandise Mart, His Honor the Mayor had lamely explained to the ambassador that his intention, in pressing for the vice-presidential nomination, was to get young Jack a little bit of exposure for the future. In his gratuitous report to this reporter, the Guatemalan, when he came down with the dishes, said: "All the talking was, well, about the *next* time and mucho friendly; you could tell, though, it was like the father talking to the son, the father being wiser about these things. You understand?"

Sure, anybody could understand. Joe Kennedy was simply telling the mayor of Chicago that there was no room for further bonehead plays—if they were going to put Jack in the White House in 1960.

CHAPTER 9

King-Maker

"Be of good cheer and remember, my dear friends, what a wise man said—'A merry heart doeth good like a medicine, but a broken spirit dryeth the bones.'"
—*Adlai E. Stevenson, concession speech, Conrad Hilton Hotel, Chicago, November 6, 1956*

The Democratic campaign of 1956 began on a high note at Santa Fe, New Mexico, and went downhill thereafter. The Democratic leadership, recognizing that the Stevenson-Kefauver ticket faced an impossible task of defeating President Eisenhower, decided that the wisest course was to salvage the state and county Democratic candidates in various parts of the nation.

In Chicago, Mayor Daley was outwardly the soul of optimism—but his intelligence from the ward committeemen was that it would take some doing to carry the city for Stevenson-Kefauver. In Chicago, the Democrats were courting disaster, and Daley knew it—but all he could do was keep slugging, hoping for the best.

Daley held his celebrated torchlight parade for the Democratic presidential candidate, thousands of ward organization people obligated to glut the Madison Street route of the motorcade from downtown Chicago to the Chicago Stadium, two and a half miles to the west, the captive cheering sections waving flags and shouting encouragement to a beaming Adlai Stevenson. The enthusiasm was a sham; this was a candidate the party workers did not like and—worse than that—there was hardly anyone who thought he had the slimmest chance of winning. At the Stadium, His Honor the Mayor shouted an introduction of the party's choice, and then Stevenson, facing the mob of faithless partisans like a gallows bird who clings to the faint hope that in some miraculous way he will avoid getting hanged, made his usual high-minded speech that, come Tuesday, the common sense of the American people would prevail.

Never, in Illinois, has a Democratic candidate for president been clobbered as Eisenhower clobbered Stevenson in 1956. For the first time since 1928, when Herbert Hoover defeated Alfred E. Smith on the Roman Catholic religious issue, Chicago turned its back on a Democratic candidate for the nation's highest office. Eisenhower carried the city, despite the best efforts of the Daley Machine, by 42,000 votes. In 1952 Eisenhower had carried Cook County by 16,000 votes; in 1956 his Cook County plurality was a staggering 315,000. Statewide, Eisenhower's plurality was 847,000, with more than 4,000,000 votes cast. Everett Dirksen won reelection to the U.S. Senate by a margin of 350,000. Governor Stratton, with the Orville Hodge scandal chasing him, squeaked by Judge Richard B. Austin, who, rumor had it, was a Daley set-up candidate—Stratton was to get elected and Daley was to get much-needed tax money for Chicago—with an advantage of 37,000 (which works out to less than 1 percent of the votes cast, giving substance to the belief that the judge had been "trimmed," as the professionals say when they fail to make a sincere effort for a man on their own ticket).

Objective study of the 1956 election returns rebuts the suspicion that Daley was party to a deal with Stratton. Judge Austin was the victim, not of a sellout by Daley, but rather of President Eisenhower's enormous popularity over the weak Adlai E. Stevenson. The Daley Machine managed to scrape up a plurality for Austin of 265,000—the candidate for governor running more than 300,000 ahead of presidential candidate Stevenson in the city. Having been put in the race by Daley as a substitute candidate when there was little time remaining to mount a downstate campaign and being virtually a stranger to the voters living outside of Cook County, Austin had nonetheless come within 37,000 votes of beating a Republican governor who was generally suspected of concealing inside information on the Orville Hodge scandal. Further evidence that Daley had made a good effort for Austin can be deduced from a comparison of his vote with that of other Democratic candidates in the 1956 disaster.

Although it was Mike Howlett who had exposed Hodge, Howlett's plurality in Chicago was a meager 203,000 over Hodge's relatively unknown replacement for state auditor of public accounts. All other Democratic candidates for state office in 1956—secretary of state, state treasurer, attorney general—and even most Democratic candidates in Cook County, the Daley candidate for coroner for example, ran more poorly than Mike Howlett. The evidence that the Democrats had taken a beating in the first general election that Daley had responsibility for is overwhelming. Not even his critics in the organization, however, considered it to be Daley's fault that the party had taken such a whipping; defeat, they believed, had been unavoidable—with Eisenhower getting a mammoth vote, dragging the lesser lights of the Republican ticket to victory that they did not particularly deserve.

Richard J. Daley said only: "It isn't the first time we lost." Stephen Mitchell, the former national chairman of the Democratic party, blamed Daley's ineptitude for Judge Austin's defeat by Stratton, an opinion that Austin, since made a federal judge, shared. The worst of Daley's troubles was that his arch-enemy Ben Adamowski, Republican candidate for Cook County state's attorney, wiped the floor with the regular Democratic opponent and the incumbent state's attorney, "Judge" John Gutknecht, who happened also to be the brother-in-law of Henry Crown. Adamowski ran virtually as well as President Eisenhower in both Chicago and the suburbs of Cook County. Somewhere down the track, Daley knew, his erstwhile pal Adamowski would be waiting to take him on in a fight for control of the city. But both men were aware that the time was not now.

The bad news for the Democrats in the presidential election of 1956 was that Eisenhower had swept forty-one of the forty-eight states. The good news was that the Democrats had control of Congress. The best news was that they wouldn't have to run against Eisenhower in 1960. Meanwhile, with four years to go, the big city bosses drew back from potential candidates who would be circulating,

testing the ground, as the second prosaic term of Dwight
D. Eisenhower ran its course. Stevenson, Senator Hubert
Humphrey, Senator Lyndon B. Johnson, Senator Estes
Kefauver—all made the rounds. In Chicago, each got a
cordial reception at City Hall, but if he did not know the
meaning of noncommittal when he hit town, he surely had
reason to know it when he left.

National politics did not concern Chicago in the late
1950s. It was only the quality of government Chicago was
getting that mattered. And much to its surprise, the establishment increasingly found itself placing quixotic faith
in the proposition that Daley was working hard at being
a good mayor. No doubt it helped La Salle Street's trust
in him to hear reports that he began each day at mass; no
one could remember when it was that Chicago had had a
mayor who prayed.

The growing affinity was not without strain, however.
For example, in 1958, the business community chartered
a jet and flew Mayor Daley up to Detroit, for an exchange
of views on big city problems. That was fine. But at a
civic luncheon in Detroit, John S. Knight, publisher of the
Chicago Daily News, introduced Daley with a joking reference to the fact that the *Daily News* had been an anti-
Daley newspaper in his mayoralty campaign. Instead of
passing off the remark as lightly as it had been intended,
Daley made something of a fool of himself with uncompli-
mentary remarks about the *Chicago Daily News.*

But such conflicts grew increasingly infrequent. In 1959,
in fact, Daley didn't require much support from anyone.
He was too popular to be beaten.

Not that everything was fine—on the contrary. But the
things that mattered were fine. Thus, although crime was
on the increase, the statistics located half of it in the five
police districts in the South and West Side ghettos, and
no one took much notice of that. State's Attorney Adamowski had raised a storm over a chronic policy of ticket-
fixing in the Democratically controlled traffic court, the
venerable court clerk, Joe Gill, taking the heat on that,
but nothing much came of it. The state's attorney complained that most of the important cases in criminal court
were being defended by five particular attorneys and tried,
almost exclusively, by a few judges. One such judge, Judge
Joseph A. Pope, who reputedly served at the pleasure of

the crime syndicate's boss of Chicago's First Ward, presided at approximately half of the big cases, and the defense ran up an impressive score of acquittals in his court.

More important to Chicago's establishment was the architectural reawakening that was occurring in Chicago. Set off in Mayor Kennelly's second term by construction at Randolph and Michigan of the Prudential Insurance Building, the boom brought a flood of jobs for Daley's friends in the building trades and money for traditionally Republican interests. Crown's Material Service trucks were weighing down the pavement of Chicago streets with their loads of ready-mixed cement, and Crown was always pressing for an okay to haul heavier loads in bigger trucks. Spending was on the increase in Chicago as Mayor Daley's payroll increased, and the Civic Federation of Chicago, the taxpayers' watchdog, had to be content to bay at the moon.

There was hardly a civic function at which Daley did not appear, and people seemed to draw reassurance from the frequent sights that it got of him. There was some clucking of disapproval over the year-by-year rise in Daley's budget and the gradual increase of real estate taxation to cover it, but, on balance, business was good, unemployment was moderate—except for the last-hired, first-fired blacks—and, while there was a flickering of scandal in the police department and a spectacular gangland murder or two, Richard J. Daley was proving to be a quite acceptable mayor.

So respectable, in fact, that the Republicans couldn't find a candidate to run against him in 1959, and their county chairman, Timothy Sheehan, had to make the race. The results were a calamity for the Republicans—Daley defeating Sheehan 778,612 to 311,940 for a plurality of 466,672. By way of explaining what had happened to him, Sheehan said that Republican business people had walked right past him to contribute their names and money to Daley's campaign. Also, the defeated Republican candidate said remorsefully, there had been no scandals of any importance in Daley's first term.

With his reelection out of the way, his militant enemy, Frank Keenan, in prison on a conviction for nonpayment of taxes on income derived from shakedowns as Cook County assessor, and with dreams of political grandeur dancing in his 56-year-old head, Richard J. Daley had reason to wonder what other wonderful things life had in store for him. He was flattered to get periodic phone calls from Ambassador Joseph P. Kennedy and delighted to scratch his engagement calendar and hustle over to the Merchandise Mart for a private lunch with Kennedy when it suited J.P. to fly into Chicago. Indeed, it was not altogether a coincidence that J.P.'s son-in-law and manager of his Merchandise Mart, R. Sargent Shriver, was "elected" president of the Chicago Board of Education, doubling as liaison between the man who ran City Hall and the man who owned the world's then largest commercial building.

J.P.'s third son, Robert, proved less popular with Daley than were J.P. and John F. As counsel of the U.S. Senate rackets investigating subcommittee, chaired by John L. McClellan, Robert Kennedy was making a few aggravating waves for Daley, who had to suffer the petulant complaints of labor leaders, by his grilling of crime syndicate figures about their infiltration of such Chicago unions as the taxicab drivers, the garbage collectors, the barbers, the bartenders, and restaurant workers. Carefully, Daley suggested to J.P. that Bobby's persistent interrogations for the Senate select committee had produced nothing more than new national records in the taking of the Fifth Amendment, but the old man brushed aside His Honor's complaint with a laugh.

J.P. could laugh, but if he figured that Bobby wasn't doing any great harm in baiting the likes of Joey Glimco, a crime syndicate man and pal of Jimmy Hoffa of the Teamsters, into hours of taking the Fifth, Chicago Democrats began to see the Kennedys as people who made up their own rules, saying to hell with anyone who did not approve.

There were signs, indeed, that political sentiment in Chicago was running heavily against Daley's infatuation with the Kennedys. Otherwise Daley's new finance chairman, Alderman Tom Keane, would hardly have had the temerity to tell the mayor that the continual investigation of Chicago unions that had been taken captive by the syndicate was bad for the reputation of the city. Of course, Keane did have sort of a working interest in this matter; an attorney of note, or at least of great influence, Keane had been retained by the Chicago Restaurant Association, a trade group that had endured much violence and intimidation. One of Keane's predecessors had been an old syndicate hand named Abe Teitelbaum, the former attorney of Al Capone. In fact, it was the employment of Teitelbaum by the association that had put an end to the restaurant window-smashing and general harassment that had plagued association members. Likewise, when Abe Teitelbaum ran out of magic and somebody started putting the torch to Chicago eating places, including some expensive ones, the Chicago Restaurant Association found it wise to hire Anthony V. Champagne, attorney for Sam ("Mooney") Giancana, heir apparent to the leadership of the Chicago mob, as its labor relations counsel, and a Capone gangster named Sam English as assistant labor relations expert.

Alderman Keane, in short, had an intriguing client, and he no doubt was displeased that young Bobby Kennedy was making life miserable for friends of people highly placed in the Chicago Restaurant Association. Yet Keane and his friends, though vocal, could do nothing. Though Daley deplores investigative tactics that hint of something scandalous going on in his city, his concern over Bobby's sniffing at syndicate-related matters was restricted to the effect it might have on the presidential hopes of brother Jack.

Alderman Charles H. Weber was openly disparaging of the Kennedys. Weber was a long-time pal of such syndicate people as Murray Humphreys, who influenced Charlie Weber to take a negative view of all Kennedys, supplying him with gossip on the mating habits of J.P. and his clan, the syndicate keeping a john-book on what famous people are sleeping with whom. Weber, in fact, even floated a trial balloon in 1960 for the presidential candidacy of Lyndon B. Johnson, printing 80,000 copies of his local newspaper, the 3,000-copy-circulation *Lake View Independent*, and distributing them as widely as possible.

Mayor Daley never acknowledged Weber's activities, and so long as Daley stood firm for Kennedy, Hy Raskin, the former vice-chairman of the Democratic National Committee and the only true professional in the Kennedy camp, only grinned when he heard what crazy Charlie Weber was doing. Hy Raskin's eyes did not wander from the target, and so long as Dick Daley stood firm, with most of the sixty-nine Illinois votes locked up, Raskin was not about to be disturbed by any Weber theatrics.

Joseph P. Kennedy had personally recruited Hy Raskin early in 1960. A Chicagoan, Raskin had a solid political background; he had begun, virtually as a kid, ringing doorbells for an aldermanic candidate named P. J. Cullerton, in the far northwest side of Chicago; he had been identified with Jake Arvey; he had been deputy director of the Regional Office of Price Stabilization under Mike Howlett, succeeding to the directorship when Mike stepped out; he was an early Adlai Stevenson man who, when Chicago attorney Stephen A. Mitchell surfaced as Stevenson's campaign manager, was Mitchell's right arm. When Mitchell became national chairman of the party, Raskin became Number Two. When Paul Butler took over the chairmanship, Raskin stayed on as Number Two. He knew everybody, and he had no political enemies. With it all, Raskin was an attorney-at-law, sharing offices in Chicago's Board of Trade Building with Steve Mitchell.

Joseph P. Kennedy recognized that this was the backroom man that he had to have if Jack was to be nominated and elected. And it is a chronic weakness of all the books that have been written about the emergence of John F. Kennedy that the vital role played by Hyman B. Raskin is grossly underplayed or totally ignored. It was Hy Raskin who had dropped in on old Democratic friends everywhere, using the soft sell that it would have to be Jack Kennedy at the convention or they would never make it in November, cashing in the chits he held for past favors, picking up a few delegates here, the promise of a few delegates there. The payoff came in the Los Angeles Arena on the night of Wednesday, July 13, 1960, when—on the first ballot—the forty-three-year-old John F. Kennedy was nominated. There had been some horrific moments. The Lyndon B. Johnson people, driven by Speaker of the House Sam Rayburn, had put the whip to many of the delegates the Kennedy people were depending on. Then Adlai Stevenson created near-panic in the Kennedy camp in a last-minute, nearly hysterical effort to win the nomination for the third time.

Of the Illinois delegation, all but an inconsequential few were solid Daley, and, therefore, Kennedy, delegates, and they showed nothing but contempt for Stevenson. Daley was adamant. On several occasions, when the private telephone lines at the Illinois standard brought calls from influential people who wanted to plead Adlai's cause, Daley would not take the calls. When a reporter asked Daley if, on the roll call, he didn't plan to toss a respectable number of votes to Stevenson—just to make things look good —Daley snapped off a reply that if Stevenson had planned to be a candidate, why hadn't he said so? Jake Arvey, seated near Daley, winced.

When, finally, the Stevenson demonstrators were allowed into the convention and Stevenson himself appeared, looking frightened as a crush of security guards literally pushed him to his seat alongside Daley—the walls echoing with curses and yells and cries of "We want Adlai!"—Daley ignored his former benefactor, and Stevenson, after trying vainly to engage Daley in conversation, aware perhaps that the television cameras were concentrated on him, struggled to look cheerful in the face of certain knowledge that he was through.

The timing was impeccable. Daley even called the correct delegate count. Kennedy was nominated.

Alderman Charles H. Weber remained unhappy at Daley's Kennedy liaison, and feeling that he was not alone, after the Democratic convention he decided to invite vice-presidential candidate Lyndon Johnson to be the guest of honor at the annual Forty-fifth Ward kid's party at Riverview Amusement Park. It was an entirely typical scheme, with extra flourishes. For example, Weber's letter of invitation was typed by his "girl in Daley's office," a plant who reported on Daley to Weber—Weber had someone planted in all important offices.

But, unfortunately, Weber never lived to find out how Daley reacted or if Johnson would have accepted. A few days later, he and his wife died, under highly suspicious circumstances, his letter unmailed.

The fact is that the Kennedys were not popular among Chicago politicians and Weber knew this. The Kennedys were not "our kind of people"—in the judgment of many of the Chicago pros. Like him or not, though, Daley cracked the whip with a fury they had never seen before —and if, as is generally believed, the election of John F. Kennedy tottered on the question of whether Richard J.

Daley could deliver the electoral votes of Illinois, Daley delivered. Just barely, but sufficiently.

There is no doubt that Kennedy's success in 1960, especially outside Illinois, was in great measure his own doing. For example, he could not have won without the electoral votes of Texas; nor could he have won Texas, despite the strength he drew from Lyndon B. Johnson, if he had not—in defiance of the advice of his old man—courageously carried the religious issue into Texas, defusing his Roman Catholicism in full view of anti-papist clergymen who had gathered in a state convocation.

The fact is, however, Kennedy *needed* Illinois' electoral votes, and given his unpopularity in the Illinois Democratic stronghold, Chicago, the role played by Daley was crucial.

Daley's special talents, though not widely recognized as such, are his extraordinary abilities in organization and compromise, the special ability he has to bring people of divergent points of view together in common cause. To Daley the fundamentals of running a city involve winning elections—and winning elections demands working at the precinct level to place the man of his choice in the White House. And this is how Daley contrived the election of Senator Kennedy. In this case, however, Daley also resorted to the use of some unprecedented strategems on election day. The combination—Daley's precinct level effort and his electoral cunning—was sufficient to give Kennedy the Illinois victory he needed.

An analysis of election results is always suspect, or should be. Satan could make a good case for the joys of paradise if it suited his purposes to do so. A vital significance does attach, however, to Kennedy's victory in Illinois. For one thing, an amazingly high percentage of the eligible voters in Chicago, 89.3 percent, cast ballots in the election of November 8, 1960, compared to the mediocre 64.55 percent nationally. Many Democrats, repelled by the alternatives of voting for a Roman Catholic or voting for a Republican, refused to vote for either.

Thus, in Chicago, Daley had to overcome religious prejudice toward Kennedy as well as ward boss indifference to pile up the 456,312-vote plurality—nearly four times Kennedy's national plurality. Yet Daley also was acutely aware that the vote would go heavily against Kennedy in an overwhelming number of downstate counties and that he therefore would have to squeeze every possible vote out of Chicago if his man was to have a chance of carrying the state.

In only one area—but an important area—was the Kennedy name an advantage to Daley in Chicago: the black vote. Blacks held Kennedy in high regard, certainly higher than they have ever held Daley, who was and is rightly seen largely as a white Horatius at the racial bridge. The young senator had given evidence that he had genuine empathy for blacks, making a deep impression upon them for example, with a spontaneous phone call to Mrs. Martin Luther King, Jr., promising his support, when her well-known husband had been jailed during the campaign for having had the audacity to ask for something to eat in an Atlanta, Georgia, restaurant.

In 1960, Congressman Dawson's five ghetto wards alone produced a plurality for Kennedy of 81,554, while the best that Dawson had been able to do for Daley, when the Democratic Machine was desperate for votes in 1955, was a plurality of 49,363.

Yet the black vote alone did not get Kennedy out of Chicago with his plurality. Subtracting the black plurality from the total Chicago plurality, one is left with 374,758, and therein lies the story of the political miracle that Daley performed on that election day. Daley's accomplishment for Kennedy—surpassing anything he has ever been able to do for himself—becomes awesome when you study the charts and discover that, in this election, the Machine could not get by on the pluralities that pertained in the Machine's automatic eleven wards.

As it happened, the eleven dependable wards gave Kennedy a plurality of 168,611—almost 44,000 more than they were able to produce for Daley in 1955—yet this fantastic advantage would not have been enough. Daley had to come up with a far greater plurality if his man was going to take Illinois, and the additional votes—287,701 as it turned out—had to come from the thirty-nine other wards, few of which were trained to jump through the hoop on orders from Democratic headquarters. How, then, did Daley manage to pile up a plurality of 456,312 for Kennedy—and what did he do with it when he got it?

As a starting point, Daley had ample intelligence, well in advance, of how desperate Kennedy's situation would be in Illinois on election day. It is standard political practice in the best-run centers of both Democratic and Republican strength for those in charge to make continuous, objective samplings of voter sentiment, and Daley's polls, while secret, are said to be accurate to a degree that would shame Dr. Gallup, Lou Harris, or any of the professionals in this field. Adding to his intelligence, giving him an advantage over the professional poll-takers, Daley constantly receives from his committeemen the accurate reports of their precinct captains. Daley reduced the problem to the equation of how much damage Kennedy would suffer outside Chicago and how big a vote he would need in Chicago to recover from it. In his final tabulations, checking over the projected vote of each of the 102 counties and coming down finally to a bottom line of what the cumulative vote for Nixon was almost certain to be, Daley realized that he would have to provide Kennedy with an edge of at least 400,000 in Chicago and that a plurality of 450,000 was probably what it would take to save Illinois for his candidate.

At no time, in the many elections that Daley had run since the first one in 1954, had the Democratic ward bosses been subjected to the pressure he applied for Jack Kennedy. The leverage a political boss can exert on his lieutenants is directly in ratio to the patronage and other benefits that he can grant or withhold from them. And in Chicago, Daley controlled, absolutely, all such matters. Indeed, when he had become mayor, as we have seen, he had caused considerable resentment by stripping the ward bosses of many of their customary perquisites. For example, Daley recovered control in the matter of the choice of police captains in their districts, making private deals with department heads, and such small but profitable grafts as the granting of driveway permits. Simultaneously, though, Daley expanded the area of public enrichment where control remained his. For example, he permitted the aldermen and committeemen to enjoy other dubious fringe benefits —autonomous control, for instance, of heavily budgeted City Council committees in which opportunities abound to make a buck in the granting of approval, say, to such franchise matters as might concern utility companies.

Some City Council committees—the committee that deals with local transportation, to cite one, headed by a raspy-voiced, tough old Italian, Alderman Vito Marzullo—rarely hold meetings and serve no visible purpose other than to supply cushy spots on the payroll for such deserving loyalists as Vito's son, William.

The clout that Daley was in a position to exert on behalf of Jack Kennedy is self-evident. In 1974 Marzullo's do-nothing committee had a budget, approved by Daley, of $343,092; and this is but one example of the weapons available to Daley in demanding and getting a superior effort on election day in Vito's Twenty-fifth ward. He used every weapon he had.

For a start, there was not the slightest doubt in the minds of the ward bosses, in advance of the 1960 election, that the man who failed to deliver a massive vote was going to be permanently maimed politically. The theme was to get every conceivable voter registered. Some ward bosses supplemented their lists with the names and addresses of constituents who were long dead or who had never lived, and post-election vote fraud investigations bore evidence that many a ballot was cast for Jack Kennedy in the name of someone in the grave. This is not to say that Daley espoused the practice of vote fraud; he merely let each ward boss understand what was expected of him. The incredible outpouring of registered voters (90 percent of those recorded in Chicago went to the polls) is a rather good indication that Daley's message got through.

On election day, on the third floor of City Hall in the offices of the Chicago Board of Election Commissioners, Chairman Sidney T. Holzman calmly puffed on a stogie as he made his periodic reports of the heavy vote that was being cast—a sampling of one precinct in each of the fifty wards being tabulated after the first hour the polls were open, at noontime, and twice during the afternoon. It is the solemn function of the Chicago Board of Election Commissioners to conduct the election, handing out credentials to the judges in each election precinct, maintaining the integrity of the count and all of that. It was the practice of Chairman Holzman to bristle with indignation at charges that he specialized in running crooked elections. He might have been, as he maintained, a faithful and uncompromised administrator of the election that saw Jack Kennedy pick up in Chicago a most extraordinary volume of votes, but he laughed when Mrs. Richard M. Nixon bitterly remarked later: "If it weren't for an evil, cigar-smoking man in Chicago, Sidney T. Holzman, my husband would have been president of the United States." Holzman, a sardonic little man from the Jake Arvey school, retorted to allegations that the election had been stolen on orders from Daley with a patient comment that that was the most ridiculous accusation he had ever heard—which was powerful retorting, in view of the frequency with which he had heard similar charges over the years.

All the same, never had the Chicago vote swung so unexpectedly, and so heavily, as it did for Kennedy in 1960. Nixon carried only three of the fifty Chicago wards, barely getting by in one of them—the late Alderman Weber's Forty-fifth. Nixon was clobbered in the so-called Independent wards—losing by 11,000 in the University of Chicago's Fifth, by 20,000 in the Tenth, by 13,000 in the Thirteenth. Kennedy's strength showed most breathtakingly in Machine-controlled wards outside the automatic eleven: 14,000 from Daley's Eleventh, 13,000 from the old McDermott-Wagner Fourteenth, 15,000 from Dan Ryan's area, the Seventeenth, 14,000 from Vito Marzullo's Twenty-fifth, and so on. Customarily, the low-income river wards are Democratic, but never before had the vote piled up in such volume as in 1960. The power of the Daley Machine was evident throughout the city, only the two crime syndicate wards, the First and the Twenty-eighth, delivering a low count, fewer votes for Kennedy in 1960, in fact, than they had delivered for Daley in 1955. The Machine interpreted this disappointing performance as a mild rebuke by the syndicate people who had been mercilessly pounded by the presidential candidate's brother, Robert.

Kennedy needed virtually every vote Daley got him. Going out of Chicago with an advantage of 456,312, he lost 137,576 votes to Nixon elsewhere in Cook County, leaving him with a net plurality of 318,736. He lost 309,878 votes downstate, winning in only eight of the other 101 counties of Illinois. And the bottom line gave Kennedy a plurality over Nixon of an almost insignificant 8,858 votes out of a statewide total of 4,657,394. Little wonder, then, that the other side complained bitterly that Nixon had been cheated, although the Daley camp put down the complaint disdainfully.

The Republicans, election chairman Holzman sneered, were crying because their man had lost. Holzman probably was right, but that does not detract from the fact that vote fixing is common in much of Illinois. The point is that vote fraud is not confined to Cook County. Apart from Daley and Holzman, most professional Democrats in Chicago will concede, if you press them on it, that their polling place judges sometimes put their thumbs on the scale when they weigh the votes. But, they claim, their activities are justified by the not preposterous counter-charge that the polling place people in such Republican counties as Du Page, Kane, and Lake are likewise guilty of favoring the home team on the count. The consistent reluctance of Republican clerks in some of these counties to report their returns until after a substantial share of the Chicago vote is in would seem to support the Machine's suspicion that the Republicans are not above rigging their vote-counts to win an office.

Evidence that vote fraud was working both ways in the November 8, 1960, election came about midnight when Senator Paul H. Douglas, appearing on NBC network television, grimly charged that whereas the Cook County returns had been posted, virtually in full, for two hours, few reports had been filed by many of the Republican counties of Illinois.

"I serve warning on you," Senator Douglas declared, wagging his finger at the live cameras, "the federal district attorney has been ordered to investigate immediately the apparent refusal of the clerks in these counties to do their duty and comply with the election laws. Those who are refusing to comply are to be arrested and prosecuted."

It was not a bluff. The senator, running for a third term, had exacted from the district attorney a promise that federal agents would be dispatched immediately to investigate the complaint, making arrests as necessary. Even before the senator and Mike Howlett, his campaign manager, had had a cup of coffee and left the Chicago newsroom, almost complete returns were pouring in from counties that had not previously been heard from. Stealing votes, apparently, is one thing; running the risk of being arrested for it is something else again.

It is probably safe to assume that, in close elections, neither political party is free of deceptive practices. There are polling place judges in both camps who misuse the facts. If suburbanites were appalled at the news that Dawson's ghetto gave Kennedy an advantage of 81,554, was not the Chicago Machine entitled to look askance at the plurality of 101,729 that the Republicans reported for Nixon in Du Page, Kane, and Lake counties?

Both sides cheat; it is simply that the Democrats, having had more practice, are more artful about it. And Daley planned to use every artifice available. Indeed, phase two of his campaign strategy was geared precisely to Republican expectations of Democratic vote manipulation.

The strategy was simple: (1) get out a massive vote; (2) report it quickly. The series of luncheons he had for the Machine's army of precinct captains—with the mayor thundering about the "great victory" that he demanded, blatantly threatening the payrollers that they would be jobless if they failed—made his intentions clear. But that was only part of it. The torchlight parades Daley staged for Lyndon B. Johnson and then John F. Kennedy, emptying City Hall even of charwomen at midday so that everyone could swell the evening throng, were mere preliminaries to what Daley planned to do on election night, when the votes were being counted. It did not concern Daley that Richard M. Nixon was a dirty campaigner, unjustly calling Kennedy a liar for having said that Nixon, if elected, would wreck Social Security. It didn't bother Daley that the *Chicago Tribune* had tossed a touch of social gravel into the works with a pre-election day editorial—RICH MAN-POOR MAN—that said: "The Democratic precinct captains tell you that Kennedy is for the little man and Nixon is for the rich and powerful. They don't offer to prove this and they can't prove it because it isn't true. The Kennedy family fortune is reckoned at $400,000,000 and includes ownership of the Merchandise Mart in Chicago, worth $75 million. Candidate Kennedy and each of his brothers and sisters got a $1,000,000 present from their father, and some day they'll share the rest of the enormous fortune. In contrast, the Nixons started poor and to this day have never climbed far enough up the money ladder to be called more than comfortably well-off."

None of this bothered Daley, or figured in his plan. The great stroke he was planning did not so much involve getting out the Kennedy vote—he knew he'd do that—but, rather, what he meant to do with it when he got it. And the crucial fact is that Daley meant to win the nation with his ploy, not just Illinois.

Daley's stratagem was simple, though never before tried. He aimed to get on the record *quickly* with the Chicago vote, with, he hoped, a consequential psychological death blow to Republicans who were still voting in the West. He planned deliberately to milk the city dry and throw his winning hand on the table, and he did so at an early hour on election night in 1960. This time, there was to be no holding back a large number of precincts in the river wards, allowing for the count to be beefed up late in the night if it proved that a heavier Democratic vote was needed to win, though holding back is the safe —and, most important, the expected—way to play it in Chicago on the ground that if the Republicans start playing games with their tallies in such areas as Du Page, Kane, and Lake counties, the Democrats must have something in reserve to counter whatever cheating the Republicans are guilty of.

Daley crossed them up the night that Jack Kennedy was elected president. His plan simply was to psyche the Republicans into believing that their case was hopeless, that their man Nixon was lost—that there was no way, in the face of the staggering Kennedy vote in Chicago, to reverse any adverse tide elsewhere, and to discourage Republican voting in the West.

It was a daring ploy. It meant going for broke in Chicago, holding back no "reserves" for later emergencies. But Daley thought his potential reward worth the risk, and while the true effect can never be measured, certainly the networks bit Daley's bait hard—and almost choked on it.

At an early hour, the network election teams were conceding that Illinois was safely tucked away for Kennedy. How could it be otherwise, with Daley's heavy vote—not identified as predominantly the Chicago vote—showing Kennedy with a lead of 200,000–300,000 in Illinois? Surely, if he were winning a weathervane state like Illinois by such a margin, he must be winning substantially elsewhere. That was the message put out, and the one Daley wanted put out. Long after Nixon was declared defeated, it was realized that he was far from defeated. Finally, it was not until about twelve noon, eighteen hours after the polls had closed, that it began to appear that Kennedy, who had actually fallen behind Nixon at one point, was going to win, by a razor's edge.

Looking back on it a decade and a half later, pondering the question of why Daley, on that particular election night, employed strategy that he had never before chanced —and never tried again—it may seem to be asking too much to concede brilliance and imagination of such magnitude to a mere political boss from Back of the Yards in Chicago. However, persons can attest that exerting an influence on the vote-counting of downstate Illinois and the vote-casting in the western states was the carefully thought-out second phase of Daley's planning and that he, more than any other man, was the decisive factor in bringing about the election of a president.

The compelling evidence that Daley's strategy worked was Kennedy's incredibly thin margin of victory in Illinois. In the first compilation of how the votes were cast nationally in the 1960 presidential battle, California— which Nixon had been expected to win—was listed with the states that Kennedy had carried; it was not until the following week, after California's absentee ballots had been counted, that it was determined that Nixon had won California—although, at this late date, Kennedy having sufficient electoral votes to be president, the outcome there was of no great consequence.

Certainly, the voting pattern in the vital state of California showed an unusually sharp tailoff in last-hour balloting, when the astounding Chicago results were already flooding the television screens. Better evidence than that: consistently and unashamedly on his not infrequent visits to Daley's Chicago, President Kennedy, smiling broadly, acknowledged his debt to the Daley Machine.

The president, his cunning old man, Bobby Kennedy the plotter, Hy Raskin the inside man, and a very few others knew how ingeniously Mayor Daley had diverted precious votes from Nixon. Small wonder, then, that those who knew nodded in silent approval when the young president insisted, shortly after taking up residence in the White House, that Daley come and spend the night there, dining privately with the Kennedys, the president and his first lady, chatting away the evening, and then being led off to a tastefully decorated bedroom reserved for only the most regal of guests, to dream whatever dreams a kingmaker from Back of the Yards might dream when he rests his head on satin-covered pillows.

CHAPTER 10

High Water Mark

"From wherever men look out, in Eternity, to see the working of our world, John Kennedy must beam with new pride."
—*Richard Cardinal Cushing, Archbishop of Boston, President John F. Kennedy memorial mass, November 24, 1963.*

John A. McDermott, executive director of the Catholic Interracial Council of Chicago, was in a grave mood when he called his small staff together on the morning of Tuesday, November 13, 1962, to break the bad news that it did not appear that Mayor Daley would be at the speakers' table that evening, at the council's annual fund-raising dinner at the Conrad Hilton Hotel. The announcement caused consternation among his staff, because the honoree was to be Vice-President Lyndon B. Johnson and it was incomprehensible to them that Daley would cavalierly ignore a quasi-official visit of a vice-president. There was even a murmuring of rancor, but McDermott waved it off in the patient manner of professionals in the field of civil rights. City Hall had been kind enough, he said, to send over a check for $750; that was a nice gesture. "God knows," McDermott said, "we need the money."

There had been a serious question as to whether even the guest of honor would show. It had been only eleven days since the Kennedy administration showdown with the U.S.S.R. on the matter of Soviet missiles in Cuba, and security had been tightened up noticeably. Not only had the Secret Service demanded a complete list of all who would attend the dinner, agents were already combing the list of hotel personnel who might get anywhere near the vice-president, searching the Conrad Hilton ballroom and the Imperial suites on the top floor, where $100 contributors had been invited to a reception for Johnson.

The Interracial Council staff was as grim as the agents. The dinner was not going to be a financial flop, but only 800 tickets had been sold, at $25 each. "My God," one of the staff members cried, "the vice-president and we can't sell even a thousand tickets!" The Catholic Archdiocese of Chicago had frequently proved to be proficient in the area of fund raising, but no help had been extended from that quarter; the Catholic Interracial Council had prided itself on its independence of the chancery office, and except for a few individual priests who felt a personal commitment to racial justice, no help was forthcoming from His Eminence, the Cardinal, nor his assigns.

The council had naively counted upon the Richard J. Daley Democrats to suspend the segregationist convictions that were attributed to them and make a respectable showing for the vice-president. After all, Lyndon Johnson was one of them and he had done nothing grievous to offend them. Why was it, then, that the Daley Democrats hated him so? Was Daley jealous that Johnson, who had fought Jack Kennedy for the Democratic nomination, was now closer to Kennedy than Daley was?

Daley never explained what the basis was for his obvious dislike of Lyndon Johnson; there is ample evidence, however, that the Daley Democrats do not dally with forgiveness—when they hate you, it is with seething and gloating that they hate you. For his part, Lyndon Johnson was too knowledgeable a politician not to have understood where he stood with the mayor of Chicago, and the wonder was that, when fate changed the balance of power in November 1963, and Johnson had the option to stick it into Daley and break it off, as the saying goes, he was too clever to take revenge in this fashion—putting the pressure on Daley, instead, to get out a whopping vote for him in November 1964 as the price of avoiding excommunication.

A Catholic Interracial Council dinner in Chicago in 1962 would have to be cataloged as a tiny political battleground, except that the circumstances of this affair —measured against the two previous fund-raising dinners of this Catholic civil rights group—provide an insight of how things work in the guts of Chicago's political machinery.

Turn the calendar back to a Sunday in May, 1960. Place the name R. Sargent Shriver, son-in-law of Joseph P. Kennedy and president of the Catholic Interracial Council of Chicago, on the $100 and $25 benefit tickets. Add to this the urgent need of a substantial sum to finance the council for the ensuing year—money for headquarters, money for staff, money to pay expenses of those who were dispatched to march with the likes of Dr. Martin Luther King, Jr., in such places as Alabama. Don't exclude the desperate need there would be for an outpouring of black voters in Chicago six months later if, as Joe Kennedy planned, Jack Kennedy would then be running for the presidency. Gather all of these things together and seat Joe Kennedy, a brash, super-confident, and essentially pragmatic rich man, in a place of prominence and examine the indispensable contributions he made to the success of a fundraiser for a cause toward which he was personally apathetic, namely, white involvement in racial justice.

Back then, in 1960, although Daley had felt reservations about Sarge Shriver's becoming head of so nonestablishment an agency as the Catholic Interracial Council—at one of their private luncheon meetings in the Merchandise Mart, Kennedy brushed aside the objections; votes were votes—the word went out to even white-backlash ward committeemen that the Interracial Council's fund-raiser was to be supported. Thus it was that the Imperial suites of the Conrad Hilton were jammed with $100 givers, many of whom were there solely because the message had come through that, for some unexplained reason, Daley wanted them to be there.

And they got their money's worth, on this occasion in May 1960, when Joe Kennedy, offering dinner and then a glittering show at the Civic Theatre, surfaced in Chicago as the undisguised advocate of the presidential aspirations of his son, Jack.

The following year, on the night of June 1, 1961, the Interracial Council of Chicago went back to the same well —instituting on this occasion its man-of-the-year award. The first honoree—would you believe it?—R. Sargent Shriver, President John F. Kennedy's director of the Peace

Corps. This time, with no Louis Prima or Keely Smith, the stars of the 1960 Civic Opera House show, in sight, the festivities consisted of another elaborate evening of drinking and eating for a worthy cause, and Democratic politicians were again very much in evidence. In the space of one year, Sarge had become a man to know—pretty good going for a man who, as Chicago school board president, had escalated the wages of the racially controversial superintendent, Ben Willis, to the fourth highest remuneration of all public servants in the nation.

Still it was the Daley Machine that clearly had played the most important part in turning out an overflow crowd to honor the brother-in-law of a U.S. president. And for John A. McDermott, the council's executive director, the fund-raising dinner of June 1, 1961, was a triumphal evening.

The event of November 13, 1962, even better demonstrates the way Richard J. Daley plays the game.

Vice-President Johnson had the look of a man who didn't quite understand why he was there as he shook hands with the $100 contributors who stood in line to meet him on the night he had flown out from Washington to be honored. There was an embarrassing surfeit of space in the Imperial suites for the relatively small number of guests, so there was a feeling of relief when announcement was made that the time had come for all present to get into the elevators and descend to the huge banquet hall, the International Room of the Conrad Hilton, for the award dinner. Already McDermott had had to ask that a sizable section of the International Room be curtained off and that the tables be spread out, with generous amounts of space in between, to encourage the impression that the number of guests was far greater than was the case.

If the practiced eye of Lyndon Johnson did not detect that the crowd was thin, and if he had not noticed that not a single politician of consequence had attended his reception, it had to be strikingly clear to him that he was getting the back of the Daley Machine's hand when he was escorted to the speakers' table. The seven or eight hundred persons who were present got to their feet and warmly applauded the vice-president as he entered the hall —but there was a gap, conspicuous as missing front teeth, of three empty tables located directly in front of the podium. The Interracial Council had assumed that Daley would have selected thirty politicians of some sort—fifteen, maybe, with their wives—to sit in those well-placed chairs. But council staff members should have checked to make certain that there would be no such affront as this to the vice-president. At least they should have known that with President Kennedy safely in the White House for six more years—his reelection in 1964 taken for granted—the Daley Machine couldn't care less about paying homage to a twangy vice-president from Texas.

Daley played politics seriously, and Johnson did not rate attention—vice-president or not. So he didn't get it. It was as simple, and as embarrassing, as that.

In any case, Daley was having his own problems in December 1962. His onetime close friend and presently bitter enemy, Benjamin S. Adamowski, had for three months been threatening to run against Daley for mayor in April 1963. Having been bedeviled by Adamowski during the latter's term as state's attorney of Cook County —1956–1960 (he had been defeated because of the heavy Kennedy vote in Chicago)—the Democrats wanted no more of Adamowski. He had a power base, the Poles, and he promised to be a more vocal, convincing, and charismatic campaigner than anyone else the Republicans had in sight.

Too, Daley had plenty of reason to hate Adamowski. It was Adamowski, for example, who had brought down on Daley the police department scandal of 1960 that led to importation of O. W. Wilson as superintendent of police and brought about drastic readjustment of the administration. Moreover, Daley felt a trifle alone in 1963. Some of the old Machine bosses were gone by 1963— County Board President Dan Ryan died in 1961 and John Duffy, who succeeded Ryan, in 1962.

Conversely, Adamowski felt these departures improved his mayoralty hopes, which he thought were already strong. Even though he had been a secondary victim of the Chicago vote for Kennedy when he sought reelection as state's attorney in 1960, he had carried Chicago in 1956. What he had done once, he could do again, he thought. In other cities, perhaps. But Adamowski should have been smart enough to realize that running against a

John Gutknecht while tailgating on the popularity of President Eisenhower in 1956 was a far less perilous adventure than running against a Mayor Daley without the help of an Eisenhower. But Adamowski was confident that he could defeat Daley and Daley recognized that Ben was a formidable opponent, especially because Adamowski saw victory in 1963 as just recompense for his 1960 defeat; in common with Nixon, but with more reason, Adamowski felt he'd been robbed in 1960. This was to be his revenge.

Thus, the 1963 campaign was rightly characterized by many as a grudge match—and the opponents treated it as such. The usual campaign charges were hurled at the opponents. Adamowski, in particular, was hurt by charges made by his 1960 successor as state's attorney, Dan Ward, that Adamowski had not accounted for the expenditures of $833,984 in discretionary payments during his term of office. Daley also was affected adversely by Adamowski's countercharges that Daley had misappropriated his discretionary funds and, more to the point, that Daley was proving to be too expensive a mayor.

The chief Adamowski weapon, however, was the Summerdale District Police scandal uncovered by Adamowski while he was still state's attorney. The affair involved the apprehension, trial, and conviction of half a dozen Chicago policemen who had been revealed, early in 1960, to be in league with a young burglar named Richard Morrison.

Unmistakably the springboard of Adamowski's campaign against Daley in 1963, the scandal, which had broken at the tag end of Adamowski's term as state's attorney, had proved sensational. Secretive raids, carried out simultaneously on the residences of the cops Morrison had named, turned up caches of stolen merchandise, all easily tracing back to the shops from which Morrison said he had pilfered it.

The scandal of the burglar cops had an immediate demoralizing effect upon the department, all ten thousand members of the force becoming suspect. His Honor the Mayor was visibly mortified and, shunning public appearances, in despair over the damage the burglars in blue had done to his city's reputation, suffered the gossip that he was hitting the sauce—Scotch—in the basement bar of his home in Bridgeport. (The recreation room of his residence is one of the two places to which Daley repairs for relaxation; the other is the steam room of the lily-white, non-Semitic Lake Shore Club on Lake Shore Drive, where he sometimes expounds on the subject of what he is attempting to do for the city.)

Daley clearly overreacted to "Summerdale." It was uniquely embarrassing, but the affair was not the cataclysmic disclosure of police corruption that Daley and others thought it to be. Fortunately for Daley, panic is a feeling he encounters seldom. It takes exceptional stimuli. However, when he does panic—when, during the 1956 convention, he irrationally dumped County Treasurer Herbert Paschen as his candidate for governor; when, during the black rioting of 1968 that followed the assassination of Martin Luther King, Jr., he screamed his order that he wanted his police to shoot to kill; when, in the convention troubles of 1968, he magnified the disorders he had done so much to create—his surrender to panic gets him in worse trouble.

This is not to say that Daley did not have reason to be afraid early in 1960. With Adamowski riding the Summerdale scandal for all it was worth, Daley was confronted by the fact that Adamowski could win another term as state's attorney. Having had four years to line up his investigative forces and prosecutive artillery, Adamowski would, after his reelection, be in a position to decimate the Daley Machine with four years of indictable exposures. As a former corporation counsel—under appointment of Mayor Martin Kennelly—and as a onetime intimate of Daley and most other Democrats, Adamowski knew where the bodies were buried, how the deals had been made. Worse than that, he would likely have no compunction—rather, he would take delight—in unearthing all manner of scandalous things. In short, for the first time since he had been elected in 1955, Richard J. Daley was in a serious jam.

As Daley recovered his wits, having found that the world had not after all fallen in, he decided that what he needed above all, to put an end to Chicago's agony over the police burglars, was the services of the most qualified police administrator in the nation—a man of style and ability and impeccable reputation who could take charge of the Chicago Police Department and, whatever it might cost in tax dollars, cleanse the department of its multifarious sins. However, he had not the slightest idea as to where he could find such a man; nor did any of the politicians, union bosses, or financial advisers in his coterie. Then someone brought up the name of Fred Hoehler. Hoehler, who had served the Stevenson administration, had taken appointment from Daley as superintendent of the Chicago House of Correction, the overcrowded city jail. Hoehler suggested that Daley approach Orlando W. Wilson, head of the criminology department at the University of California in Berkeley.

With a polite show of reluctance, Wilson accepted a request to lend his assistance to a committee of men loyal to Daley who had the assignment of finding the perfect police chief. He was made comfortable in a suite of rooms at the University Club on Michigan Avenue, and agreed to serve as committee chairman. When, at last, the search ended, O. W. Wilson modestly emerged as the perfect chief—at double the wages paid the chief who had been sacked after Summerdale and with various attractive side benefits.

Most important, Wilson got Daley's public promise that he, Wilson, would be the sole voice of authority in the Chicago Police Department and that funds without limit would be available for whatever improvements he might deem necessary.

Cynics say that there was more form than substance to O. W. Wilson's reorganization, and that it was, in any case, unbelievably expensive. But there was general approval among the citizens of Wilson's methods. Daley, consequently, was credited with a stroke of genius in finding so special a man. Not least, the appointment forced even State's Attorney Adamowski to hold his tongue. That was all that was necessary, it turned out, to recover from the Summerdale debacle and assuage the people's ire. Having done that, Daley was able to relax, run the city, dominate the Democratic Machine, hold clandestine meetings with Joseph P. Kennedy, and give the necessary thought to the matter of maneuvering Ben Adamowski out of the state's attorney's office, come November— which, as we have seen, he did, handily, by putting all of his effort into getting Kennedy elected.

Wilson's appointment gave Daley an added advantage.

Thereafter Daley bragged to the point of nausea in Chicago and on visits to other cities about how Chicago now had the finest police department in the nation, perhaps the world. In the judgment of some, His Honor the Mayor was guilty of wild exaggeration.

All the reforms cost money, a lot of money. Everything cost more money, Daley found. No doubt a case could be made for the escalated pay scales and the expanding of the top-salaried command staff that Superintendent Wilson insisted upon, but such moves had Daley gasping. A multimillion-dollar restoration of the police headquarters building, the installation of the most modern communications system, the introduction of expensive computers into which Wilson dumped the same information of crimes committed and crimes solved that the districts had always supplied to headquarters involved expenditures that hit the city hard. Little wonder that Chicago politicians were groaning and cursing when they observed that the police department, which had been budgeted for $72,000,000 in 1960, gobbled something like $200,000,000 in Wilson's first year, continuing at that pace thereafter. As Alderman Paddy Bauler remarked in awe, "Jesus, can that Wilson spend!"

As for the qualitative return on Wilson's surgery, Daley's shoot-to-kill order of 1968 and the police rioting that characterized the 1968 Democratic convention indicated structural weaknesses in the department—and Chicago's police "reform" looked like a con job when, in 1974, the U.S. district attorney indicted some seventy policemen, including Daley's chief of traffic and four district commanders, on charges of extorting money from whores, gamblers, and saloonkeepers—most of those indicted winding up in prison.

Indeed, events after the fact indicate that O. W. Wilson was enchanted almost exclusively with redecorating the externals of the Chicago Police Department. If a chief wants squad cars that look like taxicabs, if he prefers a whirling blue light to the traditional red Mars light, if the wailing of sirens grates on him—who cares? If he needed the additional two thousand policemen that Daley let him have, the day is not now far off when, perhaps, Chicago will need not 12,000 policemen but 24,000. But unless there is also a qualitative improvement—and events indicate that such has not taken place—cosmetic improvements hardly are justified.

O. W. Wilson was long gone, of course, when the tapestry of integrity he had woven for the Chicago Police Department started to unravel. After seven years of 9:00 A.M. to 4:30 P.M. work days, with an hour or two off for lunch at the University Club, he retired in 1967 to San Diego, California, on the comfortable pension he had worked out for himself when he took the job, leaving behind as his successor his deputy superintendent, James B. Conlisk—a man far less sure of himself than Wilson and a man who did not dare to dream that City Hall would let him have the independence that had been Wilson's basic condition of employment.

Of course, 1967 and subsequent events were far in the future in 1963. And in 1963, too, Adamowski had been out as state's attorney for three years. But that spring Daley still faced a finish-fight with Ben Adamowski for the office of mayor.

Daley was perhaps more concerned in 1963 by the thought that Adamowski would knock him off than he had been back in 1955, when his political future hung in the balance in his doubleheader showdown with Martin Kennelly and Robert Merriam. After eight years as mayor, loving it most of the time, Daley was losing favor with the Chicago newspapers, with the financial community, and, alas, with an increasing number of homeowners. The solvency of Daley's Chicago was predicated almost exclusively upon a base of real estate taxation, and brag as he might about what a miracle O. W. Wilson was performing, by 1963 Wilson's extravagant spending was killing Daley. The more Wilson spent, the more Daley had to raise in real estate taxes. By 1963, the pressure from property owners was was becoming unbearable and Daley was feeling vulnerable.

The irony in Daley's assiduously digging ever deeper into owners of real estate was that, by legislative intrigue, he had arranged to get his hands on the shovel. By stipulation of the Illinois Constitution of 1870, power to set the real estate tax levy on all municipalities was vested in the state legislature. Historically, it was routine business at every biennial session of the Illinois General Assembly to set the ceiling on what the tax rate for various governmental bodies throughout the entire state could be. Recognizing immediately that to cover the cost of what he planned, Chicago would have to have a higher rate than the legislature would be willing to grant, one of Daley's first acts as mayor, in 1955, was to importune his old Bridgeport pal, State Senator William J. Lynch, now a federal judge, to kill the ceiling that applied to Chicago. The Constitution of 1870 having been made seemingly invulnerable to this kind of shenanigans, it took a bit of doing, but Lynch was a man of legalistic brilliance and he got the job done. Thereafter, Chicago was free to set its own tax rates.

Many efforts have been made to reinstitute the legislature's control over the limit on real estate taxation in Chicago; all have failed. To this day, Lynch admits: "I did it for Daley, of course. But I cautioned him to be exceedingly judicious about increasing taxes. I warned him that if he imposed exorbitant taxes on property in Chicago, the people would rise up and run him out of office—and he followed my advice to the letter, which is why he kept getting elected time after time. He had home rule on taxes and he did not abuse it."

Mayor Daley has generally practiced restraint in the imposition of real estate taxes. But when a man like Daley is dependent upon patronage and big payrolls to run a city like Chicago, the temptation to spend is great, and inevitably he has succumbed. In many ways, Daley, after he brought O. W. Wilson to Chicago, was like a wealthy man who finds himself married to a profligate wife. Daley's financial advisers, like the rich man's personal accountant, sought to caution Daley that the tax base, widen it as he was now free to do, simply could not support Wilson's spending.

The end result was predictable. By 1963, voters were grumbling, and the papers were up in arms.

Daley took to brooding over the hypocrisy of the newspapers, praising him for what seemed to be a masterful cleaning up of the police department, and berating him, simultaneously, for imposing the higher taxes that were needed to pay for it. The Marshall Field papers, the *Chicago Sun-Times* and *Chicago Daily News,* came down hard on Daley for his fattening of the city payroll and his seeming disregard for the small homeowner. Then, capping everything else, two days after the aldermanic and city primary elections of February 26, 1963, one of Daley's figurehead ward bosses—a black named Benjamin Lewis—was discovered sitting dead in his chair in his private office at Twenty-fourth Ward headquarters. Lewis, who was referred to by those who had inherited control of the ward from Jake Arvey's crowd as their "house nigger," had just been reelected to another four-year term as a Daley alderman. The ward was actually run by a white hustler, Irwin Horwitz, from his Lake Shore Drive digs. Alderman Lewis had expired in an unappetizing way: handcuffed to his chair, cigarette burns on his arms and legs, and three .38 caliber slugs in the back of his head. "Thank God," the downtown Democrats said, "that Ben Lewis wasn't a white guy. Christ Almighty, can't you see what it would have done to Daley's chances if Lewis had been a white guy?" Even so, black or white, it was one hell of a thing to have on the doorstep when you are trying to get reelected mayor.

All things considered, if ever the signs had been "Go!" for a mayoral candidate running in Chicago against Richard J. Daley, never had a challenger's chances looked to be so sanguine as when Benjamin S. Adamowski took on the undefeated champion on April 2, 1963. With the assassination of Alderman Lewis unsolved; stories of the political petulancies of Sam "Mooney" Giancana, crime syndicate boss, who had shuffled no fewer than three of his flunkies into and out of the First Ward aldermanic seat in the space of a few weeks (Daley protested that this peculiar business was none of his affair); black outrage over the rape of their neighborhoods by Daley's urban renewal bulldozers; South Shore's protests over Daley's plans to violate Jackson Park, a major recreational site, by running a six-lane expressway through it; the financial community's growing concern over Daley's fiduciary indifference; and the constantly soaring real estate taxes all to make hay with, never had a candidate against Daley had so impressive an arsenal.

By no means was Adamowski favored to win, but even impartial observers conceded that his chances to win were not hopeless. Yet Adamowski had been overrated. Not only was he defeated, he fell a bit short of doing as well as Robert Merriam had done in 1955. Unlike Merriam, who couldn't quite understand how the Republicans had let him down by refusing to vote, the more professional Adamowski understood quite well the cause of his defeat; Daley didn't beat Adamowski—the Democratic Machine beat him. Clout beat him. Adamowski had the advantage of the white-backlash vote that had only then begun to stir in Chicago, and Adamowski got impressive pluralities in the Polish and other ethnic wards, piling up, for example, an eye-popping plurality of some 11,500 in the late Alderman Weber's Germanic Forty-fifth. Adamowski had decided advantages in wards on the periphery of the growing black areas, his vote running almost exactly parallel to the white count in racially changing wards. Yet he lost simply because Republicans who were registered to vote did not do so in the same proportions as the Democrats who were registered to vote.

In 1963, as had been the case with Merriam, who had won twenty-one of the fifty wards, Adamowski's strength was anchored in the white, anti-Machine wards (the fact that Adamowski won only eighteen wards reflected the census figures that showed that the black enclave in Chicago was expanding). The unexplained part of all this, the contradiction that jumps out of these arithmetical comparisons, is that the blacks remained loyal to Daley despite their disappointment in his performance. Yet this is explainable, too: the blacks do not love the Machine so much as they distrust the anti-Machine element. Bad as things might be under a Daley, in other words, their lot was likely to be even worse if there were a changing of the guard at City Hall. You hear wry jokes in the ghetto about Daley before, after, and during his reelection campaigns. The blacks have the situation pegged, thus: since they are getting ripped off in every conceivable way, in turn they try to rip off the whites whenever they can. As Reverend Jesse Jackson might say, blacks would rather be in compliance with some sonofabitch of a whitey that they can get a little something out of than with some sonofabitch of a whitey who won't give them anything more substantial than a patronizing smile. Daley would not be surprised by this evaluation. As a Bridgeport white, he has acted with regard to blacks in accordance with that view.

The way Daley's strategy in the ghetto has succeeded

can be seen in a comparison of the pluralities that the
Dawson wards produced for Daley in the 1955 and 1963
elections. Against Merriam, Dawson gave Daley an advantage of 49,363. Against Adamowski, a candidate more
closely identified with the whites than Merriam, the five
Dawson wards produced an astonishing plurality for Daley
of 69,466, an increase of 20,103 votes. Even more clearly
indicative of the black vote, perhaps, is the fact that the
Twenty-fourth Ward returned a plurality for Daley of
16,461—the best showing for His Honor the Mayor of any
ward in the city—suggesting that Horwitz and his cronies,
the absentee bosses of the ghetto-poor Twenty-fourth, are
not constrained by the inconvenience of having their alderman mysteriously murdered when it comes to the practical matter of getting out a big vote without him.

Overall, the April 2, 1963, count had Daley winning by
a plurality of 138,792. Daley's total vote was 679,497—
the only time in five mayoral elections that he has slipped
below 700,000. As always when Daley runs, the automatic
eleven wards carried the day for him. Table 3 substantiates
this.

Table 3

Ward	Daley	Adamowski	Plurality	Control
1	13,238	4,697	8,541	Crime syndicate
2	15,796	2,906	12,890	Dawson
3	22,334	3,482	18,852	Dawson
4	15,312	2,985	12,127	Dawson
6	15,494	4,917	10,577	Dawson
20	19,198	4,178	15,020	Dawson
24	17,429	968	16,461	Machine/Arvey
27	14,518	2,122	12,396	Machine/Sain
28	10,390	5,228	5,162	Machine/Syndicate
29	16,561	1,958	14,603	Machine/Horan
31	15,250	7,747	7,503	Machine/Keane
	175,520	41,188	134,132	

The Field newspapers took Daley's victory with bad
grace. On April 4, 1963, having digested the results, the
Sun-Times sniffed: "If the Republicans had put up a more
substantial type candidate, one with appeal to the business
community, the Republican vote may have been greater.

The routine Republican turnout may only indicate that the Republicans had once more nominated a routine candidate." The *Chicago Daily News* said: "A public official, running for a third term, is climbing above the snow line; gains are slower and harder won, the crevasses are deeper and the missteps more perilous. Mayor Daley made the ascent handily. Considering his burdens, his reduced majority should be a greater pleasure to him than his earlier landslides." The *Daily News* couldn't quite let Daley go without giving him the elbow, however: "The weight carried by Daley included a rise of almost 100% in the corporate tax rate since 1955. Neighborhood renewal was another source of resentment. Scandals in the Police Department and in the sanitary district—for which Daley, as County Chairman, was held to account—also reduced his popularity." In the end, though, the *Daily News* surrendered with the conclusion: "Daley is a dedicated man, with a proved ability to lead the city forward in many fields."

As for the reelected mayor, he cooed: "My thoughts are one of humility, gratitude, and appreciation. As I said in 1955 and 1959, I will try to embrace charity and walk humbly with my God."

The skies were blue and the birds were singing and the future of Richard J. Daley was good. Richard J. Daley, confidant of a president—receiving warm congratulations from the president by telephone on the night of his victory—and ready to plan now for the renomination of John Fitzgerald Kennedy in 1964 (in Chicago perhaps?) and to play a big role in Kennedy's reelection (possibly getting rid of the objectionable Lyndon Johnson in the process). The dreams had all come true for the boy from Bridgeport, and life was *grand*. Until . . .

Until that gray afternoon of November 22, when having been incommunicado for several hours, Daley marched into Democratic headquarters, shooting a curious glance at his personal secretary, Mary Mullen, who seemed to be sitting there transfixed, and heard her say those horrifying words, tears flooding her eyes: "Dick, President Kennedy is dead."

Shocked to the depths of his mind though he was by the assassination of President Kennedy, Richard J. Daley had had a foreboding for three weeks that this ultimate disaster was impending. Three weeks earlier, alert Chicago police had picked up a highly suspicious potential assassin during a Kennedy visit to Chicago, and although the police and the FBI acted quickly to make assassination impossible, Daley was never able to eliminate the prospect from his mind. Thus, the assassination was as much a confirmation of his fears as a shock.

In any case, life, especially political life, had to go on, and practical man that he is, Daley rather expected to be called into conference with the new president, despite such breaches of political good manners as the 1962 Catholic Interracial Council dinner. There was precious little sympathy between Johnson and Daley, yet each respected the other as a professional who accepted the necessity of tending to public business. The new president certainly did not underestimate the influence that Daley exerted upon Daley Machine congressmen, and both men understood that they now were dependent upon each other. Thus it was, when President Johnson made his first address to the Congress and the nation after Kennedy's funeral, he asked Daley to be present. If Chicagoans are sometimes inclined to underestimate the political power of Daley, Johnson was too knowledgeable a politician to fall into that error of judgment.

Daley, for his part, found that he needed all his political power just to keep his head above water, as the movement for social change that typifies the 1960s began to have a major effect on Chicago.

There had been many indications prior to the assassination of President Kennedy that the time had come for social change in the comfortable order of the white man's world. By the very early 1960s there were indications of nonwhite rejection of white privilege in the areas of housing, education, and employment opportunities, and the movement was so strong that no one—not even the capricious followers of the Honorable Richard J. Daley, nor the leader himself—could hope to hold a line of defense against the "encroachment," manipulate the blacks in the old accustomed way as they might.

The signs of change were everywhere. President Kennedy had been but one year in office, Richard Daley basking in the glow, when unknown to the Daley Machine a little man in a black silk suit, a bejeweled overseas cap on his head, was conducting a meeting of an organization that he called "The Black Muslims" in the historic but dilapidated Chicago Coliseum on South Wabash Avenue. It was here, in decades past, that U.S. presidents had been nominated. In this place, in February 1962, where the rafters had grown old in the echo of grandiloquent oratory, Elijah Muhammad—née Elijah Poole of some no-account little place in Georgia—gave new meaning to a word in the American language: black. In his squeaky, tinny voice, addressing a congregation that he proudly claimed to have converted from the evil professions of thieving and whoring, the Messenger of Allah—as he chose to be called—spoke at length on a theme that the only white man in the place, an NBC reporter, had never heard before: "Black is beautiful."

"You are black," Elijah Muhammad proclaimed. "You are not knee-grow. Knee-grows are the result of the violation of our beautiful women by the white devils; knee-grow is a mixture of the bloods and now we must be purified because we are black."

Had Richard J. Daley been sitting there, through the two-hour diatribe, he might have turned purple—as sometimes he does in moments when his sensibilities have been abused—though he would have been consoled by Elijah Muhammad's disclaimer of violence. In City Hall's way of thinking, if someone is not intending to cause trouble, it matters not what he hollers about. Thus, it did not seem that there was much for City Hall to fear from a new racist religious group that seemed to find strength in merely condemning all whites to eternal damnation. After all, Elijah Muhammad seemed to be playing the Daley Machine's game—advocating black segregation, supporting the organization with heavy tithes on his flock, creating in the South Side ghetto an unimportant conglomerate of retail shops. Black Muslimism, close up, had the mark of the new world. But, Daley could hardly have thought that his world was the one whose days were numbered. The strength of the Daley Machine, shored up with timbers of patronage from the Congressman Dawson people who delivered the votes, would hardly allow for City Hall to take the slightest notice of a black racist religionist. Yet in this Daley and almost all the other whites in power were wrong, and their error was to cost them and their cities, states, and nation dear. True, the Black Muslims had little effect on the crises that were to confront Richard J. Daley in the 1960s, but a large measure of Daley's troubles in the 1960s reflected the subtle hatred that was promulgated by the Messenger of Allah.

At the bottom of the mountain of controversy and violence that was Chicago in the 1960s, two volcanic craters, at least one of which still is bubbling, are to be found in what otherwise was largely a political paradise. The first, of course, was racial discord; the second was the price that Chicago paid for U.S. involvement in the Vietnamese war.

If Martin Luther King, Jr., and his followers weren't on the march or making impassioned demands for better housing, jobs, and education, the long-haired, bearded, disheveled anti-war protesters were demonstrating in the heart of the city. If anything, the Vietnam war was contributing to Chicago's economy, much war matériel being produced by the city's diversified factories, but Daley was among those who felt revulsion and foreboding at the sight of the protesters who reviled the nation's leaders, especially President Johnson, for continued U.S. involvement in the war. The long-term threat of serious trouble in the area of racial injustice should have been the priority concern of the Daley administration, but the near-treasonable display of disenchantment with the nation's sacrificing its youth in a useless, far-off war was the thing that aggravated Daley—the interesting thing about this being that his sons were not in military service, nor were the sons of anyone with good connections.

Whether the Daley Machine could have done something to soften the fear and the agony of the racial hatred that Chicago endured is debatable. Half a million whites— 505,000 by the U.S. Census count; 18.6 percent of the city's white population—simply packed up and got out, fled to the suburbs, during the 1960s. And while this was no different from what happened in Washington, D.C., Newark, Atlanta, Detroit, St. Louis, Birmingham, and most other metropolitan cities of the nation, and while, further, in some areas—financial solvency, for example— Chicago made a remarkable showing in giving ground grudgingly, Chicago was nonetheless indifferent under Mayor Daley toward the demonstrable injustices that existed in the areas of education and employment opportunties. Not only did the Daley administration lack interest in alleviating racial inequities, City Hall was allied with those who worked to preserve the status quo—in public education, for example.

In the early 1960s many civil rights groups made efforts to establish the fact that the Chicago Board of Education had a deliberate policy of segregation. Benjamin J. Willis, the autocratic superintendent of Chicago's public schools, coldly denied that this was so. Mayor Daley put his hands together like a mantis and said it was not his policy to interject himself into Board of Education affairs. This, of course, was a cop-out. The mayor had not employed Willis—who was then paid $48,500 per year, with such perquisites as a chauffeured limousine, making him the fourth highest paid public servant in the nation—but Daley had appointed the seven school board members who hired Willis, so it was not entirely truthful to say that Daley exerted no influence.

Moreover, Daley, who had given his mild approval when Philip J. Hauser of the University of Chicago, a sociologist of some renown, was named by the federal court to head a five-member "integration study group" of the Chicago school system, had no comment when the Hauser study group reported: "Quality education is not available in Chicago to the [black] children who are in greatest need of it."

This news can hardly have come as a surprise in a city that, while spending billions of dollars on education, has produced, citywide, a consistently low record of achievement in the basics of reading and arithmetic. Eighth graders in Chicago, for example, function at no better than a sixth-grade level (the national average running at plus-eight). The dropout rate of kids in the inner city of Chicago has never been disclosed, but a vast number of inner-city children simply quit, and nothing is done about it. If Daley does not choose to acknowledge the fact that Chicago's ghetto schools are the poorest equipped and the most inadequately staffed in the national public school system, it is nonetheless the case.

In specific areas, the Hauser study group surprised many citizens of Chicago—especially those who claimed that the blacks simply do not want to find jobs in, say, such fields as the building trades—with a charge, not particularly a secret, that Superintendent Willis was more or less in league with the AFL unions in denying training to blacks. The study group reported that black students were denied admission to the apprenticeship training program of the Washburne Trade School solely because the trade unions of Chicago—not the Board of Education, which supposedly ran the institution—decided which student applicants got in, and the trade unions, run by close friends of His Honor the Mayor, were lily white. Daley could not possibly not have known about the unions' exclusionary policies. In the first place, this policy could not have been implemented without the tacit approval of Superintendent Willis and Daley's Board of Education. In the second, Daley's personal friend, Thomas J. Murray, vice-president of the Board of Education, was president of Local 134 of the Electrical Workers Union, AFL, and president of the Building Trades Council of Chicago.

Charges and countercharges were flung around; Daley sat impassively by. Ben Willis did little more, though he claimed the accusations were spurious. Willis indeed was a match for Holzman, the man who ran Chicago elections, in turning away accusations, and as the years passed he had more and more charges to deny—for example, when a brilliant black lawyer, Paul Zuber, who had already won a historic school desegregation case in New Rochelle, New York, documented his charges that not only was the ghetto plagued by inferior teaching in overcrowded schools but there was an untold number of empty classrooms. As Zuber said, if overcrowded classrooms contributed to the difficulty of instructing ghetto children, why couldn't additional teachers be put into the vacant classrooms, thereby reducing class size? Willis was adamant in refusing to concede the logic of Zuber's argument; indeed, Willis refused to reveal the total number of empty classrooms in the ghetto schools, grimly procrastinating when even members of Daley's captive Board of Education urged him to render an accurate report on this.

So the struggle went on, Zuber next embarking on the tedious chore of trying to make his own count, at the same time seeking to prepare documentation satisfactory to the federal court to show that Willis had deliberately con-

trived to effect school segregation by arbitrarily gerry-
mandering school district boundary lines to ensure that a
child attended classes "with his own kind." Zuber argued
that the boundary making was patently ridiculous, that the
arbitrarily set school boundaries were beyond question de
facto evidence of segregation. The judge who heard the
case—Abraham Lincoln Marovitz—did not dispute Zuber's
contention; he simply suggested that reasonable men
should be able to work this thing out without hurting anybody.

Zuber had not expected such a response from a judge
who was expected to give a ruling. But as an NBC reporter
explained over lunch one day: this is Chicago and this
Judge Abraham Lincoln Marovitz was a buddy of His
Honor the Mayor in the state legislature, a longtime confidant of the mayor, bought the mayor neckties, sometimes had drinks with Daley in the mayor's basement, had
a habit of showing up as an interested observer in the Illinois delegation at Democratic party conventions.

"Who put him on the federal bench?" asked Zuber.

"President Kennedy," the reporter replied.

Paul Zuber shook his head in disbelief. "God Almighty,"
he said, "what kind of a city is this?"

Zuber, of course, was not alone in his fight against
Willis. Many civil rights groups were active at the time,
though rivalry often kept them apart. For example, come-
dian Dick Gregory was leading black and white marchers
on Daley's block on South Lowe, ignoring the obscenities
and water that the mayor's God-fearing neighbors rained
on them. Saul Alinsky's Woodlawn Organization in the
South Side ghetto was busy practicing the master's radical
techniques. On the West Side, in the Lawndale area, in
Jake Arvey's old bailiwick, activists also were busy.

The aim was always the same, though the techniques
differed. In one instance, when an NBC reporter passed
on reliable information to Sears Chairman Gordon M.
Metcalf that certain young blacks were planning to put
the torch that very night to Sears, Roebuck's massive mail
order building, a fixer from Sears was passing out money
within the hour on nearby Roosevelt Road. There was
no fire that night.

And if the techniques used differed, the effect was cumulative. Gradually, the city and its mayor realized that

movement was necessary. Progress, however, was slow. For every two steps forward, there was a good step and a half back.

Thus, when the civil rights umbrella organization in Chicago, the Coordinating Council of Community Organizations (CCCO), organized school boycotts in 1963 and 1964, Congressman Dawson suffered the first boycott, yet denounced the second. Judge Marovitz gratuitously offered to adjudicate the dispute and then assumed that there was no justification for such boycotts.

Yet progress was discernible, Marovitz's decision notwithstanding. Richard J. Daley was getting heat from all sides. Although Dick Gregory and his marchers were arrested for disorderly conduct when Daley's Bridgeport neighbors got vehement in their counter-protest, even conservatives could see that the police had grabbed the wrong offenders. The police explanation—that the Gregory libertarians had been hauled to the pokey to avoid letting Daley's neighbors start a riot—was seen to be utterly ludicrous. Daley felt the pressure, and reacted typically. Backed into a corner and angry over the extensive press coverage, he snarled, "Is it 'news' when a few people assemble in front of a man's home?"

Former Governor William Stratton, a Republican, was standing trial for income tax evasion, but that didn't give Daley much of a breather. The old-time residents of the Sicilian settlement southwest of downtown were raising holy hell with Daley over his destruction of their neighborhood, which Daley "needed" for the site of a Chicago branch of the University of Illinois. Daley was catching hell for his urban renewal plan to start ripping up the western reaches of Lincoln Park in the upper-income area north of downtown and from the University of Chicago crowd for his plan to run a six-lane expressway into the south Hyde Park section (Daley's police arresting upper-class whites who chained themselves to the trees in Jackson Park to prevent crews' cutting down hundreds of trees).

Even outside Chicago, Daley was getting into trouble. Although he had his own man—Otto Kerner, Jr.—in the governor's chair, a brash young legislator who professed to being a Democrat, Paul Simon, wrote an article for

Harper's magazine charging that 20,000 of the 60,000 state jobs had been dished out as patronage. There was no end to the revelations. On June 1, Daley was revealed to have purchased a seven-acre lakefront summer home on the Michigan shore, an hour's drive from Chicago; an automobile dealer sold it to Daley for $41,000, making it, it was said, one of the best buys of the year in Chicago area real estate.

No matter what Daley said, or tried to do, public attention kept swinging back to protest marching and anti-Ben Willis demonstrating. And Willis did not help himself when, for example, he crowed that the highest incidence of violence had been occurring in the school districts where the boycott had been most effective. That he wasn't bright enough to discern the connection was hardly an excuse, although it was characteristic of him to reject criticism of his attitude and his methods. His greatest strength was that Daley thought Willis was great.

Daley fought back, accusing the news media of creating and exaggerating Chicago's troubles, in the school system and other areas. Yet the news media could not be blamed for the unconscionable effort of the U.S. Steel Corporation to grab off 194.6 acres of submerged Park District land, at a price of $100 per acre, in a deal engineered—but not yet, twelve years after it surfaced, consummated—by Edward C. Logelin, regional vice-president of U.S. Steel, who happened also to be chairman of Daley's Chicago Plan Commission. Likewise, the news media had nothing to do with the fact that although Chicago boys were being inducted to fight in Vietnam or were being tried and sentenced in federal court for refusing to bear arms in Vietnam, Daley's sons were not inducted, nor were the sons of Daley Machine politicians.

In 1964, in fact, Daley seemed to be slipping, failing to sense the fear and despair of the American people. He was not alone in this of course. But in Chicago, posturing as the leader of all the citizens of a great city, he was supremely alone, and apparently not accountable.

At year's end, it suited the pleasure of School Superintendent Willis to answer the hoary question of Paul Zuber. Willis had at last completed the seemingly uncomplicated task of toting up the number of empty classrooms in the public school system of Chicago. His answer: 422. Unfortunately, his staff simultaneously released its count and, surprisingly, the staff said the number of empty classrooms was 703. Before anyone could press him for an explanation of this interesting disparity in the counting of classrooms, Willis held a press conference to announce his recommendation that $1,000,000,000 be spent forthwith on the refurbishing of Chicago's public schools. Coincidentally, the Federal Office of Health Education and Welfare announced that it was embarking on an investigation of charges of racial discrimination in the public schools of Chicago—drawing a protest from Board of Education President Frank Whiston that HEW was being unfair, that it should be willing to take Chicago's word that racial discrimination was nonexistent in Chicago.

In the circumstances, especially since a Democratic victory was not in doubt, the 1964 political conventions were of little moment to the Richard J. Daley Democrats. The late-August Democratic convention in Atlantic City was a lark. Johnson was to be nominated, and Daley was privately committed to a vice-presidential candidate he didn't particularly like, Senator Hubert H. Humphrey of Minnesota. The trouble with Hubert, Congressman Daniel Rostenkowski of Chicago, Daley's man in Washington, explained, was that he gave long-winded answers to questions no one had asked. In any case, out of family loyalty Daley favored Robert F. Kennedy, who was anathema to Johnson and who did not make much impression upon the Daley delegates in Atlantic City when the recently resigned U.S. attorney general was invited by the mayor to address the Illinois delegation.

Such reactions made little difference. Johnson and Humphrey were the ticket, because Johnson chose Humphrey. Daley, always the loyal Democrat in the end, did the necessary thing in Chicago on November 3, 1964, coming up with pluralities for a presidential candidate that no major American city had ever before seen. Table 4, showing the voting in Chicago's automatic eleven wards, tells the story.

Lyndon B. Johnson carried the State of Illinois in 1964 by a plurality of 890,887, even though Senator Barry M. Goldwater had the advantage in twenty-three

Table 4

Ward	Johnson	Goldwater	Plurality	Control
1	18,044	3,148	14,896	Crime syndicate
2	22,238	1,276	20,962	Dawson
3	33,851	982	32,869	Dawson
4	26,399	3,443	22,956	Dawson
6	34,000	1,034	32,966	Dawson
20	35,016	807	34,109	Dawson
24	21,662	304	21,358	Machine/Arvey
27	20,241	1,142	19,099	Machine/Sain
28	19,966	2,705	17,261	Machine/Syndicate
29	27,172	596	26,576	Machine/Horan
31	19,970	5,266	14,704	Machine/Keane
	278,559	20,703	257,756	

of the 102 counties. Daley delivered for Johnson in Chicago a mountainous plurality of 674,852. When one recalls Daley's refusal to break bread with Johnson at the Catholic Interracial Council dinner less than two years before, if there is a better way of saying "sorry," the politicians of Chicago are not aware of it. President Johnson accepted the apology with a happy chortle: "Dick Daley is the greatest!"

If Daley's display of political power gave him a nice, glowing feeling, little else did in 1964 or 1965. In 1966 Johnson did Daley the kindness of nominating Daley's old chum from Bridgeport and his ex-law partner, William J. Lynch, to the federal bench despite Lynch's total lack of judicial experience, but Johnson did nothing to call off the dogs of federal welfare agencies that were snapping at Daley's Chicago. And the pressure was still building. There was already speculation that federal agency efforts would compel the Chicago Board of Education to cease holding hands with the trade unions—from maintaining, for example, the all-white apprentice training school, Washburne. Daley pal Tom Murray, head of the trade union group, snorted, "If the Board of Education interferes in union membership practices, the trade unions will pull out of Washburne and start their own school"—quite a remarkable thing for the vice-president of the Chicago Board of Education to say.

Everywhere he turned, Daley was at bay. For example, Daley was accused of using massive war-on-poverty funds —$140,000,000 were administered by the Chicago Urban Opportunity Committee, a Daley-created subsidiary of City Hall—in ways that contributed little toward winning the poverty war. Anti-Ben Willis marches continued. Willis was consistently supported by Daley, who also said that no one appreciated how hard Willis and Dr. Deton Brooks, head of the Chicago Urban Opportunity Committee, were working.

But eventually even Daley appeared to be becoming rattled. At mid-year 1965, discontent increasing, Daley declared that he had "proof" that Communists had infiltrated the anti-Ben Willis movement. When pressed for specifics, he ignored the question. Two weeks later, forty-eight prominent Chicago citizens addressed a letter of inquiry to the Board of Education, asking for a statement of policy, with reference to the validity of the allegation and marches of the various civil rights organizations. The prominent citizens got no reply.

As far as Daley would go was to summon a Conference on Race and Religion. During the much-publicized conference, the city's religious and civil rights leaders and leaders of the business community came up with various nonspecific assurances. But about all that actually came out of the conference was a perfunctory acknowledgment of the first self-evident truth of the Declaration of Independence, namely, that all men are created equal.

On July 30, 1965, the *New York Times* advanced an editorial theory that, black unemployment in Chicago having reached a sobering 17 percent, many of the blacks were marching because they had nothing else to do. Martin Luther King, Jr., and his Southern Christian Leadership Conference followers were making quick hit-and-run attacks on the Chicago establishment by mid-1965. King's intentions were to lead the blacks into the promised land, but he seemed oddly out of his element in Chicago. The white people regarded him as nothing much more than a curiosity, another nuisance, and the street-wise blacks of Chicago had misgivings about him, as if fearful that he would stir up trouble rather than resolve it. In addition, some black organizations resented the intrusion of the

SCLC. Where, they seemed to be asking King, have you been while we have been fighting the battle?

- In the circumstances, it was understandable that King thought Chicago might prove to be his toughest challenge. He got a taste of Daley's power when on October 5, 1965, the U.S. Office of Education declared that the Chicago Board of Education was in violation of the Civil Rights Act of 1964 and consequently would not receive a federal grant of $30,000,000—only to have the decision miraculously reversed the very next day.

On January 4, 1966, independently of Martin Luther King, the CCCO filed a federal suit demanding that Superintendent Willis respond to the charge of John Coons of the U.S. Office of Education that the public school system of Chicago was clearly in noncompliance with Title VI of the Civil Rights Act of 1964. Willis declined to respond, just as he had refused to cooperate with Coons during a four-month investigation—denying the federal agency complete access to information. Martin Luther King cried out against the "plantation politics of Chicago's City Hall"—hammering Daley for coming up short in providing Chicago blacks with adequate education, housing, and job opportunities, while subjecting them to economic exploitation. In late March 1966 the Chicago Board of Education naively released a report that its white schools were staffed almost exclusively with white teachers, and that the reverse of this was true of the black schools. Superintendent Willis at length replied to the federal charge of segregation, denying the charge—but it was now clear that Willis had finally become too hot. In short order, he was out, and a former Chicago school administrator, the more tolerant James Redmond, was brought in.

Benjamin Willis, an autocratic educator whose tenure as superintendent stretched back to Mayor Kennelly's time, had long enjoyed favor as the establishment's man. When, however, in July of 1965 some forty-eight prominent, pro-Daley citizens issued a statement of policy that implied strong criticism of Willis, it seemed unlikely that his contract would be extended beyond its August 31 expiration date. An informal newspaper poll of the nine board members supported the expectation that Willis was through, despite the desire of School Board President Frank Whiston and Vice-President Thomas Murray to give him a new contract. In a matter of days, the black community was shocked and cried "Betrayal!" when three board members regarded as being close to Daley changed their minds and voted to retain Willis, rather than sack him—explaining that the superintendent had promised to be cooperative in the future and that he had given assurances that he would retire, as he previously had promised to do, upon reaching his sixty-fifth birthday in December of 1966. He did not last that long, as James Redmond was brought in to take his place on October 3, 1966.

Having taken a resolute position that segregation simply did not exist in the schools, Willis had blunted and frustrated all efforts to demonstrate, in the courts and in the streets, that he was following a racist line. Even the mighty giants of the Chicago press got embroiled, the *Sun-Times* demanding the ouster of Willis, and the *Tribune* stoutly defending him. Dr. Eric Oldberg, the renowned neurosurgeon who headed up a search committee called the Mayor's Commission on School Board Nominations, went about the business of interviewing likely prospects for appointment to the board by Daley—the task of finding candidates becoming more difficult as the controversy swirling around Willis intensified. In early 1966, Willis aggravated board members who were displeased with him by losing his temper when one of them accused him of being needlessly belligerent. He reacted also to the almost inflammatory attacks that were now being made against him by Reverend Martin Luther King, Jr., King having put his roots down in Chicago—addressing himself to the job of finishing off what others had begun, namely, the ouster of Willis. Despairing, but unbowed, Willis finally quit, leaving Chicago to suffer its torment of segregated schools.

It was a little late for Redmond, an advocate of creating equal educational opportunities by busing school kids, to do anything about easing Chicago's tensions—especially so when Redmond's planning intensified the white blacklash. Demonstrators were arrested outside Mayor Daley's home one evening in early May for walking down public sidewalks, while Daley's neighbors were watering the sidewalks with their garden hoses. On June 6, Martin Luther King started "Operation Breadbasket," and the twenty-seven-year-old Reverend Jesse Jackson was placed in charge. The idea behind the foundation was that the blacks would not trade with and would picket merchants who took their money but would not give them employment.

On July 10, 1966, King had stepped up the pressure on Daley by holding a protest rally in Soldier Field on the lakefront. Normally, Chicago's Park District would have denied a permit for such use of this huge facility, but King's national stature meant that Daley couldn't chance denying him use of the place. It was a warm Sunday, in a hot summer, and many thousands of people were there—perhaps 40,000, although King's people claimed 100,000 —as the remarkable preacher recited a litany of racial injustices. He spoke with characteristic brilliance of the usual things, winding up with a list of "demands" and two basic threats: blacks would invoke sanctions on all Chicago businesses that practiced discrimination and would knock out of office all blacks who did not wholeheartedly support the cause of civil rights. Chicago's City Hall was sullen.

The week of July 11-15, 1966, has been described as the worst week Daley ever experienced. There was rioting and arson and looting in the Lawndale ghetto. Daley called upon the governor, Otto Kerner, Jr., to bring in the National Guard, and only then was quiet restored. Racial discord was now plainly of such magnitude that Daley's police force could not contain it.

In the first week of August, Martin Luther King grimly led leaders of the black organizations into a summit meeting with the white power structure, including the newly arrived Catholic archbishop of Chicago, John Cody, reputed to be a liberal. The summit meeting, which was intended to stop the marching of civil rights people in the streets of Chicago, especially those who assembled at Buckingham Fountain in Grant Park and walked to City Hall, ostensibly was a conference on open occupancy, and agreement on the issue was announced, though there was no clear statement of what the terms of agreement were.

Alderman Tom Keane, Daley's City Council leader, sneered that there was no agreement and, when it became clear to the militants that they had been tricked, the demonstrators resolutely resumed their marching—to the

Wacker Drive building where main offices of the Board of Education are located, to the Civic Center in the heart of the downtown area, to Daley's Bridgeport.

Characteristically, Daley fought back. On September 28, 1966, Daley put a major share of the blame for Chicago's racial troubles on the doorstep of the media. Speaking to delegates attending an international conference of the Radio and Television News Directors' Association, Daley assailed the media—especially television—for giving publicity to the "haters, the kooks, the psychotics" through "crisis coverage" of the civil rights demonstrations and other protest movements. Daley blasted the newspapers along with others of the media for giving coverage to "frivolous and irresponsible individuals who, in many instances, represent groups so small in number as to be practically nonrepresentative." Daley had his usual trouble reading the speech, but though the phraseology was foreign to his style, the message that the media was "managing" the news, "distorting and misrepresenting," allowing "irresponsible persons to make outrageous statements" was very much Daley's own. Two months later, on November 3, there was yet another sign that His Honor the Mayor was taking the offensive; he angrily denounced Martin Luther King, Jr., for "trying to undo the Democratic party." Chicagoans hardly noticed that Jim Redmond was now officially in Ben Willis's seat.

There was a cooling off of tempers in Chicago as 1966 ran out, but the new year, 1967, did not begin auspiciously. The Chicago public schoolteachers were forestalled in a serious strike threat by Daley's promise that he would provide $17,500,000 for pay increases—the interesting aspects of these heroics being that Daley had no idea where he would get the money and, in making his offer, was forgetting his claims that he never intervened in Board of Education affairs. The sixty-million-dollar McCormick Place on Chicago's lakefront was gutted by fire. Republicans in Springfield firmly said no to Daley when he went to the legislature seeking authority to tax liquor and cigarettes. It was not a good start to the year, all in all.

The only consolation was Daley's mayoral victory in April 1967. If Daley was a glutton for punishment, his opponent, John Waner, was a Republican party setup. His Honor the Mayor beat Waner, 792,238 to 272,542, and Daley can hardly have failed to notice that, with civil rights discord still unabated, his vote total was the highest he had ever received in a mayoral contest—and that Waner's was the worst showing of a Republican candidate since 1935. Waner, a Republican ward committeeman who owned a heating and air-conditioning business, carried not one of the fifty Chicago wards.

The anomaly of Daley's extraordinary victory, in the atmosphere of interracial hatred that prevailed, was emphasized by the vote that was accumulated for him in the Dawson wards and the other predominantly black wards of the Machine's automatic eleven, the white wards of the automatic eleven not figuring in this chart (see Table 5).

Race problems or not, the Chicago Democrats were doing business as usual. Indeed, the lopsided vote for Daley in early 1967 seemed to suggest that Daley's abandonment of conciliation in 1966 and his attack on the media and Martin Luther King, Jr., had been a ploy predicated on the accurate assessment that the blacks would continue to vote Democratic, even in the face of Daley's open appeasement of the whites.

By mid-summer of 1967, however, hell was breaking

Table 5

Ward	Daley	Waner	Plurality	Control
2	11,654	1,760	9,894	Dawson
3	19,160	2,281	16,879	Dawson
4	13,998	1,857	12,141	Dawson
6	12,268	2,657	9,611	Dawson
20	15,770	2,743	13,027	Dawson
24	15,208	926	14,282	Machine/Arvey
27	16,780	842	15,938	Machine/Sain
29	15,570	1,209	14,361	Machine/Horan
	120,408	14,275	106,133	

loose again in the West Side ghetto, particularly in the old Arvey-Sain-Horan wards. Many retail businesses were put to the torch in Lawndale. Looting followed the arson, and City Hall was frustrated by the inability of the police department, now headed by James B. Conlisk, Wilson's deputy, to stop the torchings or discover who was responsible.

In response, the Chicago City Council in mid-1967, crossed its fingers and voted open occupancy—and then was irked when King got credit for forcing this historic change in Chicago policy.

Taking advantage of the initiative that now appeared to be his, King infuriated Daley further by issuing a call to all blacks to unite in acts of massive civil disobedience—thundering his battle cry, with customary emotion, at a jam-packed Operation Breadbasket meeting in a South Side church on July 12, his new challenge dominating the front pages and spilling over into the national press.

Not surprisingly, as the local situation deteriorated, Daley turned for solace increasingly to his national reputation. Yet he was not so foolhardy, public opinion to the contrary, to risk his reputation with a Chicago Democratic Convention, in 1968.

Far from importuning Johnson to award the 1968 convention to Chicago, Daley did his utmost to avoid the selection of Chicago. National Committeeman Arvey and the Chicago business community—the State Street merchants and the hotel people—made a pitch for the 1968 convention, but Daley said nothing to Johnson about it, presuming that the president would interpret his silence as a rejection of the honor. Things were simply too tight in Chicago to allow for the gamble of hosting an important nominating convention that would have world attention, with Robert F. Kennedy already denouncing Johnson's continuing involvement in the Vietnamese war. Daley had declared emphatically that he would not stand with Bobby in a denunciation of LBJ. Who knew what manner of hell Bobby Kennedy would create at the 1968 convention? Enough, perhaps, to forewarn a wise old head like Daley that this was a monkey that no smart big city boss would want on his back. In short, it simply is not true that Daley sought the 1968 convention for Chicago. Equally, it is true that Johnson had not caught the sign. Daley, in turn, was not in a position to reject the convention when Johnson placed it in his hands.

For Daley the decision was a surprise. He had loaded

his confidants onto a chartered plane on Saturday, October 7, 1967, and headed for a $500-per-plate fund-raising dinner in Washington, D.C., by way of a world series baseball game in St. Louis, Missouri. With the Cardinals leading the Boston Red Sox, 5 to 2, in the seventh inning, Daley and his coterie got up and headed for the airport.

At the black-tie dinner four hours later in Washington, LBJ had arranged that Daley and his congressional leaders —Daniel Rostenkowski, John Kluczynski, et al.—occupy a table alongside his own. This was the night that the president was to promise that the war in Southeast Asia would be won in 1968, that America had reason to be proud that it had sacrificed in the defense of liberty, and so on. Prior to the speech, LBJ did some table-hopping, and Daley's table was his first port of call. He was standing behind Daley and was reaching to give His Honor the Mayor a bear hug before Daley knew the president was there. "The greatest of them all!" the president declared, squeezing Daley's well-tailored shoulders. "Mr. Mayor," President Johnson said, in a congratulatory tone, "I've decided the best place for the '68 convention is Chicago! You are the one who can handle it!"

Stunned, Daley ceased struggling to get to his feet. Instead, Daley gave Johnson a sickly smile; all others at the table blanched. And then the president moved on. "Dick," Rostenkowski cried, "we can't take that convention. For Christ's sakes, those civil rights people will crucify us!" Others at the table quickly picked up the argument. Daley looked miserable. Finally, he said: "He gave it to us. We've got it. We'll take care of it." Listening, a few minutes later, to Johnson's talk about how the United States, next year, would win its most unpopular war was, Rostenkowski later said, pure agony.

Back in Chicago, Martin Luther King, Jr., jeered. How was it, he demanded, that a national administration that ignored the miseries of its black minority could put the burden of fighting its war on this minority? "How do you rationalize," cried King, "that a nation which will not tend to the housing, education, and employment of its Negro citizens has a disproportionate number of Negroes serving and dying in Vietnam?"

Glowering at the television clips of the defiant King as

they gulped their drinks in Bridgeport taverns, Richard J. Daley's friends and neighbors were united in their hatred. "Why don't somebody tell that bastard to shut up?" someone said.

CHAPTER 11

1968

"The mistakes of the past should be warnings for the future. There can be no reasonable fear lest any plans shall prove too broad and comprehensive. Therefore, no one should hesitate to commit himself to the largest and most comprehensive undertaking."
            —*Daniel H. Burnham,* Plan of Chicago

Calendar 1968 was a year of three calamities: the assassination of the Rev. Dr. Martin Luther King, Jr., in Memphis, Tennessee, on April 4; the assassination of U.S. Senator Robert F. Kennedy, in Los Angeles, California, on June 5-6; the agony of the confrontation attendant to the Democratic National Convention, in Chicago, August 25-30. These were national tragedies, bursting out of the social agonies of troubled times. The common denominator of all three, as far as Richard J. Daley and others who thought that they were the ultimate targets of this violence were concerned, was *fear*.

The murder of Martin Luther King, Jr., even though it occurred in Memphis, created an immediate response that terrorized the establishment in Daley's Chicago. Daley's overreaction to what seems now to have been nothing more than the noisy, obscene threat of revolution on the part of a small and disorganized mob of anti-war protesters contributed to the shame that fell upon Chicago during a presidential nominating convention. The murder of Bobby Kennedy, while universally abhorred, had no noticeable effect upon conditions or the scheme of things in Chicago. Possibly the assassination of Bobby inspired some part of the raucous protesting in the heart of the city at convention time; more likely, however, the absence of Bobby as an anti-Vietnam candidate diminished the discord, for he almost certainly would have played to the gallery of discontented youth had he lived—providing the demonstrators with the savior-figure that they lacked. Apart from any grief he might have felt personally, the assassination of Bobby created no special problems for Richard J. Daley—nothing even remotely resembling the West Side ghetto violence that occurred immediately after the assassination of Martin Luther King.

With the advantage of hindsight, it is easy to see that in 1968 Daley had to deal with two crises, not three, and it is likewise obvious that the West Side ghetto rioting was of much greater social significance than the highly exaggerated disorders of Democratic convention week. Characteristically, it is the rioting of convention week that sticks in Daley's craw. Yet the sad business of ghetto people's torching and pillaging, and Daley's mad cry that he wanted them shot, is the thing that he should never forget.

In misery and bewilderment, Daley surveyed the gutted West Side ghetto—safely, from a helicopter—and softly spoke the lament: "I never believed that this would happen here." The wonder of it is: Why didn't he? What did Daley think the marching was about? The court battles over adequate education, housing, and jobs? At the time that King was assassinated, there was not a single black person in charge of any of the twenty-four departments of city government in Chicago. There was then but one black among the nine congressmen elected in Chicago— Dawson, who was subservient to the Daley Machine—and the worst of the violence in April 1968 occurred in the ghetto wards, all-black, that were represented in City Council by white, Daley-Machine aldermen or by blacks who served in City Council solely as the functionaries of absentee white ward bosses who lived in costly apartments on Lake Shore Drive or comparable avenues of luxury and affluence.

Daley had boasted in the early 1960s that he would eliminate the slums of Chicago by 1967; at the time that King was killed, the slums were more wretched than when Daley had made his promise. Public housing, funded by the federal government, was confined by the Daley administration to those segregated ghetto sites that Daley's friends in the real estate business did not want for more profitable development; indeed, it was Daley administration policy that all federal housing must be built in the ghettos.

When at last the American Civil Liberties Union went to court to compel the Chicago Housing Authority to cease perpetuating segregation with federal money, the CHA whimpered that it had no options—as a creature of Daley's City Council it had to build on sites, in the ghettos, that the council approved and purchased for public housing. When, after hearings that stretched across several years, Federal Judge Richard B. Austin determined that it was a fact that deliberate segregation had been a policy of CHA and ordered that federal funding be denied CHA until such time as it ceased this practice of confining low-income housing to low-income neighborhoods, of keeping poor blacks with poor blacks, the response to this ruling came not from CHA but from Daley, who snarled that the federal government could keep its money. Chicago, Daley declared, would find its own, rather than accept Judge Austin's formula for spreading the construction of public housing throughout the city.

This answer, of course, was an idle boast—the city lacked the millions of dollars that would be needed—but Daley's retort served to underscore his eagerness to neutralize a federal court ruling that would alienate vast numbers of white voters who strenuously objected to locating public housing projects in "their" neighborhoods.

It is typical of Daley to get himself out of sight in controversial situations. Thus it was that the burden of fighting Judge Austin's order that low-income housing must be built in all-white parts of Chicago fell not upon Daley or the City Council but the CHA. Even though from 1969, when Austin decreed that 750 federal housing units be built immediately in nonghetto neighborhoods and that, thereafter, three-fourths of the vastly greater number of dwellings for which funding was available must likewise be built in white areas, it has been the CHA, a creature of the Daley government—and not Daley—that has had to bear the onus of defying the federal court. Judge Austin has been at pains to specify that the CHA is merely implementing policy over which Mayor Daley has control;

yet, in appeals that have reached to the U.S. Supreme Court it is the CHA—not Daley—that is cast in the role of espousing segregation.

Daley fulminates against intermittent charges that Chicago is the most segregated of all northern cities (the not-for-profit Council of Municipal Performance restated the charge in a national survey released in November 1974) yet the evidence that this is so is irrefutable. As a consequence of the Judge Austin order of 1969, to cite but one item of evidence, not one public housing unit has been completed in Chicago—the CHA thwarting federal housing programs (thereby denying adequate housing to those who need it) with a continuing legal argument that, if Austin's decree is valid, the CHA does not have to abide by it until such time as its powers extend to the building of low-income housing in the suburbs (the issue that is presently delaying a building program that has been dormant for five years).

Public housing for the poor might provide great social and economic advantages; the extension of such housing into the better neighborhoods is held by Daley to be politically untenable, because it would vitiate control of the ghetto vote—and, in all things, political considerations are paramount in Chicago. Desegregated public housing had been one of Martin Luther King's demands; it supposedly was part of the agreement reached in the 1966 summit meeting. But the facts are that whereas the bulldozers of Daley's Department of Urban Renewal crushed thousands of slum dwellings, the choice cleared sites were sold at bargain rates to such real estate developers as Arthur Rubloff and other Daley friends. The displaced residents merely caused the population density of the ghettos to soar. Pierre de Vise, a De Paul University sociologist and a recognized authority on population movement, says that, typically, the population density in the worst of Chicago's slums, such as the area where the April 1968 rioting occurred, is twice what it is elsewhere in the city.

In short, it should hardly have come as a complete surprise to the Greatest Mayor Chicago Ever Had when the West Side ghetto erupted.

Yet it did, and Daley responded in the only way he could, with vicious anger. The nation was nauseated when it saw Mayor Daley swagger across their television screens and snarl, in the best Bridgeport manner, though he would later deny that he had said exactly this: "I told Conlisk to issue an order to police to shoot to maim or cripple anyone looting any stores in our city." Daley said: "I assumed the orders had been given all policemen. I assumed that any police superintendent would issue instructions to shoot an arsonist on sight and to maim or cripple any looters. I found out this morning"—with the West Side ghetto still smoldering— "that such orders never had been given." Grimly, Daley said: "I was disappointed that orders had not been given to shoot arsonists."

Ironically, the docile police superintendent, James B. Conlisk, had refused to issue a shoot-to-kill order because his predecessor, O. W. Wilson, had issued General Order 67-14 on May 16, 1967, expressly forbidding the firing of armed weapons in riot situations, and all police personnel had been trained in other methods of riot control. It would, in fact, have been virtually impossible for Conlisk to have implemented Daley's shoot-to-kill order.

If there is a proper and apt closing to the shameful episode of Chicago's response to King's assassination, it occurred in December 1973, when the Chicago City Council passed an ordinance creating a City of Chicago holiday, January 15, to honor the memory of the slain civil rights leader. Characteristically tardy and insensitive, the council acted for a city administration that had implacably frustrated the man at every turn while he lived.

There was widespread speculation, after Richard J. Daley's shoot-to-kill remarks, that the 1968 Democratic convention would have to be located in some other city. Daley's response to this was, "By God, you gave it to us and by God, we're going to keep it!"

It was clearly going to be a hot summer. Controversies abounded. The Chicago Board of Education found itself caught in a fascinating contradiction: refusing to certify thousands of substitute teachers, on the ground that they were not qualified to teach, while employing these "incompetents" on a full-time basis. Daley's school board advisory committee, which screens candidates for the nine-member board, publicly counseled His Honor the Mayor to dump President Frank Whiston, the real estate man, and Vice-President Tom Murray, the trade union man, on the ground that they were too closely identified with the status quo side of the racial controversy. But having learned in Bridgeport that a guy sticks with his friends, Daley reappointed both.

Whiston was a personal friend of Willis, the pair of them being driven to work frequently in Willis's chauffeured limousine; Murray, head of the lily-white electrical workers, was counted among the most ardent of the Willis advocates. The pro-Willis prejudice of the top two officials of the Board of Education was such that when they stood for reelection at a contentious board meeting on May 23, 1968, they couldn't muster from their seven fellow board members the three additional votes necessary to give them a simple majority; they remained in power, leaders of the black community doing a slow burn, solely because the others could not agree on who should be elected to replace them.

The next scandal was more humorous than important, offering almost comic relief. With Daley out of town—he was down in Florida, fishing—three of his Bridgeport payrollers flew off at city expense to Tokyo, announcing that this was a "study trip" to learn what was new in municipal garbage collecting. Part of the laugh was that the three City Hallers took their wives with them, announcing that while they were traveling first class, the wives would be in economy—providing a little insight into how things work in Bridgeport. Daley, sizzling, came hustling home with his fishing pole and, with a straight face, defended his aides' scholarship in garbage collecting. Their trip to Japan, Daley said, was a serious, scientific mission.

Equally serious, but perhaps not so scientific, Dick Gregory took his black followers marching past Daley's house on South Lowe once again, explaining that, even though you can't expect them to right any injustices for you, like Martin Luther King, Jr., he was a great believer in getting out where they could see you.

The good news for Daley was the effusive statement of John Bailey, national chairman of the Democratic party, on May 27, that Chicago had the best facilities for holding a presidential nominating convention. The die was now definitely cast—although the rumors of another city's taking it started circulating one week later, when Bobby Kennedy was fatally shot in Los Angeles, and continued into July, when the telephone installers went on strike in Chicago.

The protesters started moving toward the city.

Recollections of what actually occurred in Chicago in Democratic convention week in August 1968 are so contradictory that the most effective method of examining the events involves study of the defense of the Richard J. Daley administration, as prepared by the Richard J. Daley administration. The official apologia of the Daley administration, entitled "The Strategy of Confrontation," is based on the evidence compiled by Raymond F. Simon, corporation counsel of the Daley administration. From this report it would appear that if—as Daley tenaciously maintains—the convention week violence was the greatest hoax ever perpetrated upon the nation, the tragedy was that the Daley administration seriously overreacted to the hoax.

The report is nothing if not comprehensive. And now and then one can detect items of truth. For example, it is true that the television network personnel came to Chicago in a hostile mood, but the hostility was not directed so much at Daley and Chicago as caused by the need to move everything and everyone from Miami to Chicago in one week and with no respite in between conventions.

As we move on to the convention, Daley's claims become less and less documentable; in one place, indeed, his official report contradicts itself. In "The Strategy of Confrontation," the breakdown by ages of the 641 persons arrested—including twenty-two newsmen and one delegate who formally charged that they had been assaulted by police officers—showed that 450 of the 641 were twenty-four years of age or younger (349 were twenty-one or younger). This information, which was tabulated in a chart that appeared on page 74 of the document, is at variance with the claim on page 41 of the document that only 280 were in the twenty-one-or-under age bracket. Understandably, the lower figure was cited by the Daley administration as part of an "inescapable conclusion" that those arrested were "adult trouble makers who came into the City of Chicago for the avowed purpose of a hostile confrontation with law enforcement."

Accusations were made by the Daley administration that, during the 19-minute confrontation in front of the

Conrad Hilton Hotel, on the night of Wednesday, August 28, 1968, the demonstrators had set off noxious fumes in the lobby of the hotel and in the lobby of the Blackstone Hotel, located across the street. Yet, according to "The Strategy of Confrontation," when National Guardsmen lined up to prevent a march from the Grant Park area on the east side of Michigan Avenue to the International Amphitheatre, the convention site, many miles away, "a guardsman fired two canisters of tear gas. . . . The gas drifted to Michigan Avenue and into the Blackstone and Hilton Hotels."

It might be true, as Daley boasted in a 1972 extemporaneous speech to the National Restaurant Association, that the demonstrators would have been beaten up if they had marched into Bridgeport with Viet Cong flags. The fact is they didn't try.

In the aftermath of the Martin Luther King, Jr., and Robert F. Kennedy assassinations, it was perhaps understandable that Daley was quick to reach for the panic button as the 1968 Democratic Convention neared. Thus the purported justifications contained in "The Strategy of Confrontation" support a conclusion that nothing serious occurred *only* because extreme precautions were taken to contain the anti-Vietnam protesters. More likely, however, the strident vocalizing of the dissidents—what the official document calls "psychological warfare"—led the Daley administration into a trap of national, if not international, humiliation through overreaction to a crisis that the Daley administration did much to create.

Take one telling paragraph from the introduction of "The Strategy of Confrontation": "Although publicity, largely unfavorable, was enormous, arrests and injuries were moderate. The Convention was not disrupted; the City was not paralyzed. Not one shot was fired; not one life lost."

Now the Daley administration would argue that these tranquil results would not have pertained had members of its 12,000-man police department *not* been placed on twelve-hour duty, had the Illinois National Guard, 6,000 strong, *not* been activated, had federal troops, 5,000 of them, *not* been brought in and stationed at O'Hare Airport and the Glenview Naval Air Base. But the buildup of this massive containment force had been prompted by undocumented threats that 100,000 anti-war protesters would be moving into Chicago, by a parade-permit application for the march of 200,000 protesters to the convention hall, and by a permit application that would have allowed the assembly of 150,000 persons at the Grant Park band shell. And there is *no* evidence—and never was—that so vast a number of protesters would descend upon Chicago. City Hall accepted the figures at face value simply because the career protesters who came to be known as the Chicago Seven hoodwinked the Daley administration into believing that a protest of this magnitude could be mounted.

Had the blacks of the West Side ghetto joined in the demonstrations, the problem would have magnified to dangerous proportions, But there was never the slighest indication that the ghetto blacks considered the anti-war protest to be their affair, although a disproportionate number of their boys were fighting the war. In fact, with the exception of Dick Gregory, who is a nonghetto black, the blacks largely ignored convention week.

Stripped to the bare bones of actual numbers claimed by the Daley administration's document of defense, and allowing for the participation by the same individuals in many of these marches or other unauthorized assemblies, the actual head count of those who actively took part in the acts that struck terror into the heart of Chicago's City Hall would seem to have been no more than 2,000, not the 150,000 or 200,000 that Daley had anticipated.

However, if you dress up the statistics with the earthy Anglo-Saxonisms that are quoted in the Daley-authorized version of what the frightened young policemen had to endure—and it has been well established that large numbers of inexperienced rookies were employed in what the document euphemistically refers to as "the skirmish line" —you get an accurate perspective on the emotionalism of the confrontation.

It is true, as the outraged Richard J. Daley reported to the National Restaurant Association members four years later—His Honor the Mayor never has been able to erase the memory of his darkest hours—that there were instances of the demonstrators' hurling plastic bags of human waste at police officers. But it is likewise true, although Daley neglected to mention it in his 1972 speech, that the police precipitated the battle by driving the dissidents out of Lincoln Park and into the streets. City Hall had ordered that this be done, giving no thought apparently to the question of where the dissidents might then go—no thought of what retaliatory tactics the dissidents might then employ. No one can say what might have ensued during convention week (the resulting violence and discord that developed in Grant Park, across Michigan Avenue from the Conrad Hilton, for example, brought about the calling in of reinforcements from the Illinois National Guard) if on two successive nights, Sunday and Monday, Daley's policemen had not indiscriminately used clubs and tear gas to drive a mob of grubby and unwelcome squatters out of a public park in which they might have remained peaceably confined.

The summary of the "weapons used by the dissidents" contained in "The Strategy of Confrontation" provides little basis for a conclusion that the anti-war dissidents had come to Chicago prepared for battle. The complete list of their weapons includes such "merely disgusting" armament as cellophane bags of human excrement and cans of urine and paint. The "lethal weapons" listed as having been used during five days of convention week trouble included, in toto, "rocks, bricks, two-by-fours, dart guns, glass ashtrays, golf balls with nails impaled therein, potatoes with razors hidden inside, live black widow spiders, Molotov cocktails, knives and stilettos, cherry bombs, cans of noxious chemicals, a piece of metal with tenpenny nails attached to it, aerosol can with contents which acts as a stink bomb, a piece of wood with a razor attached, golf ball with nail forced through it, one-half of a wooden rolling pin filled with lead, bottle top with a wick for use with inflammable liquid, empty beer cans, baseball bat inscribed, 'Cops are pigs,' staple nails taped together to be used as a weapon." Completing the list of "battle" supplies listed in the Daley administration document were these items reported as having been in possession of persons arrested during convention week: "Helmets, gas masks, Vaseline to protect the body from Mace, revolutionary literature and 'battle' plans, dangerous drugs."

If, as Daley told the restaurant people four years later, a disorder of this kind "doesn't happen by accident; there had to be some planning some place, there had to be some program," the conclusion seems inescapable that—whoever it was that did the planning, and Daley has never specified that responsibility—the planners did a poor job of it. And had the Daley administration had the good sense to sweat the thing out, and ignore for one week the city ordinance, routinely ignored—even now—that forbids civilian use of city parks after 11:00 P.M., had City Hall had the wisdom to live with a bad situation rather than run the risk of inciting a riot by using skirmish lines of policemen to club a motley mob into running wild in the streets, pursuing them, provoking them with verbal howls and obscenities into uncivilized conduct outside the limits of the park, the 1968 convention week morbidity might have been greatly minimized, if not avoided.

But it is not the Bridgeport way to turn from someone with a chip on his shoulder. As Daley told the restaurateurs, speaking generally of violence, "We don't have to have it that way, if we make up our minds we are going to do somethin' about it."

In "The Strategy of Confrontation" truth was distorted to justify the Daley administration's methods of dealing with its enemies—not the least of which, in Daley's vituperative opinion, was television.

It is undoubtedly true that there were instances of camera crews' staging a few melodramatics to exploit the scenes of violence. It is probably true that trash fires, featuring the burning of signs that read "Welcome to Chicago, Richard J. Daley, Mayor," were set for effect. It might be true that some of the hippies were persuaded to pose with imaginary injuries. There was, however, little need of histrionics, because the scenes of violence were available to the camera's eye in sufficient quantity to preclude the need of staging. There was a surfeit of brutality, a sickening display of American citizens—demonstrators, news media people, and "innocent bystanders"—being clubbed and Maced, injured young people being tossed, concentration-camp style, into police vehicles. There was sufficiently ghastly evidence of terror and viciousness to make unnecessary the staging or simulation of what was going on in front of the Hilton Hotel, on the third night of the Democratic Convention in Richard J. Daley's Chicago.

Yet, though Daley shouted in angry protest, livid that

such scenes as this were presented to the nation on network television—nationally prominent Democrats seizing the podium to excoriate Daley, the Daley delegation shouting back defiance and insults at those who denounced him for the ugly portrayal of his police in action—and though President Johnson, observing these horrors on television sets at the White House, calling the convention platform on a private line to demand, in anger, "What in the Goddamn hell is going on out there!"—Daley will forever hold that television, which can only see what is there to be seen, is the diabolic tool of those who would destroy him.

The Greatest Mayor That Chicago Ever Had was unable to comprehend that he could reap so vast a harvest of loathing from a mere nineteen minutes, approximately the time frame of the feces-tossing and nightstick-clubbing that so appalled the nation, of conflict in the streets and parks of his city. And the harvest was vast. Although the Richard J. Daley admiration society regrouped after the horrific convention week happenings of 1968, the Bridgeport people and his friends and industry being blessed with conveniently short memories, the scars of that sorry convention week remain.

Remarkably, Daley hung on to control of Chicago, but the sweet pleasure of his achievements was never to be the same again. Superficially, Daley appeared to have changed not at all after that exposure of himself and his city to the nation during convention week of 1968; his strut and his smug self-confidence underwent no apparent change— if anything, he seemed a trifle more arrogant and bossy than he had been previously, Periodically, however, in his explosive orations of how judiciously he acted, he reveals his inability to erase from his mind the humiliations that he is convinced were unfairly heaped upon him. Many misfortunes, more grave than those of 1968, have befallen Daley and persons close to him since that time, but his inability to eradicate from his mind the experience of being portrayed as an advocate of violence haunts him. The joy he once took in exercising political power is not the same. Methodically, he rules and delivers the vote as of old—obediently, the lesser bosses do his bidding and remain respectfully, perhaps fearfully, in awe of Daley. Yet his exuberance was crippled by the sorry events of convention week, so much so, indeed, that many times there has been confidential speculation in Democratic circles that Daley has lost his driving compulsion to rule.

Meanwhile, since Daley rules, his ward bosses continue to bring in the vote, which is the condition of retaining their fiefs. Thus in 1968 Daley delivered a plurality in Chicago for Hubert H. Humphrey of 421,199—the automatic eleven giving a satisfactory performance, producing an advantage over Richard M. Nixon of 183,605 (See Table 6).

Table 6

Ward	Humphrey	Nixon	Plurality	Control
1	13,422	3,099	10,323	Crime syndicate
2	17,250	1,483	15,767	Dawson
3	25,001	1,378	23,623	Dawson
4	20,213	1,818	18,395	Dawson
6	25,355	1,731	23,624	Dawson
20	24,994	1,585	23,409	Dawson
24	16,498	309	16,189	Machine/Arvey
27	14,011	1,678	12,333	Machine/Sain
28	14,354	2,052	12,302	Machine/Syndicate
29	19,570	507	19,063	Machine/Horan
31	14,308	5,731	8,577	Machine/Keane
	204,976	21,371	183,605	

The volume of the vote produced by the automatic eleven for Humphrey was almost 25 percent less than had been turned in four years previously for Johnson, but it was a remarkable showing nonetheless. The same could be said of the citywide vote, and even though Daley sent Humphrey out of Chicago with only half the plurality that he had generated for Johnson, in a normal presidential election this would have been sufficient to ensure the statewide election of a Democratic candidate.

One gets an idea of exactly how professional a political boss Daley is when one remembers that he had a personal dislike for Vice-President Humphrey, who, he believed, lost Illinois to Nixon, by 137,000 votes, because he ran a dumb campaign. Humphrey, for sure, had no cause to complain that Daley had not extended his best efforts.

Even in 1972, when President Nixon scored his crushing victory over Senator George McGovern, the automatic eleven delivered a plurality for the despised McGovern of 154,183. The Democratic Machine, anxious to get out a big vote for such state candidates as Secretary of State Mike Howlett, refused to "get even" with the senator when such an act would involve jeopardizing the chances of Howlett. But whereas Howlett was sent out of Chicago with a healthy advantage of 339,400 votes, assuring his election (Howlett ran dead even with his Republican opponent downstate, one million votes ahead of his presidential candidate, and one hundred thousand votes ahead of Dan Walker, the successful anti-Daley Democratic candidate for governor). McGovern hobbled out of Chicago with a meager plurality of 202,116 and got clobbered downstate, losing to Nixon statewide by 874,707.

One should also note that never in all of his years as Democratic leader had Daley's professionalism been more visible than it was in 1972, when he gave his best effort to get out a vote for the man whose followers had maneuvered him, Daley, out of his seat at the Democratic convention, only four months earlier. Being denied, along with fifty-eight other "regular" Democrats, the credentials they had won in the spring election of delegates, was a major humiliation—and the blame was placed on McGovern. Yet even then Daley did not seek retribution.

Following the debacle of the 1968 convention in Chicago, the Democrats had set up a commission, under McGovern's chairmanship, to revise the procedures for the selection of delegates to the nominating conventions. The new rules were intended to broaden the demography of those chosen to vote on party candidates for the presidency, to make provision especially for equitable proportions of women, minorities, and young delegates. Locally, having paid mild lip service to the new concept that organization Democrats should not hog the seats by electing themselves, the Daley Machine methodically lined up the organization votes to elect 59 of the state's 170 convention delegates. Opposition candidates, headed by William Singer, an anti-Daley alderman who represented Paddy Bauler's old Forty-third Ward, and Reverend Jesse Jackson, the articulate disciple of Martin Luther King, Jr., thereupon cried that the Machine was in violation of Democratic party rules and retaliated by holding caucuses in various parts of the city to renounce the "illegal" election of the

Daley delegates. The Singer-Jackson adherents, heckled by Machine Democrats who infiltrated their meeting, elected themselves on voice votes as the "valid" delegates.

All of this seemed comical, and Daley did not appear perturbed. Having gone through the motions of electing their fifty-nine delegates in accordance with Illinois election laws, the Daley delegates felt entitled to their credentials, and the state courts so held. The Singer-Jackson forces thereupon sought relief in the federal courts, which were reluctant to intervene in a matter that seemed to be solely within the discretion of the political party that set the rules. Arguments from both sides then were heard by the pro-McGovern convention credentials committee at a meeting in Washington, and one week in advance of the opening of the Democratic convention in Miami Beach, the decision was reached (by a vote of 71 to 61, with twelve committee members not voting) that the Daley delegates should be unseated and that the Chicago credentials belonged to the fifty-nine Singer-Jackson delegates. National Chairman Lawrence F. O'Brien, a survivor of President Kennedy's Irish Mafia, was caught in a trap. Committed to McGovern, or believed to be, O'Brien realized that Daley would be furious, but he simultaneously had to applaud this extraordinary demonstration that the *new* Democratic party was to be, as the McGovern commission had promised, representative of all segments of society. Reporters were waiting at O'Hare Airport when Singer stepped off the plane from Washington, a cocky, lop-mouthed grin on his face, and declared: *"We* are the delegates now." Daley exploded in anger.

Daley contended, and not without logic, that his delegates had been elected in accordance with Illinois election law. Livid, he asserted that the Singer-Jackson "challengers" had undemocratically chosen themselves—some of them indeed had been "elected" in secret caucuses. Yet the tables were turned. Having previously refused to acknowledge that a Democrat of his eminence could be stripped of his credentials after being chosen delegation chairman at a meeting in Springfield of the legally elected delegates of Illinois, Daley was now reduced to fighting the obnoxious Alderman Singer in the courts.

Attorney Jerome Torshen, as associate of Alderman Tom Keane, Daley's council leader, was instructed to ask the U.S. Court of Appeals in Washington to reverse the credentials committee action and reseat the Daley delegates. In a second action, brought by Keane's flunky, Alderman Paul T. Wigoda, Daley sought intervention by U.S. Supreme Court Justice William H. Rehnquist. All that Torshen and Wigoda got was a ruling that the Daley delegates were free to go back to the state courts in search of an injunction to prevent the Singer-Jackson group from being seated at Miami Beach.

Attorney Torshen, Alderman Keane prominently at his side, next sought justice from Circuit Court Judge Daniel A. Covelli, who ruled decisively that the Singer-Jackson delegates were illegitimate—issuing an order that forbade them to take their seats at the convention. Cheerfully defying Covelli—arguing that no court had jurisdiction over the procedures of a political party and ignoring Covelli's charge that they were in violation of Illinois election laws—the Singer-Jackson fifty-nine boarded their charter flight and flew off to Fort Lauderdale, a short bus ride from their hotel in Hollywood.

Covelli, raging mad at being defied, announced in open court that he would clap into jail at his first opportunity Singer, Jackson, and all of the ringleaders of the anti-Daley delegation if they dared take their seats at the Democratic convention. Safely within an hour's bus ride of the convention site and with the credentials in their pockets, Chairman O'Brien having delivered them, the Singer-Jackson delegates planned to take their seats. Their only worry now was a floor fight being promised by Daley's friends from other states.

Some of the Daley fifty-nine showed up at the Diplomat Hotel: City Collector Marshall Korshak, labor union bosses, Alderman Vito Marzullo, Alderman Claude W.B. Holman, a black who prided himself on being president pro tem of the Chicago City Council, empowered to preside when Daley wasn't there (which before mid-1974 happened only on extremely rare occasions). Daley's press secretary, Earl Bush, who soon was to be convicted of mail-fraud charges, stalked the crowded hotel lobby; Mary Mullen, Daley's personal secretary, occasionally was to be seen.

Rumors flew that Daley was somewhere in the area and that he intended to address the convention, demanding that his delegates be seated. Actually, Daley was holed up at his seven-acre retreat on the shores of Lake Michigan. Network film crews were staked out on the roads leading into the place, but no one had seen Daley's car, with his tail cars filled with Chicago policemen, enter, and news directors handling the convention coverage—anxious as they were to get a fix on where Daley, mystery man of the hour, was holed up—clung to the idea that he was somewhere in the Miami area, preparing to make a dramatic appearance at the hall.

In Miami, Illinois State Chairman Jack Touhy, son of a longtime leader of the Twenty-seventh Ward, was in constant touch with Daley. A former speaker of the Illinois House, brought up in politics, Touhy tried hard to line up enough delegates to reverse the decision of the credentials committee that had denied seats to the Daley fifty-nine.

In fact, the crisis over Daley's being ousted from the convention was now a matter of greater interest than the expected nomination of George McGovern. With the verdict of the credentials committee now on appeal to the full convention, Jack Touhy was following up the contracts that Daley was making by phone with old pals whose delegations were needed to send the Singer-Jackson people packing. The roll call on the question of whether the Daley delegates should be seated shaped up as the most dramatic moment of the 1972 convention; it didn't matter that, subsequently, McGovern was certain to be nominated—the professionals didn't give him a chance of defeating Nixon in November. The power of the old guard was under challenge: this was the issue.

A reporter who had the trust of Chairman Touhy asked him if Daley was in the Miami Beach area. Touhy said no, Daley was sweating it out at his place in Grand Beach, Michigan. Would Daley be flying down to the convention? "Only if we win the vote and get the credentials," Touhy replied. Vito Marzullo and Claude W. B. Holman and other Daley delegates paced the lobby of the Diplomat Hotel or sat in funeral style, glowering at the frenetic Singer-Jackson delegates (and a similar group of unsophisticates from New York, who likewise had been assigned to the Diplomat)—not knowing where their leader was or what he was doing to avoid disaster.

At the undisciplined caucuses of the Illinois delegation,
Singer seemingly in charge, a scattering of organization
delegates whose credentials had not been under challenge
—Secretary of State Mike Howlett, an ex-officio delegate, for one—observed the Singer-Jackson plotting and
planning with faint amusement. When, for example, there
was bitter dispute over a question that had been raised
regarding the garden lettuce that was part of the garni
found in the box lunches that somebody was placing on
the delegate seats at the convention hall—could the eating
of this lettuce be construed as abandonment of Cesar
Chavez' fight for better wages for the United Farm
Workers?—such veteran politicians as Jack Touhy and
Mike Howlett openly smiled.

When it was time to act, however, the smiles disap-
peared, and professionalism paid off. For example, Touhy
immediately torpedoed a suggestion made by some of the
Singer-Jackson faction that, for the good of the Democratic
party, there should be a compromise, half of the credentials to be turned over to the Daleyites. Asked why Jack
Touhy dismissed this suggestion, Howlett said: "Daley
can't give recognition; if he does, Singer and Jackson will
be hollering for the same cut on everything back in Chicago
when the convention is over." There was no room for
compromise.

The delegation vote that was watched when the convention was polled on the matter of which faction was
entitled to be seated was the group from Massachusetts.
Could Senator Edward Kennedy deliver for Daley—and
would he? A tenseness pervaded the convention when the
roll call finally got to that point. Massachusetts voted to
sustain the credentials committee, and there was bedlam
in the hall as McGovern loyalists—the sizable number of
non-organization delegates—realized they had carried the
day. Daley had lost. By morning, his people—the Marzullos, the Holmans, the Korshaks—had packed up and
gone home. Chairman Touhy remained, because he had a
job to do.

Having won their fight to cast the Illinois votes for
McGovern, the Singer-Jackson forces should have pressed
their advantage; they should have sealed their victory when
they caucused before the long night was out; they should

have voted to place their own people on the Democratic National Committee. Had they done so, the Singer-Jackson forces would have perpetuated their beachhead on Daley's area of influence. With Singer and Jackson controlling the Illinois members of the National Committee, Daley would have been forced to deal with them. But they failed to make the necessary effort. Jack Touhy, aware of the implications, outmaneuvered the rebels when they gathered, exhausted, in a pre-dawn caucus at the Diplomat Hotel. Cunningly, with the help of pro-Daley members of the Illinois delegation, Touhy got the Singer-Jackson faction confused in contentious debate over procedural matters as they endeavored to nominate and vote on those who would represent Illinois during the next four years on the National Committee. Touhy's people offered amendments to every nomination or resolution of the Singer-Jackson group, raised points of order, demanded parliamentary discussion on what issue was then before the delegation. Dog-tired from a long night at the convention hall, overemphasizing the lasting importance of having won the credentials fight, the rebels failed in their attempt to put a seal on their victory. The night ended in chaos, many of the Singer-Jackson group drifting off to their rooms. Finally, on a motion from one of the Jack Touhy people that the matter of selecting National Committee members be put off until some future caucus, to be held in Chicago, the meeting was adjourned.

As friends gathered around Alderman Billy Singer to congratulate him on his brilliance in pulling off the coup of getting Daley kicked out of the convention, Jack Touhy walked to a public phone in the lobby and placed a call to Daley, to convey word that things were now under control. A reporter asked Touhy what he had gained by the delaying tactics. Couldn't the Singer and Jackson forces assert their power later, in Chicago? Touhy smiled. No, he said, there was a lot of dissension among them and McGovern needed Daley now. Besides, he said, "Singer is going to be so busy defending himself on Covelli's contempt of court citation, he can't cause us any trouble."

Back in Chicago, Judge Covelli, blazing that the Singer-Jackson delegates had ignored his orders not to attend the convention, did indeed bring them to trial, finding them guilty—the verdict thereafter bouncing through U.S. circuit courts of appeal and the Supreme Court itself in a maze of legalistics, a final determination still not made at year's end, 1974. Meanwhile, flashing back to the post-convention period of 1972, Senator McGovern unashamedly sought rapprochement with Daley, infuriating Reverend Jesse Jackson, who declared, "McGovern may need Daley in Chicago, but he needs *me* nationally," and accused McGovern of betrayal of the blacks.

All around the rebels fell apart. When six of Daley's people were named to the Democratic National Committee, Alderman Singer remained mute, and Jackson accused his erstwhile associate of having sold out those who had fought Daley at the convention. Many of the anti-Daley Machine delegates and sympathizers were disillusioned when McGovern came to Chicago during the campaign and was praised not only by Daley but also by Senator Edward M. Kennedy, whom Daley forgave—Teddy was a Kennedy, after all—for his failure to deliver the Massachusetts delegation to Daley in the critical roll call at Miami Beach. Anti-Machine Democrats were further disenchanted when Daley gave organization backing to the anti-organization candidate for governor, Daniel Walker, who had excoriated Daley during a bitter primary contest as head of a "vicious" Machine.

But the disenchantment was not confined to the rebels. Even some of the regulars found it hard to believe that the pragmatic Daley, giving priority to need for electing Democrats, regardless of whether or not they were loyal to him, could so conveniently forgive and forget. Yet Daley was boss, and if he chose to forgive, they would follow him. They had no choice. Alone of the organization aldermen, Vito Marzullo, his Sicilian blood boiling, would not forgive and forget. Marzullo, who had stormed out of the Diplomat Hotel in Florida cursing McGovern as a "no-good, Goddamn sonofabitch!" vowed, then and later, to campaign for the reelection of President Nixon. This was apostasy of the highest order, coming from a loyal Machine boss. But the irony was that, try as he might, Marzullo could not overcome the Democratic voting habits of his constituents, and McGovern comfortably carried the Twenty-fifth Ward. Marzullo found consolation, perhaps, in the terrible beating that the senator from South Dakota received in Illinois and elsewhere in the nation.

Daley had little to say about the defeat of McGovern. He knew in advance what the outcome was going to be; yet, hating McGovern as deeply as anyone did—and with a particular reason for so doing—Daley had grimly gone about the business of trying to get a vote for the man. Getting out the vote for your party is the mark of a professional, of course, but there usually is nothing altruistic about it. In Daley's effort for McGovern, as in 1956, the motivation was that of preventing the poor vote that was anticipated for a "bad" candidate from doing too much damage to others on the party ticket. Even with this consideration in mind, however, the election of 1972 was a cheerless time for Chairman Daley. In a continuation of the manner in which the tides seemed to have turned against him, starting with the abortive convention of 1968, Daley was confronted not only by a national administration in strong Republican hands but by rebellious Democrats on his home grounds.

In 1970 he had had to slate Adlai E. Stevenson III for the unexpired term of the late U.S. Senator Everett Dirksen, the choice forced upon him not by what Adlai amounted to, personally, but rather because of the quasi-sacred name he bore. The Stevenson name just had too much to offer politically.

This was especially galling because young Adlai· had done much to cause Daley to distrust him. For a start he had turned into a person less amenable than his distinguished father, now several years dead, and had made a habit of expressing disagreeable criticism of Daley—searching for opportunities, or so it seemed to the organization, to twist a verbal knife in the mayor, as when he referred to the Daley Machine as "a feudal system that maintains itself by passing out political jobs and favors to the faithful." Stevenson tended to speak disparagingly of the "outrageous" manner in which Daley had run the 1968 convention. In an apparent desire to discredit Daley, young Adlai had told his noncomformist followers that the Democratic party would have to be "revitalized" if it were to survive, and he directed his denigration of all that Daley believed in toward those, like himself, who professed to be nauseated by the old guard—to the young people who were strictly anti-Daley and to the Eugene McCarthy, Teddy Kennedy, and George McGovern sympathizers.

In the face of this continual barrage of softly spoken criticism, Daley would only respond, when pressed for statements of rebuttal, that Adlai had a right to express his own thoughts. All the same it had aggravated Daley, to say the least, when he had found that he had no choice but to run the young man for Dirksen's vacant seat in the U.S. Senate. Typically, Daley knew he had to do this before Adlai knew it. The decision to run Stevenson for the Senate was made suddenly in late summer of 1969.

Adlai, then serving as state treasurer of Illinois, was being host to an old-fashioned political picnic on the thirty-acre Stevenson farm near Libertyville, some thirty miles northwest of Chicago, one Sunday afternoon—and Daley was the last Democrat in the state that Adlai expected to show up. All advance notice had been that this was to be an outing for critics of the Daley regime. Suddenly, however, the mayor's limousine pulled into the farm. The startled Stevenson, resorting to his endowments of good birth and breeding, made an effort to be gracious to his unexpected guest. He had not the slightest notion of what it was that had brought Daley so far out of the city on a Sunday afternoon to a beer and hotdogs party for amateur political aficionados who did not approve of him. Wearing his very best Irish smile, and ignoring the looks of disbelief on the faces of Adlai's mob of casually dressed friends, Daley knew very well what he was about: this was the overture to the business of sending Adlai to the U.S. Senate.

At the moment that Daley's car pulled in, Senator Dirksen was at the point of death in a Washington-area hospital. Frequently, the senator had been in and out of hospitals, but on this particular Sunday, just home from mass at the parish church, Daley had received a call from Washington that it was all over for Dirksen; he probably would not live out the day. This was all the notice Daley needed to get started toward Stevenson's widely publicized anti-Daley picnic.

At approximately the moment when the host was asking for quiet, in order that he could make some brief remarks and introduce distinguished members of the company, word was flashed that Senator Dirksen was dead. Hearing the news, the flag having dropped again for Daley at a most propitious time, all eyes turned toward Daley.

When Daley was asked to speak, he did so with moving reference to Dirksen and, with political wisdom, went as far as he dared to hint that Adlai would take Dirksen's place. It wouldn't be at once, of course; Governor Richard B. Ogilvie would appoint a fellow Republican to the vacancy, but Illinois law provided that there be a political contest for the unexpired portion of Dirksen's term—and that meant November 1970. It was generally understood when Daley climbed into his limousine for the trip home, Adlai and guests politely applauding, that Adlai E. Stevenson III was now in the process of being adopted by the organization he had heretofore deplored. And so it came to pass in November 1970, when Stevenson defeated the lightweight temporary incumbent, Ralph Smith. It didn't sit too well, actually, with some of Adlai's friends—especially a close associate named Daniel Walker—that he was in jeopardy of relinquishing his political independence.

Dan Walker, general counsel of Montgomery Ward & Co., author of the presidential study of the Chicago convention troubles, which he indignantly declared to have been "a police riot," was to be cochairman of Stevenson's successful election campaign in November 1970. A Daley organization man was assigned as the other cochairman, and Walker was openly hostile. Immediately after the election, as if to declare that—even though Adlai had been converted to the true faith as preached by Richard J. Daley—Walker was still his own man. Walker made announcement of what seemed to be a preposterous idea, namely that *he* would be an independent Democratic candidate for governor in 1972. Advised of this, Daley smiled faintly and said, "Everyone has a right to run for public office."

Walker's announcement of candidacy provoked little immediate interest. Daley had been furious with the conclusion of the Walker Report to the National Commission on the Causes and Prevention of Violence that the 1968 convention trouble in Chicago was essentially a "police riot." But Walker's ambition to defeat the Daley Machine was of no great moment; what was Walker, after all, but a past president of the Chicago Crime Commission, a do-good organization that stalks corruption? Daley had more urgent matters on his mind.

Public indignation was aflame, especially among the blacks, over a pre-dawn raid that State's Attorney Edward V. Hanrahan's police had made on December 4, 1969, on a flat occupied by Black Panthers—a federal grand jury finding that two Panther leaders, Fred Hampton and Mark Clark, had been shot to death in a horrible display of misguided law enforcement, the evidence indicating that Hanrahan's people had grossly abused the civil rights of the black group. Daley stewed over this for months, even though Chief Judge Joseph Power of the criminal court, a Bridgeporter, gave the appearance of trying to keep the lid on and save Hanrahan's hide, only the white backlash folks supporting Hanrahan for what his raiders had done.

Then there was the federal investigation, subsequent trial and conviction of U.S. Court of Appeals Judge Otto Kerner, Jr., the former governor. Word reached Daley at an early date that Kerner, for whom Daley had done so much, was implicated in a sweetheart deal on racetrack stock—that he had provided favors in the assignment of racing dates to Marjorie Lindheimer Everett, receiving in return a bargain basement price on Arlington Park-Washington Park Stock. This was another scandal, implicating someone close to Daley, that would not evaporate.

At age seventy-eight, Congressman William Levi Dawson died on November 10, 1970, and Daley was in a stew over how to hold the South Side ghetto together as a political force.

In December of 1970, Daley maneuvered another trade union boss, taciturn John D. Carey, into the presidency of the Board of Education, Frank Whiston having died —but the election of Carey came about in an unprecedented secret vote that did not fill Chicago with confidence. There was only sporadic demonstrating at this time against the inadequacies of the public school system, but Daley sensed that serious outbreaks might erupt at any time.

The rebuilt McCormick Place—costing $75,000,000 more than the first one, which had been destroyed by fire on January 16, 1967—was reopened in January 1971, but Daley had to endure both criticism of its cost and its box-like appearance; nothing was going right.

Federal funding had been secured for an agency called The Chicago Plan, which had the task of getting jobs for blacks in the building construction industry. Under the direction of Alderman Fred Hubbard—who had been elected as an anti-Machine alderman of the Second Ward, and who had almost at once become the willing captive of the Daley Machine—the Plan was failing dismally and this embarrassment was capped when Hubbard, up to his neck in gambling debts, vanished at almost the moment that $96,450 was discovered to be missing from the funds entrusted to his care. There was no end to the bad turning things had taken and soon Daley had candidate Dan Walker badgering him, blaming him, castigating him, insulting him; Daley was experiencing some bad years.

Critics of Dan Walker say he is too quick to smile and too eager to ingratiate himself with anyone who happens along. There is a resemblance to Don Quixote in Walker, and the Democratic Machine people were openly derisive when the new candidate, virtually unknown to the voters of Illinois, announced that he intended to repair that lack of exposure by literally walking the state of Illinois, from its lower reaches to the Wisconsin line. As he strode along the highways, stopping to shake hands in every by-way —bareheaded, a red bandanna flapping under his stubborn chin—he "pressed a lot of flesh," as the late Senator Dirksen used to say. At first, Walker the walker was a joke. Then, slowly, he became a curiosity, and small-town newspapers started to write him up, his itinerary following the placards and publicity handouts that well-drilled advance men passed out in great abundance. Finally, the arrival of Dan Walker and his entourage came to be awaited in downstate Illinois towns as the natives had once anticipated the arrival of traveling circuses. When he talked, he spewed invective on the evil Richard J. Daley Machine, though, interestingly, the worst things that he said about Daley were deleted in the press releases that flowed in on the Chicago media.

Daley was said to be doing a slow burn, never having had much use for Dan Walker, especially since the so-called Walker Report—the actual writing of it being done by a longtime Daley hater named Victor deGrazia, who surfaced as Walker's campaign manager—pictured Daley as odious. And what became clear as much from Daley's reaction as anything else, was that Walker was no fumbling amateur. Certainly, Walker's campaign was costing someone a great deal of money, and sly suggestions were dropped to reporters at City Hall: "Why don't you ask Walker who is backing him?" In time, the question was asked, but open disclosure of his campaign contributions is one area in which Walker's preachments of full disclosure of everything proved to be inoperative. He has never revealed who bankrolled his successful million-dollar-plus campaign for governor.

If it had not been for a state income tax that had been imposed during the Governor Ogilvie administration, Mayor Daley collaborating in lining up Democratic votes in the State House and Senate, it is unlikely that Walker would have been elected. Passage of the income tax, inevitably unpopular with Illinois residents, had been a bipartisan effort to save the state from imminent insolvency. But having helped Ogilvie impose the tax, Daley kept silent as his Democrats put the blame for it on Ogilvie. It was patently unfair to place responsibility solely upon the Republican governor who was seeking a second term, but the inequity of this didn't disturb Daley; Daley had a new-look candidate of his own, Lieutenant Governor Paul Simon of Troy—now a congressman from downstate—and he counted upon Simon to trounce Walker in the primary, the regular Democrats of Cook County providing the winning margin, and then to beat Ogilvie on the income tax issue.

However, in a moment of candor with reporters, candidate Simon destroyed Daley's plan. Simon had allowed himself to be drawn into a hypothetical question of whether, having to make a choice of increasing the state sales tax or the state income tax, he would hit the purchaser or the wage earner. His innocent reply was that he would favor an increase in the income tax to provide relief for low-income people who were obligated to pay sales tax on everything they bought. This translated instantly into headlines that screamed: SIMON FAVORS INCREASE IN

INCOME TAX. Daley was appalled. Simon protested that this was not what he had meant, but City Hall curtly told him: "That's what you said." Joyously, Walker grabbed Simon by the throat and upset him in the primary—beating him statewide by 39,000 votes, running up his big advantage in the downstate area where he had done all the walking. Daley almost retched, having to accept Dan Walker, who had attacked him so viciously, as the Democratic candidate for governor.

There were no denunciations of Daley as Dan Walker went on the attack against Governor Ogilvie, transferring to Ogilvie the scorn he had poured upon Simon for putting the burden of an income tax on the wage earners of Illinois. Simultaneously, and with a rather melodramatic flair, he cried that, in all honor, Ogilvie should make public a list of his campaign contributors, implying that shady characters were secretly funding the Ogilvie campaign. Daley groaned; he knew from his intelligence that the Continental Bank of Chicago was holding notes in the amount of $750,000—some of them signed by persons of dubious reputation—on contributions to the Dan Walker fund. But Ogilvie never attacked Walker on the subject of finances.

When the last of the 4,660,000 votes cast in the Illinois gubernatorial election on November 7, 1972, were counted, Democrat Walker had beaten Republican Ogilvie by 77,494 votes. With a somber face, Chairman Daley faced reporters to make a "victory" statement: "We all know, everyone knows, Dan Walker will make a great governor." Then he marched grimly out of party headquarters and went home.

Neil F. Hartigan, one of the Daley Machine's bright young men and Paul Simon's running mate for lieutenant governor in the primary, had outpolled Simon—defeating Walker's candidate—and consequently had wound up running with Walker. They did not like each other, Hartigan and Walker, and they avoided each other during the campaign. Congratulated on his victory, Hartigan, aware of the Daley organization's distrust of Governor-elect Walker, said, "I don't know whether to laugh or cry. All I know is that I think we are in for some rough years."

Someone asked Secretary of State Mike Howlett what

the basis of the problem was. Howlett replied: "The basis of the problem is that we have elected a governor who hates Daley and thinks this is the way to get elected president of the United States."

CHAPTER 12

The Long Descent

*"No one has the right to say that the End is
here, for Christ Himself has declared that only
the Father knows the day and the hour."*
—*Matt. 24:36*

Monday, May 6, 1974, began for Mayor Richard J. Daley
as countless other days had: the early rising, the quick
shower and shave, the carefully tied Windsor knot in his
necktie, the hasty breakfast and small talk with Sis in the
kitchen of 3536 South Lowe, a peek out the front window
for reassurance that no one other than the ubiquitous assigned cop was there, and that no demonstrators or reporters were waiting to badger him, the quick observation
that his black limousine was punctually at the curb, the
detectives in unmarked tail cars behind it, the final glance
at himself in a hallway mirror, a peck on Sis's cheek on the
way out, and the deliberate pacing down the walk to his
car, the policeman touching the peak of his cap murmuring, "Morning, Mr. Mayor."

"St. Peter's," Daley said as he climbed into his car. His
driver and bodyguard were glad to hear that that was
where the mayor would "catch mass" that morning. When
he opted for St. Peter's on Madison Street, one block
south of City Hall, it indicated that he was in an agreeable
mood and that nothing particularly was bothering him.
Daley's decision to attend mass at St. Peter's was also a
sign that the mayor faced a busy schedule. The Franciscan
Fathers, who operate the church in the heart of downtown Chicago, string their schedule of masses like beads
of a rosary—recognizing the need of Catholics who at-

tended regularly to get in and out in rather a hurry. St. Peter's is not really "Daley's church"; Nativity, out in Bridgeport, has a solid claim on that honor. Also, there were days when Daley said, "Old St. Mary's" when he came down the walk at 3536 South Lowe of a morning and got into his car. His driver and bodyguard surmised, then, that there was something bothering the mayor and that he wanted to be alone. "Old" St. Mary's, the Paulist Fathers' church, was not old but rather new, having replaced an ancient church that had existed since shortly after the Great Fire of 1871. The new "Old" St. Mary's was located at Van Buren and Wabash, at the southeastern extremity of the elevated structure that for three-quarters of a century has been referred to as the Chicago Loop. The Paulists, who made the move from their old to their new church unwillingly and only because they were ordered to do so by John Cardinal Cody, thereupon referred to their new chapel as "Old St. Mary's." Indeed, some of the priests believed that Mayor Daley's dropping in occasionally for morning mass indicated that he shared their sentiment that the old church should not have been surrendered to pharisaical real estate developers. But, sentimental attachment to old things is not characteristic of Daley; he patronized the Paulists principally when he wanted to pray in peace. Old St. Mary's is not frequented by worshippers of importance with whom he would feel obligated to exchange greetings, as generally is the case at St. Peter's.

In any event, there was not the slightest hint when Daley set out from home on the morning of the day that was to shock those who keep an eye on his temporal temple that Daley's health was anything but excellent. For three or four years now, he had been popping pills into his mouth every morning: Orinase, which is commonly prescribed for elderly persons who frequently need mild medication to compensate for a lazy pancreas that isn't putting enough sugar in the blood; and Hydrodiuril, a diuretic taken in the morning to relieve mild hypertension by stimulating the elimination of fluids. No outsiders other than Dr. Thomas J. Coogan, Jr., his personal physician, and a downtown pharmacy, were privy to this information, and his doctor was not concerned. What was known about Daley's medical condition was that he was obese but vigorous, that he had never been hospitalized in nineteen years as mayor and that only on rare occasions had he been indisposed by such minor ailments as upset stomach or flu. Looking healthy and acting fit was part of Daley's image, and the fine state of his health had been exploited by the heavy schedule of public appearances he made during his quadrennial election campaigns.

Indeed, it was Daley's history of good health that made the impact of the news, that morning in May when it became shockingly clear that Daley was human after all, felt throughout the city.

As usual, Daley was at his desk in City Hall before nine, one of his bodyguards having carried in the loaded briefcase of paperwork that he habitually took home with him every evening. He had scurried that morning almost at once to the county side of the block-square building to participate in a brief memorial service for a county commissioner, a well-known Polish woman, who had died the previous week. County Board President George Dunne, sometimes mentioned as the potential heir to Daley's throne, remarked later in the day, "The Mayor looked the picture of health."

Flanked by his bodyguards, with Frank Sullivan, his press secretary, tagging along, Daley had walked with his customary resolute step back to the City Hall side of the building, murmuring his litany of "How are ya?", raising his right hand in acknowledgment, beaming at a few of the many who deferentially expressed greetings to him. He was hardly back in his office on the fifth floor when he had to get up and take an elevator to the City Council chambers on the second, where he spoke briefly to thirty-nine boys and girls of high school age who had been selected for the vacuous honor of being city officials for a day. Daley had a pleasant word and a handshake for each—Daley really likes kids—as he passed out the certificates designating this one as Youth Day fire chief, that one as chief of police, and so on. He posed for pictures with the honorary mayor, a girl who looked to be taking this nonsense as seriously as Daley did.

As quickly as he could disengage from the ceremonies, however, Daley exited, as he always does, through the rear doors of the council chambers—pausing, as he often does when in a good humor, to stick his head in the press room to joke for an instant with City Hall reporters. Then, almost without breaking stride, he walked to the elevator that was being held for him and went shooting up to the fifth floor.

This was going to be a particularly busy day; there was no council meeting to burn up several hours, but Daley had a date to speak at the Palmer House at the civic luncheon for the junior officials he had certified, and this was not one of those occasions where he could pop in at the last moment, read his speech, and get out. Protocol insisted that he would have to be present from start to finish. Then, in early afternoon, he had a block of time set off on his schedule for a private and serious meeting with Robert Strauss, national chairman of the Democratic party; Strauss was conspicuously a pro-Daley man, and Daley was not about to slight such a person.

Suddenly, however, as he pondered how he was going to cram into a limited number of hours the many things that had to be done, Daley felt ill. He felt dizzy, and when he spoke to his secretary, his tongue was thick and his speech slurred. He experienced a dull pain in his right leg. Looking pale, he quietly informed his secretary that he had to see Dr. Coogan. The secretary hurried back to her desk and got on the phone; in a matter of minutes, the mayor—who always works with jacket on—got up and was on his way, looking straight ahead, ignoring everyone, certainly deeply worried about what it was that was ailing him.

Shortly Daley was debarking the limousine and heading into the 900 North Michigan Avenue building, kitty-corner from the Drake Hotel, where Coogan has his office. The doctor checked the mayor's blood pressure and found it elevated; Daley's pulse and respiration were irregular. Putting these findings together with the slurred speech and the dizziness and the leg pain, Coogan made a preliminary diagnosis that the mayor had suffered a stroke. Quickly Daley was en route to Presbyterian-St. Luke's Hospital, facing Congress Expressway, some four miles southwest of 900 North Michigan.

Unaided, Daley had gone to the elevator and walked to his car. At the emergency entrance of the hospital, Daley got out and walked in the manner of a man who is master of his fate. An ordinary mortal in this situation would have been transported by ambulance; presumably, Daley—ever careful about appearances—wouldn't hear of that. Allowing the mayor to walk to and from his limousine and to travel by car to the hospital was questionable medically, but it was politically wise to give no indication that anything untoward was occurring. His arrival in apparent good health—a city fireman who saw the mayor walk into the emergency room reporting later that "he looked good"—was stage one of what developed into a multistage cover-up of what his medical problem was and what was going to be done about it.

Frank Sullivan, the mayor's press aide, was already at the hospital when reporters and film crews poured in. Sullivan casually said only that the mayor was suffering a "minor ailment." A public relations woman for the hospital was more specific; she said Daley had "hypoglycemia" —low blood sugar—which could be indication of diabetes or a liver malfunction or something else. Later, apparently at the urging of Sullivan, the hospital retracted the statement. The Sullivan line seemed to be that the midday dash to the hospital was a routine thing, the importance of which should not be exaggerated: Daley was merely at Presbyterian-St. Luke's for tests and would be back in his office next morning. If this was the official story, the Democratic Machine bosses thought otherwise: Daley had hardly arrived at the hospital than Daley's top people were anxiously in conference on private telephone lines— searching for a clue as to "how bad off he is" and what was now to be done. Newspapers with big-type headlines, "DALEY STRICKEN!" were being grabbed off newsstands in all parts of the city, but the stories had precious little information about what was ailing the man.

Mrs. Daley, concealing her emotions, arrived at the hospital and was ushered immediately to her husband's guarded room on the tenth floor. The four Daley boys and his three daughters, some looking frightened, were likewise taken right up. Was it *this* bad, that the family had so quickly come to Daley's bedside? Suavely, press secretary Sullivan said that this was no indication that Daley had a serious illness: "This is a sign of the affection the kids feel for the mayor." Late that first day, however, a spokesman for the hospital told reporters that a wing of the lobby was being set off for a press room and that

Illinois Bell technicians were already installing emergency lines—feeding speculation that Daley was bedded down with something serious that would require treatment stretching over several days.

Next morning, Tuesday, May 7, Dr. Eric Oldberg, socialite president of the Chicago Board of Health—a neurosurgeon of national renown and also a close friend of the mayor—confirmed that the tentative diagnosis was hypoglycemia. The condition apparently had been brought on, he said, by oral medication for incipient diabetes. Did this mean, then, that Daley was diabetic? "You can't really say he has diabetes," Oldberg replied, "but he's been on the verge of developing it, so oral agents have been given to fend it off."

At a press conference, Frank Sullivan disclosed that Mrs. Daley had remained at the hospital in a room near Daley all through the night, and when Dr. Oldberg announced that Daley would remain in the hospital for several days undergoing tests and that nothing further could be reported until the tests had been completed, reporters continued to suspect that they weren't getting the truth. The secrecy surrounding the hospitalization of the mayor, which ran counter to the usual practice of twice-a-day medical briefings that reporters get when an important personage is hospitalized, had the press fuming and fed the fear that he was in bad shape. Front-page headlines declared: "DALEY SUFFERED STROKE." Yet not even the best informed Democrats at party headquarters knew what Daley's condition was. The question was: If it were true that the mayor was not in serious condition, why all the tests—and what was he being tested for?

The tenth floor room was isolated from all others. Even hospital personnel getting off elevators at that floor were carefully screened to determine that they were on legitimate business. The corridor was patrolled by both city policemen and hospital security guards. Reporters, frustrated in their press room, did not know what manner of doctors had been called in on the Daley case. Had they known, the story of what his problem was would have been reported days sooner than it was.

Dr. Tom Coogan, Daley's personal physician, knew very well that the mayor had suffered a stroke, and so did Dr. Oldberg. Moreover, Presbyterian-St. Luke's has a de-

partment of cardiovascular-thoracic surgery that has
earned an international reputation for innovative discov-
eries in this field, and it was to this department, headed
by the skillful Hassan Najafi, that Dr. Coogan turned for
help in diagnosing Daley's ailment. Najafi's closest colleague, Hushang Javid, M.D., Ph.D., took the case, and
after several days of waiting the media people finally were
told what was wrong with the mayor. The shy Dr. Javid
explained that there was medical agreement that the
mayor would have to undergo an endarterectomy—an
operation on the left carotid artery, which carries blood
to the brain.

The specialists had discovered that Daley had suffered
a partial blockage in this vital segment of the circulatory
system and that consequently he had suffered a "little"
stroke. The endarterectomy was necessary to clear out the
deposits, called plaque, which narrowed the channel and
reduced the flow, and to reduce the strong possibility that
the mayor might suffer a crippling or killing stroke in the
not too distant future. Dr. Javid would have to slice open
his neck, clamp the left carotid above and below the
blockage, insert a polyethylene tube to detour the flow
of blood past the blockage site as he used a delicate prong
to clear out the plaque.

The period of acute danger in an endarterectomy is
the exceedingly brief time available for the setting of the
clamps and getting the bypass in place and operative. During this procedure, the surgeon must work swiftly. "The
brain can tolerate two or three minutes of no blood flow
—particularly a brain that has been without adequate
circulation for a time and has developed some cross-
communication [which meant a brain that had created its
own means of compensating for a diminished blood sup-
ply]," Dr. Javid said.

Mayor Daley was counseled by both Javid and Dr. Oldberg, his trusted friend, that the chances of complete recovery were exceedingly good. "We are not perfect," Dr.
Hassan Najafi, head of the cardiovascular department,
cautioned a reporter, "We are not God, but we have
performed something like 2,500 endarterectomies in this
hospital alone, with an overall recovery—a completely
successful recovery, allowing for the patient's return to
his normal activities—in well over 90 percent of these

cases." And what might the mortality rate be? "Well, the element of risk is always present in major surgery, but I would say that incapacity or death would run on the order of perhaps 2 percent. This is a highly acceptable limit of risk, in our opinion."

Having gotten through a mild stroke and already recovering from its effects, Daley might have been tempted to leave well enough alone. His left carotid did have blockage, however, and while it was agreed that Daley could quickly go back to work, if that was what he decided, the prognosis was that he would suffer greater strokes of fatal or near-fatal magnitude if he did not undergo surgery.

It was Daley who made the decision that he would undergo the endarterectomy. Was he in good enough physical shape to tolerate it? "The mayor," Dr. Najafi confided to a reporter, "is in very good health. For his years I would say he is in exceptionally good health, and there is no reason to expect complications." Could he then go back to City Hall and resume his duties—run for a sixth term in 1975? "Normally, someone who has had an endarterectomy would be back at work in three weeks. As for continuing on as mayor . . . well, he surely could, and personally I would hope that he does because I think he has done wonders for this city."

Having been fed frightening headlines for days that implied Mayor Daley was seriously and permanently incapacitated, if indeed he were not at the point of death, the public was not prepared to be as sanguine as the surgical experts of Presbyterian-St. Luke's toward Daley's going under the knife. And suspicions were not assuaged when, after nearly two weeks of hospitalization, Daley was not operated upon but released.

In fact, postponement of Daley's endarterectomy was dictated not by caprice but by clinical considerations. Doctors had determined that Daley had incurred a slight cerebral infarct—an area of tissue that had degenerated as a result of having been deprived of its blood supply—and that a period of three weeks from the initial hospitalization date was required to allow this ulcerated area to heal over with scar tissue. The doctors at Presbyterian-St. Luke's would have preferred to have kept Daley hospitalized and available for surgery on an emergency basis, in case his condition should change and make quick action necessary, but he was eager to go home, and finally they permitted it. After all, he was a man accustomed to having his own way.

On Saturday, June 1, at about 1:00 P.M., the mayor secretly arrived back at Presbyterian-St. Luke's with members of his family. Safely sealed off in a ninth-floor room, the mayor agreed that the hospital's public relations people—who had been accused by the media of a cover-up on his first visit—should reveal only that he would be operated on during the ensuing week. Actually, Dr. Javid performed the operation the next morning, although the public learned about it only when the operation had been completed successfully and Daley was in post-operative care. By Tuesday, June 4—two days after the operation —Daley's recovery was so well advanced that he was allowed to walk about. A hospital bulletin said: "He is cheerful, his appetite is good. His neck wound is healing well, his temperature has remained below 100 degrees, and he has required no pain medication since surgery."

Dr. Javid smiled briefly when complimented on the success of the operation; the operation had been routine. After a private visit with the mayor, five days after the operation, Dr. Eric Oldberg agreed that His Honor had come through the ordeal extremely well. "Dick's speech is perfectly good," Oldberg said, "and he had no difficulty with his thought processes. He had been sitting in his chair and before I could stop him, he jumped up from his chair and laid his cheek alongside mine; it was very touching. We talked for about ten minutes. I tried to be light and humorous. He said, 'I feel weak,' and I said, 'Of course you feel weak.' " Dr. Oldberg seemed to be saying that Daley would need an extended period of rest. "It's going to take him a while. He has had a real bump and Dick isn't used to bumps. He thought he was indestructible." A few days later, as quietly as he had entered the hospital, Daley once again left it. The next anyone outside his immediate circle knew, he was convalescing at his place on the lake, in Michigan.

Daley's seven acres, a bit of it groomed but much of it growing wild, the main house hidden in the shrubbery and the trees, made an ideal retreat for contemplation as well as physical recovery. It is a perfectly isolated spot and rather easily guarded, allowing the mayor to walk the beach or his property in utter security. When his strength permitted it, he went off in his limousine for early morning mass at nearby towns, the natives quickly getting used to the sight of him and Mrs. Daley and making no effort to invade his privacy.

In the city, rumors were rife. Daley had suffered a speech impediment. He walked with difficulty. He was not nearly so well as friends of Daley seemed eager to have everyone believe. Daley, for his part, was aware of what was being said in the city. On a sight line his summer place is about fifty unobstructed miles from the television antennae above the John Hancock Building and the Sears Towers, and he was well aware of the news reports. He talked with his people and devoured the Chicago newspapers. Once, in a private conversation with Secretary of State Mike Howlett during the mayor's recuperative period, Daley mildly remonstrated with Howlett over a published report that the secretary of state had said there was not the slightest possibility that he would be drafted to serve as mayor; Daley told Howlett that he shouldn't be saying things like that, because the Machine might want to draft him—to which Howlett replied, "Oh, bullshit, the only one who is going to be drafted is *you*." Daley giggled. Mostly, though, amid his walking and reading and taking the sun, duffing around on a nearby golf course, Daley used his time to recover his physical strength and to meditate upon current problems and future ones.

There was both sadness and anxiety in many of the things that occupied Mayor Daley's mind during the four months he remained in self-imposed exile, his only ventures into Chicago being for medical checkups—the quickly executed trips generally being carried out without detection by the news media. It pleased Daley exceedingly to read in one of the Chicago papers that Mayor Kevin White of Boston, on a brief stopover at O'Hare airport on June 24, had referred to him as "The nation's superior mayor. He's like the great baseball hitter who generates excitement, even after he might strike out eight times in a row." Mayor White was not only confident of Daley's physical recovery, he said: "Beyond question, Daley will be a major force in the selection of our presidential candidate in 1976." He must have had a wry reaction, reading the reports that his detractor, Governor Dan Walker, had been at pains to praise Daley's courage and dedication to principle.

Other news was less good. One unsettling thing had followed another in Daley's well-ordered world since the ghastly convention of 1968. Seeds of discord and occlusion of his powers seemed to have been implanted in his political garden, and Daley had been aggravated by his inability to uproot the poisonous sprouts that seemed continually to be cropping up. The damage inflicted upon the Democratic party by Nixon's smashing defeat of McGovern in November 1972 had hardly been inventoried —Daley's major concern being that his prestige had been hurt nationally—and no estimation had yet been made of how to contain the self-proclaimed white knight—but essentially opportunist—Dan Walker, who had defeated the Daley Machine in the gubernatorial primary, when something far more foreboding shocked the Greatest Mayor Chicago Ever Had: Otto Kerner, Jr.—son-in-law of the late Mayor Anton J. Cermak, former county judge, federal district attorney, and now distinguished member of the U.S. Circuit Court of Appeals—named to the bench near the end of his second four-year term as governor in the summer of 1968—was indicted on charges of mail fraud, conspiracy, bribery, income tax evasion, and perjury before the grand jury. Daley, who had been aware that the widely respected Kerner was under investigation in connection with a sweetheart deal on the purchase of stock in the Arlington Park-Washington Park racetracks, was nonetheless stunned by Kerner's indictment.

Otto Kerner was a political figure by inheritance. His father, who had ended his days as a federal appeals court judge, had been the boyhood friend and longtime crony of Tony Cermak. They were Bohemians who shared common interests. Young Otto, educated at Brown University and in England thereafter, major general in an Illinois National Guard division that saw service in the Far Eastern Theater in World War II, governor, head of President Johnson's commission on urban violence, could only loosely be identified as a member of the Daley Machine. The "regular" Democrats had an open dislike for the suave, slightly overbearing Kerner, whose speech is slightly nasal and eastern. "He ain't one of us," the Vito Marzullos would say. Even so, he had been brought along by

Daley; indeed, in the damaging trial testimony of William S. Miller, the state racing board chairman who set up the stock deal for which Kerner eventually went to prison, it had been Daley who importuned him to raise $150,000 in 1960 to get Kerner's first gubernatorial campaign off the ground.

Daley knew a good deal more than he has been credited with regarding the multimillion-dollar racing enterprise of Marjorie Lindheimer Everett, operator of the highly prized Arlington-Washington thoroughbred and harness operation that was dependent for survival upon having a working accommodation with the state racing board, which, in turn, was under Governor Kerner's executive control. For a start, Daley's boyhood pal and ex-law partner, William J. Lynch—a present-day federal judge—had emerged in those years as Mrs. Everett's legal counsel, winding up with 150 of the thousand-dollar-par shares (3,000 in all) of her enterprise. It would have been uncharacteristic of Daley not to have sought from Lynch, whose holdings were worth perhaps three-quarters of a million dollars, the details of what Kerner's financial involvement in the racetracks was. Personally, Daley, being highly circumspect in avoiding conflicts of interest, would not have had an investment in the racetracks. Reading the indictment, Daley was struck, no doubt, by Kerner's lack of discretion in treating his $150,000 profit in the racetrack stock as capital gains, rather than ordinary income. As an attorney, however—even though he has never argued a solitary case—Daley was appalled at the allegations that Kerner, a member of the second highest legal tribunal in the land, had recklessly lied to the grand jury.

During the summer months of 1974, while Daley was convalescing at his Michigan retreat, Kerner, having exhausted all avenues of appeal, had surrendered to serve his three-year sentence at the Federal Correctional Institution at Lexington, Kentucky. But that was but one of many disasters that had occurred to persons in close proximity to Daley, and there were many substantial rumors of worse things impending to trouble Daley's mind as he took the sun and pensively weighed the situation that would confront him when finally he returned to City Hall.

The most immediate of his problems was the imminent federal trial of Earl Bush, Daley's fifty-nine-year-old press secretary during the first nineteen years that Daley had been mayor. Bush, sacked in August 1973, was subsequently indicted on twelve counts of mail fraud and one count of extortion in connection with his secret ownership of a firm that had, since 1962, had an exclusive contract with the city of Chicago for all advertising and display promotions at O'Hare Airport—the specific charge being that Bush had received net profits of $202,000 as a consequence of having deceived Mayor Daley while cheating the city.

Because Bush had concealed his ownership of the advertising firm, altering the ethics statement he was required by law to file—obliquely admitting his outside interest in the sworn statement, eliminating this admission in the "duplicate" that he gave the mayor—Daley was scheduled to be a government witness at the trial. Clearly, there was no way in which Daley could avoid giving damaging testimony against Bush. It was equally obvious that Daley was eager to avoid testifying, and when he offered to produce an unsworn statement supporting the government's charges of deception, U.S. District Attorney Thompson's office indulgently agreed that this would be an acceptable alternative to a court appearance—the inference supposedly being that the mayor was still too weak to be subjected to testifying in open court. Daley was relieved to have this chance to escape appearing as a witness, yet the fact that his trusted media man and speech writer was to be tried on criminal charges depressed Daley, Thompson's explorations into corruption never before having come so close to the mayor as this.

Earl Bush had been indicted on February 21. Even more staggering for Daley was the fact that sixty-nine-year-old Alderman Thomas E. Keane, chairman of the City Council finance committee and generally regarded as the second most powerful man in Chicago government, had been indicted on May 2—four days prior to Daley's having suffered his stroke—on seventeen counts of mail fraud and one count of conspiracy, the charges being that he had used his powerful City Hall connections to purchase 1,900 parcels of tax-delinquent real estate, selling off much of this property, at enormous profit, to such public agencies as the Sanitary District, the Chicago Park District, the Chicago Department of Urban Renewal, and the Chicago Housing Authority. Daley feared the worst was waiting for Keane—and, therefore, politically for himself—when he read that the boss alderman's secret business partner, John A. Hennessey, Sr., had been granted immunity from prosecution on his promise to testify for the government—as William S. Miller had done in the Kerner case—about the land deals that Keane had slid through City Council, presumably under Daley's nose. It made Daley's Irish blood race when he reflected upon District Attorney Thompson's device of building his cases against politicians by asking immunity for nonpolitical rogues who obviously had shared the guilt for whatever crimes the indicted politician was accused of having committed. Daley had been heard to ask indignantly: "Where is the justice of this?"

In between the indictment of Bush on February 21 and that of Keane on May 2, yet another prominent Daleyite of status, Alderman Paul T. Wigoda, associated with Keane in legal matters, had been indicted on April 5. The charge against Wigoda, who seemed always to wear an apprehensive look, was that he had extorted $50,000 from a real estate developer and that he had evaded payment of income taxes on this money—the principal government witness in this case, granted immunity, being Robert E. Haskins, an attorney who specialized in securing favorable City Council action on rezoning ordinances. Where in God's name, Daley wondered, was all of this going to end?

Unfortunately for Daley the news in mid-1974 was only part of a continuing series of bad news items. For almost eighteen months prior to his stroke on May 6, 1974, Daley had been under tremendous pressure. Calendar 1973 had hardly begun when press secretary Bush had fumbled an embarrassing disclosure by one of the bright young men Daley had brought into city government, namely, that virtually all casualty insurance on city buildings was now being written by an Evanston, Illinois, firm named Heil & Heil—which had had the wisdom to employ Daley's son, John Patrick, as agent.

The mayor stoutly maintained that there was nothing irregular about this and promised full disclosure of his reasons for personally ordering that the Evanston firm get $2 million in Chicago's business. Additionally, Daley's

son got the insurance of the theoretically independent
Chicago Park District and Public Building Commission.
There was, of course, considerable grumbling in high
Democratic circles; operating insurance brokerage companies is a time-honored ploy of well-placed Democratic
politicians, and there was private griping because Daley
had taken from these old pros the high-premium business
that he had given his son's employer; Heil & Heil records,
subpoenaed by the county grand jury in February 1974,
revealed that son John received commissions of $100,000
from mid-1972 to mid-1973. Daley compounded the frac-
ture in his relationship with lesser Democratic bosses when
he announced, in July 1973, that son John and William,
his youngest son, had formed a partnership to sell insurance—the sardonic reaction of City Hall people being
that, just possibly, John and William might prosper. It
was, incidentally, in pique over published criticism of the
boys' getting hooked into this profitable venture that the
Greatest Mayor Chicago Ever Had snarled at a closed
meeting of his committeemen that his critics could "kiss
my ass" if they held it was wrong for a father to help his
sons—the upper level Democrats laughing in approval of
Daley's naked display of the fact that he was second to
nobody in the implementation of clout.

Next, County Clerk Edward J. Barrett, a free-spending
old Democrat, who had been selected to take Daley's place
as Cook County clerk in 1955, and who had consistently
been elected every four years thereafter, was found guilty
in federal court in March 1973 of charges that he solicited
and got a payoff of $180,000 from a company that got a
contract to sell 900 voting machines to Cook County.

The Chicago Transit Authority, which Daley had
worked to set up when he was a state senator, tottered on
the brink of bankruptcy—frightening Daley with the possibility that public transportation in Chicago would col-
lapse—largely because of high wages that the mayor had
engineered with the operators' union that was threatening
to strike.

Daley got locked in a conflict with the brash new
governor, fifty-year-old Dan Walker, over whether or not
a federally authorized billion-dollar expressway should be
built in the western reaches of Chicago. The mayor, anxious to give the city a whopping economic shot in the arm,

insisted that it would be built; the governor declared: "Never!"

Then there was the matter of Alderman Keane's and other parties' being disclosed as participants in a land acquisition deal for Colonel Henry Crown's Material Service Company, the ready-mix cement and building supply firm, the Crown family having supplied Daley with both financial and vocal support. The arrangers of this deal turned a quick profit of $375,000—the most delicate revelation being that William P. Thompson, a Daley son-in-law, now divorced, was the real estate man of Material Service and that he had received a stipend of $20,000 for his efforts in this transaction. Daley was not personally implicated, but the deal looked suspicious and allowed for an inference that he had tacitly approved a dubious arrangement that permitted parties close to him to make a killing.

The sequence of bad news for Daley in 1973 was unending. One high point was the conviction of Traffic Chief Clarence Braasch and eighteen vice detectives who had served under Braasch in a Near North Side police district on federal charges of having extorted on a regular basis sizable sums from tavern owners and night club operators.

To repair the image of the police department, Daley had sacked the inept Commissioner James B. Conlisk and replaced him with a tough realist named James Rochford, who had immediately staggered Daley by unilaterally demanding that the seventy top officers of the department submit to lie detector examination by way of establishing that they were not corrupt. When some of those tested failed the test, Rochford arbitrarily downgraded the assignments of those who failed but declined to resign.

It was small consolation that National Democratic Chairman Robert Strauss came to town and lavished compliments on Mayor Daley at a party gathering to which Governor Walker had not been invited. There was some pleasure for Daley, perhaps, in the inability or unwillingness of Dan Walker to explain who had provided the money for his successful 1972 campaign and how he figured to pay off an estimated campaign deficit of $750,000. The huge Continental Bank held a fistful of personal notes on loans, some signed by persons of dubious background, to support Walker's cause. The "new look" governor lamely explained that he did not know who the contributors were nor what his deficit was and that he did not care to know because it is "bad policy to know." This information, he solemnly explained, had the potential of influencing an elected official's judgment in the awarding of contracts and the granting of other favors. Daley grimaced at the disclosure that Governor Walker, who had piously denounced patronage during his inauguration speech in January 1973, was conniving, at year's end, to get his hands on five thousand state jobs that were protected by Civil Service— "deputy governor" Victor deGrazia, Walker's most influential adviser and an anti-Daley man of long standing, reportedly having the mission of shaking loose this patronage.

It was Victor R. deGrazia, with the title of assistant director, who was credited with having written the Walker Report on street violence in Chicago during the 1968 Democratic convention—the document that infuriated Daley. It was deGrazia who was credited in the Daley camp with having seized upon the controversy over plans to construct the Crosstown Expressway as a device to damage the Daley Machine's standing with voters on the far western side of the city—Walker building up a big following in this area by thundering that the 22-mile, billion-dollar expressway would never be built when *he* was elected governor. Daley had accepted neighborhood opposition to the plan, residents and business people located along the route fearing they would suffer serious economic and social losses if it were built because traffic congestion was becoming acute in highways leading to downtown, and the Crosstown was regarded as imperatively needed if through traffic was to have a bypass to keep it out of the inner-city area. Standing above all of the lesser disputes between Daley and Walker was this serious battle between them, unresolved at year's end (with Walker winding up two years as governor), over Crosstown. Not for an instant was Daley ready to abandon his position that it must be built, nor could Walker retreat from the opposite stand without appearing to be a traitor to the west siders whose cause he had espoused and a fool who capitulated to Daley. Of all the aggravations that Walker gave Daley—his clumsy, ineffectual efforts to build his own power base, his thinly veiled remarks about "the evil politicians"—it was Walker's refusal to go along on the building of Crosstown that annoyed Daley the most.

If 1973 proved bad for Daley, 1974 was far worse. For one thing, nonorganization Democrats for whom he had little use resumed their efforts to nibble him down to their size. Senator Adlai Stevenson III, speaking in his customary monotone, volunteered a prediction, following Daley's stroke, that Daley would not run for a sixth term in 1975—allowing for the inference that in Adlai's opinion, Daley was through. Daley was annoyed and likewise nettled when Jake Arvey was quoted as having said he would not run—again, the implication being that he could not. The flamboyant Governor Walker apparently had decided that the time had come to challenge Daley's grip on Democratic members of the state legislature, most of them having an accommodation with Boss Daley, and came flapping at Daley, early in 1974, with a nonorganization cluster of candidates. With his trusted associate Victor deGrazia plotting the anti-Daley strategy, he went to the people on television commercials with the pitch: "I am Governor Dan Walker, urging you to choose candidates for the state legislature who will work for *you*, not for the politicians." Then, on March 12, in advance of the primary election, someone in the Walker administration leaked a story that youthful William Daley, the mayor's son, had failed to pass his examination for a state insurance broker's license and that he had been certified on the basis of someone's having filled in the answers for him. Daley sizzled.

Walker's candidates didn't perform well in the primary, and some who lost privately complained that they would have been elected if they had not received Walker's "support." Walker claimed his side had made a good showing. Daley was too professional a politician to make an issue of Walker's persistently giving him the prod, although the primary results reinforced Daley's confidence in his Machine, and his thoughts continued to turn to the question of how he might neutralize or obliterate a "reform" governor who was riding high in public esteem. Having assailed Daley in his campaign to get elected as an independent Democrat, Walker's periodic efforts to patch up their differences brought little response from the wary Richard Daley. As he strolled and pondered during more than three months of convalescence at his place on Lake Michigan, it is hardly likely that he ignored the problem of how to contain Dan Walker.

The governor was clearly the worst of Daley's enemies —much more serious an adversary than, say, Alderman William Singer, the young reform alderman who became the city's liberals' hope in 1968 when he defeated the organization aldermanic candidate in Committeeman Eddie Barrett's Forty-fourth Ward, later redistricted into Paddy Bauler's Forty-third. Having stumbled onto a formula to keep Daley out of the presidential convention of 1972, Singer had boldly announced, in mid-October 1973, that he intended to be a nonorganization candidate for mayor in 1975. Daley had private plans to flatten Alderman Singer. Since Singer had no weapons of patronage with which to fight back, dealing with Singer would be easy. Dealing with Walker, who was superior to Daley in the matter of having more favors to dispense, was a much more complex problem. To make matters worse, Walker worked the state as an apostle of righteousness—forever on the move like a traveling evangelist—and it annoyed Daley that Walker never seemed willing to take a position on an issue, state the merits of his case, and then slug it out with him, as a political enemy is "expected" to do. Walker was too elusive to suit Daley.

Walker still was beyond Daley's reach when the mayor returned to City Hall on Tuesday, September 3, 1974— the day after Labor Day—for the first time in four months. Daley looked about twenty-five pounds slimmer than before he had taken ill. Comments on his physical fitness ranged from good to fair; his articulation was excellent and he was as alert as ever. He was at his desk at 8:20 A.M. the first day, spent a busy hour and a half on paperwork—taking few phone calls and receiving few visitors. Promptly at ten, picking up a coterie of aides and Democratic officials who had gathered in his outer office, he left City Hall—walking briskly one block south on La Salle Street to a meeting in the La Salle Hotel of the state Democratic platform committee, meeting privately with the committee for five minutes, then took off in his limousine for the funeral of Judge Harold G. Ward, who had served on the circuit court for thirty-three years.

Daley spent half an hour in the early afternoon at his

Michigan Avenue tailor's, got back to his office for another hour of work, and took off for home in midafternoon. Officially now, the mayor was back on the job.

Next day, Daley made his first public utterance since the operation. Speaking to the one hundred members of the state platform committee of his party who had gathered to approve the Democrats' bland 1974 state platform, Daley said: "I am very happy to be back with you and I will be available for the rest of this campaign, to encourage and to help and assist." All speculation over who might succeed Daley vanished; there was no mention now, as there had been for four months, of the chaos that would ensue when Daley was gone. Like a Don Corleone, recovered from the near-fatal wounds of an assassin, the Godfather of the Chicago Democrats was safely home and in charge of The Family again. Indeed, in the crowd of well-wishers who pressed in upon Daley, one woman held his hand and kissed it.

Almost at once, having finally gotten back to work, Daley was back in the middle of things. There was precious little slack, actually, in the administration of Chicago government; at an early point in his convalescence, the mayor had been in telephone communication with Deputy Mayor Kenneth Sain—nephew of the alderman of the Twenty-seventh Ward, Harry Sain—his department heads, his budget director, and his outside financial advisers. He had trained them well; as one of his administrative assistants said: "We have well-established guidelines and we all know what they are. We never took every single problem to him anyway; you get the feel of how he wants things done and you do it that way." Daley's budget director, speaking obviously for Daley, made a point of telling reporters that he was preparing a "hold the line" budget for 1975. The practice of publicizing Daley's policy of frugality had been characteristic of the administration on the four previous times that Daley had stood for reelection, and the reprise of the budget director in the autumn of 1974 was taken in some quarters to mean that the man was planning to run for yet another term in 1975.

On September 6, Daley was given a long standing ovation at a private luncheon meeting of Chicago's top labor union bosses. "Everyone was absolutely in favor of another term for Mayor Daley," declared Patrick E. Gorman,

head of the Butchers Union. Daley delightedly had acknowledged the pledge of Labor's support, but he gave not
the slightest hint of what his plans for 1975 might be. In
another quarter, Alderman Vito Marzullo announced at a
seventy-seventh birthday party he held in his honor at
City Hall that *he* intended to run for a sixth term in 1975
and that Daley would do likewise. Informed of this, Daley
smiled noncommittally.

The consensus of knowledgeable people was that Daley
could have a sixth term for the taking despite the continuing series of scandals and quasi-scandals that would
have been the ruination of most big-city mayors. The
accusing finger that had been pointed at so many of
Daley's people had even been turned toward Daley himself. On July 11—with the mayor still in convalescence at
his Michigan retreat—a copyrighted story in the *Chicago
Sun-Times* virtually accused him of being yet another
public servant who had been indiscreetly piling up wealth:
"*$200,000 nest egg*—MAYOR DALEY'S SECRET FIRM." The
story said: "For 17 years of his tenure as mayor of
Chicago, Richard J. Daley has kept secret his ownership
of a real estate and holding company that now has assets
of $200,000. The mayor's secret nest egg is called Elard
Realty Co. Its assets and transactions have been concealed
in a thicket of secret land trusts, nominees and close-
mouthed agents." Chicago was stunned, and the wire
services spread this disclosure over the nation.

In subsequent exposés, the *Sun-Times* reported that
Mayor Daley's longtime Bridgeport friend, Chief Judge
Joseph A. Power of the criminal court, had admitted involvement in the purchase for an insignificant $20 of a
parcel of vacant, tax-delinquent South Side property,
which, the newspaper claimed, was worth $7,500. The
transaction was carried out with "elaborate secrecy" by
agents of Elard Realty. The newspaper claimed that it
had exploded the myth that the politically powerful Daley
was financially poor, Elard Realty having cash of $40,056,
securities worth $31,431, receivables of $26,987, and real
estate estimated to be worth $127,000. The big scoop
elicited not a peep from Daley.

The only illegal aspect of the whole affair, actually,
was the apparent violation of a state statute that forbids
public officials from *knowingly* buying up tax-delinquent

property at scavenger sales. In its original story, the *Sun-Times* had conceded: "The existence of Elard, and Mayor Daley's interest in such a holding, violates no law." The most damaging part of the continuing story, picked up by the other Chicago papers, was that Peter M. Shannon, the mayor's personal accountant, who set up Elard and fronted as its president, had received city contracts for his own firm of "nearly $500,000 since 1972" and that a data-processing firm in which Peter Shannon was associated with his son, Daniel, had received more than $130,000 in nonbid city contracts. Peter Shannon's auditing firm had received fees totalling $144,186 from the Chicago Park District between the years 1959 and 1967, at which time son Dan, a former Notre Dame football player, was named by Daley to be a Chicago Park Board commissioner.

Further evidence of how the Bridgeport folks had kept things in the family in Mayor Daley's long reign was the discovery that Dan Shannon was the registered agent of County Clerk Matthew Danaher's Garden Realty Co. (Danaher being the original Lowe Avenue protégé of the mayor), and the discovery that the Elard Realty tax bills were funneled through Morgan M. Finley, Inc. Finley, a former state senator of the Bridgeport area, was yet another Daley protégé. In addition to his son Dan, Peter Shannon had yet another successful son, Patrick, a lawyer who did part-time legal work for the Chicago Transit Authority.

In further illustration of how the Bridgeport inbreeding works, the CTA legal department, which parcels out some $500,000 a year in attorney fees, was headed by a man named O'Donohue, who was related to the mayor by marriage. O'Donohue's predecessors in the job were two other Bridgeport boys: William J. Lynch, who is now a federal judge, and George Schaller, who is now a circuit court judge. Both Lynch and Schaller were former law partners of Daley's.

With reporters scratching in all directions for new developments in the Elard Realty case, inquiry was made of U.S. Attorney James Thompson as to whether his office had started an investigation. Thompson calmly responded, "No comment"—which did not seem to be much of an answer from the celebrated corruption fighter who was expected to run as the Republican candidate for mayor in 1975.

In fact, Jim Thompson had plenty of things to occupy his talents without getting into the Elard Realty matter. First, a second trial for Earl Bush was in preparation. The jury that had acquitted Bush of extortion charges had been unable to reach a verdict on the question of whether Daley's former aide had used the mails to cheat the city of the $200,000 profit he had realized from his secret O'Hare Airport advertising contract. Second, Thompson's office was ready for trial in the matter of whether Alderman Thomas E. Keane had recycled tax-delinquent property back to city agencies, using the mails in a conflict of interest scheme that brought him sizable profits. Third, Thompson's office was ready to go against Alderman Paul T. Wigoda on charges that he bled somebody for a $50,000 rezoning payoff and had neglected to pay income taxes on the proceeds. In short, Thompson had a good many things bidding for his attention. He even shared with the mayor a problem of what to do about County Clerk Matt Danaher, who was awaiting trial on charges of conspiracy and income tax evasion growing out of a real estate development deal that had netted Matt and his brother-in-law a reputed profit of $400,000. The problem was that Matt had been drinking so heavily that Daley despaired of straightening him out and Thompson couldn't figure out how to bring such a defendant to trial.

When the forty-seven-year-old Danaher had been indicted on April 10, the erstwhile confidant of the mayor remarked, "I know in my heart I'm not guilty." Daley had said, "It's a sad day for him and his family. An indictment is not a conviction." Daley's remark teed off prosecutor Thompson, who was already annoyed over a remark made the previous day by Daley that Thompson was carrying on a "vendetta" against the Democratic organization of Chicago. In reply to Daley's two statements, the prosecutor snapped, "I agree with the mayor that an indictment is not a conviction. My regret is that the mayor quickly comments after an indictment, but never after a conviction. If Daley's associates had worked with the same fidelity as the citizens serving on federal grand juries, we wouldn't have the problem we have today. He ought to reflect on that."

A tentative trial date for Matt Danaher had been set for January 1975, and there was some apprehension in Democratic circles that something nasty might spill over onto Daley if, indeed, Danaher could be brought to trial. Speculation ceased on Sunday, December 15, when Matt Danaher was found dead, dressed in an undershirt and pajama bottoms, sprawled on the bedroom floor of the suite he had occupied for six months in the Ambassador West Hotel, as he marked time waiting to be divorced by his wife, Maureen Joan. Daley became one of the six Bridgeporters who carried Danaher's casket into church and then to the grave. The Democrats grunted when their friend, the coroner, announced that an autopsy had shown that Danaher had died of a heart attack. They grunted again when the circuit court judges of Cook County selected Morgan M. Finley, forty-nine, to take Danaher's place as clerk. Finley, who lived in the same block of South Lowe as Daley, had been appointed by Daley in 1967 to the Cook County Zoning Board of Appeals and had become chairman, passing judgment on the disputes of property owners; interesting work, considering that he was a real estate man. Finley became the Eleventh Ward's third circuit court clerk in succession to hold the office, Matt Danaher having succeeded Joseph J. McDonough when Joe died in September, 1968—Joe being the son of the late Big Joe, who had been Daley's mentor.

Even in Bridgeport, however, there are some things a man must take care of for himself; so, on the mayor's return to City Hall, after four months, it remained for Daley to deliver the coup de grace to the great exposé of the Elard Realty Co. On his first day back at work, September 3, the mayor told reporters that his total assets were in Elard Realty and in his mortgage-free home at 3536 South Lowe. "After I became mayor of Chicago," he said, "I was advised by the late corporation counsel, John Melaniphy, that undoubtedly I would be named as a defendant in suits against the city, both individually and as mayor. Mr. Melaniphy pointed out that in order not to cloud the title of property I might own, it would be best to have a corporate entity established. After checking that advice, I followed it."

Accepting this explanation—how could you argue with it?—reporters moved on to something more promising.

Did Daley plan to run again in 1975? "The doctor said I should try to work not as hard as I did in the past." What was the state of his health? "Very good." Question: "If you had to decide today, Mr. Mayor, you would run, wouldn't you?" Answer (laughing): "You've answered it." Question: "Mr. Mayor, as of this moment, is there any medical reason you know of why you should not be able to run?" Answer: "None whatsoever." Question: "If you were strong enough, then, you would run?" Answer: "Right."

Daley subsequently proved himself strong enough to lead his troops to a smashing victory in the November election. Adlai Stevenson III was reelected to the U.S. Senate with an overwhelming vote in Chicago over Republican George Burditt, a diehard Republican attorney, who did not even come close to carrying a single Chicago ward. It was a reasonable guess that, in a popularity contest, Stevenson could not beat the Democratic committeeman in any of the wards that make up the automatic eleven; nevertheless, the automatic eleven gave him a plurality of 102,905 in an utterly lackluster election in which victory was taken for granted and the only problem was forcing the people to get out and vote. On election night, as he delivered his customary spiel about how the public had once again wisely spoken, Daley had all the reassurance he needed that the Machine could get him a sixth term, if he decided that that was what he wanted; if the Machine could deliver a plurality of 450,000 for Adlai, it certainly could deliver a comfortable edge for Daley. The lingering question, then, was—did he want it?

Plenty of others did, especially on the Democratic side. Republican District Attorney James Thompson, on the other hand, bowed out of the 1975 mayoral race on September 23, 1974, citing a variety of reasons why duty compelled him to continue his search and prosecution of corrupt public officials. The fact is that Thompson studied Chicago election returns dating back to 1931 and concluded that he simply could not beat Daley and would hardly have a chance against any other Democratic organization candidate if Daley chose not to run. The clincher of Thompson's decision was the consistency with which the automatic eleven brought in pluralities of never less than 100,000, regardless of who the organization candidate was or what office he was running for. The automatic eleven had slipped a little in 1971, when it gave Daley an advantage of "only" 103,000 over Republican Richard Friedman, but Daley had swamped Friedman with a citywide plurality of 424,000—taking 70 percent of all the votes cast—and there was no rational reason to believe that even a giant of law enforcement of Thompson's stature, able to pick up the careers of corrupt Democratic officeholders and rip them apart in open court, was likely to alter a voting pattern that had remained unchanged for four decades.

Although Alderman William Singer had been a declared Democratic candidate for more than a year, objective political observers found it impossible to perceive that Singer would have a chance against any Democratic organization candidate in the primary of February 25, 1975. Apart from Singer, several blacks announced their candidates, and Congressman Ralph Metcalfe, a one-time protégé of the late Congressman William L. Dawson and the former faithful Machine alderman of the Third Ward, toyed with the idea of running for mayor. But none of the anti-organization candidates—including the apostate Metcalfe, who had quarreled with Daley on the issue of police brutality in the ghetto—posed a serious impediment to Daley's winning a sixth term. On December 4, however, with Daley apparently poised to spring for an unprecedented sixth term, the sixty-four-year-old Metcalfe withdrew—assailing Daley for exerting pressure on black businessmen to discourage them from making contributions to a $500,000 campaign fund that a Metcalfe committee had been attempting to raise. Metcalfe accused Daley of "extracting a pound of flesh" from black businessmen for whom City Hall had done favors. With voice quavering, eyes moist, the gray-haired congressman said, "The people in the black community who have wealth do not have political freedom." The chairman of his fund-raising committee said, "At this point we do not know of another black man who would have a chance of beating the incumbent." With Thompson out of it, the Republicans likewise appeared to have no one with the remotest chance of beating Daley. Yet Daley bided his time in making the announcement as to whether he would run again in 1975.

In November, it annoyed Daley to learn that Governor

Walker considered the idea of supporting the hated Alderman Singer, and that there were exploratory conversations between Walker's man, Victor deGrazia, and Singer. By disavowing Singer, Walker could immediately have erased the implication of treachery, but he did not do so. Indeed, disclosure that a New Yorker named David Garth, who produced anti-Daley Machine television commercials for Walker, had been retained for Singer served to increase the suspicion that Walker was weighing the possibilities of wresting from Daley control of the Democratic party. But Daley was no more worried about losing the election to Singer than he was to Edward Hanrahan, who, also in November, announced his candidacy. Daley had merely grunted, "Everyone is entitled to be a candidate," when the racially sulfurous Hanrahan announced that he was now a candidate for mayor. The fifty-three-year-old Hanrahan, who had lost to a Republican in a race for Congress on November 5, was striving for a political comeback. Politically unpredictable, he had been state's attorney of Cook County on December 4, 1969, when policemen assigned to his office had shot their way into the West Side pad of the Black Panthers, leaving two Panther leaders dead—one of them found dead in bed. Once regarded as a Daley favorite and possible successor to the throne, Hanrahan had destroyed his political future with a quarrelsome effort to justify the murderous expedition of his men —stormy litigation, involving both state and federal investigations, dragging on in the courts for several years (there is still a civil suit, the families of the assassinated Panther leaders seeking damages of $1,000,000). Renounced by the Daley Machine when he sought renomination for state's attorney, Hanrahan had beaten the Machine candidate in the 1972 primary—only to be clobbered by a vast outpouring of outraged black voters, the only time in all of Daley's reign that they united to beat a Democrat. By November 1974, Ed Hanrahan had no visible political future, and Daley took his mayoral announcement in stride.

It wasn't Hanrahan that bothered Daley in November 1974. What choked him was that, in quick order, federal juries had found Earl Bush, Tom Keane, and Paul Wigoda—three men who had been exceedingly close to Daley —guilty as charged. Keane, the second most powerful man in Chicago government, was the first to go. He sat grimly as the court clerk read the verdict: guilty on seventeen counts of mail fraud, one count of conspiracy. Looking tough, the sixty-nine-year-old Keane, a reputed millionaire, sneered at a reporter who had braced him with a question as he stalked out of the courtroom: "Sorry? What's there to be sorry about?" At the moment that the Keane verdict was being read, Mayor Daley was testifying in another courtroom of the Dirksen Federal Building that no, he had not known of Bush's secret ownership of the firm that had an exclusive city contract to sell advertising at O'Hare Airport. Emerging from the Bush trial, Daley glumly declined comment when asked about the Keane verdict, ducked into a private elevator that took him to his limousine in the underground bowels of the building. Alderman Vito Marzullo fumed over the guilty finding on Keane. "I think it's a Goddamn shame. He's innocent," Marzullo snarled. Alderman Singer cheered, implying that Daley should share the guilt. "Keane is part of the system; he is what the system is all about. The mayor has to be held responsible in these convictions." Thus went Chicago's biggest news on Wednesday, October 9, 1974.

Next day, October 10, Alderman Wigoda, who shared law offices with Keane, was found guilty of failure to report in his federal income tax return a $50,000 payoff the government had charged that he had received in connection with a 1969 rezoning of the former Edgewater golf club in his ward.

Next day, October 11, Earl Bush sadly shook his head as he was found guilty on eleven counts of mail fraud, stemming from his secret ownership of the firm that had a lock on all advertising at O'Hare, the world's busiest airport.

A seasoned reporter, speaking with some reverence about District Attorney James R. Thompson, said, "He's the toughest gun we've had around here since Al Capone."

Tom Keane swaggered into the court of Judge Bernard Decker to hear his sentence, on Monday, November 18. The judge was seated, calmly waiting for the tardy Keane to make his appearance. Did Mr. Keane have anything to say? Gruffly and insolently, as if making reply to an inferior, the defrocked City Council leader said, "I have nothing to say." Judge Decker had quite a good deal to say: "Defendant Keane for a number of years was entrusted with almost unlimited power. The spectacle of public officials standing before the bar of justice for sentencing is becoming altogether too common. In almost all of these corruption convictions, the result has been the misuse of power of office for personal aggrandizement." The judge then proceeded to give Keane a verbal scourging. He referred to Keane's "Machiavellian cover-up scheme to hide from the City Council and citizens of Chicago the facts of his personal financial involvement in a number of actions on which a council action was required." Keane, the judge said, had displayed "an arrogant disdain" of his duty to disclose his land deals.

Mayor Daley looked sorrowful at the news that Keane had been sentenced to the maximum of five years, the terms to run concurrently, on each of the eighteen counts. Asked to comment, Daley said, "I think it's an unfortunate thing that such a fine public official and a fine friend . . ." and his voice trailed off, the comment unfinished. Swallowing to clear his throat and regain his composure, Daley then expressed hope that the U.S. Court of Appeals would reverse the sentence, defending this position with the further comment: "Keane is one of the outstanding municipal authorities in the country. And he's done a good job." Daley was asked if he would continue to ask Keane for advice. He replied: "He will always be a friend, he and his family. I served with him in the [state] senate and saw him do some wonderful things for the people of Illinois and the people of Chicago."

Next day, November 19, Daley had to go through much the same inquiry when Earl Bush, fifty-nine years of age, was sentenced by Judge Philip W. Tone to serve one year for mail fraud.

Sentence on Alderman Wigoda was delayed until December 2, Judge Abraham Lincoln Marovitz entertaining a defense motion that one of the prosecuting attorneys had introduced extraneous references during his closing argument in violation of the defendant's rights to a fair trial. Many recognized that, as the close pal of Mayor Daley, the case had been painful for Marovitz. Only a few knew how painful; it was not widely known that Paul was Abe's protégé.

The Greatest Mayor Chicago Ever Had had managed,

rather miraculously, to escape contamination during a lifetime of exposure to political corruption. He had worked and he had prayed, and if many of those who had been closest to him were winding up their public service imprisoned and disgraced, victims of their injudicious use of the Chicago weapon that is called clout, well, as Daley himself occasionally had said, "Every man must account for his own actions." Though Daley is Chicago's potentate, he has always deferred to higher authority the matter of passing judgment on what punishments should be exacted from those whose evil doings surfaced in the political stream. Daley was deeply saddened by the earthly accountability that federal courts had demanded of the Kerners, the Barretts, the Wigodas, the Keanes, the corrupt police captains. So many public servants of power and influence in Chicago had been exposed as parasites on the body politic that Daley grieved and perhaps even got on his knees and thanked Providence that he had remained pure in a profession in which most men, alas, seemed vulnerable to the infection of greed. Daley's simplistic faith had led him safely through an inferno, hardly allowing him to be scorched. In one sense, however, Daley had reason to feel betrayed; what others had done, even though each man is accountable for his own sins, reflected poorly upon Daley—for, after all, he had been the leader of those who had been caught and tried. Thus, it was as 1974 closed that Daley pondered the dilemma of whether he should run again in 1975—demonstrating that the voters held him to be more virtuous than the others—or whether he could safely step aside and expect public gratitude that his work was now honorably done. To run or not to run— that was the question. And not the least of the pressures driving him to seek a historic sixth term were the political considerations:

• Settling scores with Alderman Singer.

• Forcing a confrontation with Governor Walker.

• Pushing the Democratic National Committee into selecting Chicago as its presidential convention city in 1976, giving Daley a chance to restore Chicago's reputation as a civilized place.

But, on the other hand, Daley did not know what further damage the unabated investigations of the U.S. District Attorney might do to the still-invincible Democratic Machine. All he knew was that the federal people were pressing on, determined to wreck thoroughly what they called "the Chicago system"—exposing corruption with savage joy that allowed not a shred of sympathy for the powerful men and their families who were being stripped naked and destroyed. The objective of the prosecutors was to destroy the evil political structure that the decent Daley had dominated for twenty years, and the choice that faced him was whether to regroup and fight on, accepting the appalling casualties that the U.S. attorney's office had fixed as the price of continuing his leadership of the Democratic Machine—or whether to bow out with whatever grace he could summon, spending his remaining years God knows how.

Daley had one other alternative: He might decline to run for mayor in 1975 but simultaneously retain authority as chairman of the Chicago Democrats. Yet as he himself had said—in an impassioned, off-the-cuff speech in May 1972, to the National Restaurant Association members. "I say this in all sincerity, the question of party politics: how can you control the city, unless you're the leader of your party?" If his conclusion was valid then, might not his successor as mayor insist that he must also replace Daley as head of the Machine? What would be left, then, for Daley, except to fade out and wait to die? Would Daley be content, as Jake Arvey has been, to live out his years as an elder statesman—pretending to be powerful when he was in fact politically impotent?

In the month following his highly satisfactory victories in the November 5, 1974 election, his Democratic party candidates cutting deeply into the Republicans—the Democrats winning control, among other gains, of both branches of the Illinois legislature—Daley remained coy as members of his adoration society gently pleaded with him to declare his candidacy ' for a sixth term. With plenty of time remaining to make his great announcement, not having to file petitions supporting his candidacy until December 28, Daley was both coy and flirtatious. Then, on December 3, it became virtually clear that Daley would run, when leaders of labor, industry, and finance made their quadrennial pilgrimage to his office to kneel at his feet and petition him to run.

Just as the swallows return each St. Joseph's Day to

Capistrano, every four years representatives of Chicago's power structure show up in Daley's office to make their pleading. They gather in an outer office—bankers, financiers, and merchants in one group: Roger Anderson, board chairman of the Continental Bank; Henry Crown of Material Service and General Dynamics; Arthur Rubloff, the real estator; et al. Fashionably tailored, manicured labor bosses are in another delegation: William A. Lee, president of the Chicago Federation of Labor; Louis Peick, head of the Teamster Union's Joint Council No. 25; Robert Johnston, director of the United Auto Workers' Region No. 4; et al. All vigorously applaud as His Honor the Mayor makes an appearance, pretending that this visitation his trusted aides have arranged is a complete surprise. This plea to Daley that he remain in charge of Chicago government has become part of the liturgy, the ceremony being performed in much the same way every four years. Even the wording of the petition remains pretty much the same: "We told him," said the Continental Bank's Roger Anderson, "that we're a nonpartisan group representing a broad spectrum of the city who have great respect for the progress the city had made during his tenure. Chicago has made such great progress under his leadership, we'd like to see it continue." The Greatest Mayor Chicago Ever Had flashed his noncommittal "gee whiz" smile, as the likes of Dr. Preston Bradley, well-known pastor of the People's Church, Dr. Morris Fishbein of the American Medical Association, and Edward C. Logelin, midwest vice-present of U.S. Steel Corporation beamed. Nobody mentioned that most of those who petitioned that Daley make the sacrifice of remaining as mayor of Chicago did not live in the city, but in fashionable suburbs to which they fled when the work day was done.

As sort of a spiritual leader, Daley undoubtedly was pleased to be the subject of this obeisance. It was balm for the wound he had suffered the previous day when an old pal, Judge Abraham Lincoln Marovitz, had felt compelled to drop a one-year prison sentence on his protégé, Alderman Paul T. Wigoda, wrapping up the conviction of Wigoda on charges that he evaded payment of income taxes on a $50,000 bribe he took—claiming to the last that he was innocent—on an important zoning ordinance that had sailed through City Council with his name on it. The expectation had been that the probation-prone Marovitz would have suspended sentence on Wigoda, and cynics said the alderman got a year because a suspended sentence would have appeared unseemly, with Daley on the verge of announcing for reelection. In any case, excoriating the federal attorneys who have a habit of granting immunity from prosecution to equally guilty witnesses who agree to testify against the likes of Wigoda, Judge Marovitz sugarcoated his lamentation with a statement: "I am particularly saddened and disheartened to see additional scorn brought to the term 'politician.' I yearn for the day when a 'politician' will once again be a person who serves his community, rather than a dirty word."

One thing was certain as various other people (one group of women, another of "house" Latinos, a third of black clergymen who did not wear the Democratic organization collar) formed processionals and filed into Daley's outer office in the first week of December to beg his favor of running for another term: Daley would carefully choose his moment. It would have been indelicate for Daley to have replied to the business chiefs: "O.K., if you want me all that bad—I'll run." The ceremonials required that Daley give the impression that he was taking the matter under advisement and that, after further cogitating, he would try to reach a decision. Secondly, by way of getting the fullest publicity when he did make the grand announcement, Daley had to pick a day when he stood a good chance of dominating the local news.

Wednesday, December 4, would have been a bad day because this was the day that U.S. Attorney Thompson announced the indictment of eight legislators on the grounds that they had ripped off the ready-mix concrete industry for $31,000. The crime dated back to a piece of legislation in the 1972 session that would have permitted the ready-mix companies to increase vastly the weight of the loads that they carry to construction sites over public streets and highways. Thompson said that at least twelve other legislators had been involved in getting passage of this bill; he regretted that the government did not have sufficient evidence to support indictments of these others. The legislators were charged with having demanded a payoff of $50,000 from the ready-mix interests and continued to demand it, even after the then-Governor Richard B. Ogilvie, alerted to the damage that the heavily-weighted trucks would do to public pavement, had vetoed the bill. The $31,000 they got was a compromise figure, the ready-mix companies reluctantly agreeing that the legislators had certainly done their part in approving a bill that was clearly not in the public interest.

Not the least of the reasons why the news media gave this latest bomb of Thompson's a big play was his disclosure that seven industry executives had been designated unindicted coconspirators, the presumption being that they had agreed to testify against the lawmakers. The best known of the unindicted coconspirators was Lester Crown, forty-nine, socialite son of Henry Crown—a millionaire in his own right, president of Material Service Co., part owner of the New York Yankees, board member of such giants as Continental Bank and Trans World Airlines. With Lester Crown's smiling face on the front pages of Chicago newspapers, December 4 was not a day that Daley wanted his to be there, also.

There was yet another reason that argued against a hasty announcement of candidacy by Daley: On the night of December 4, Alderman William S. Singer, anti-organization candidate for mayor, was holding a fund-raising dinner at the Hyatt Regency-Chicago Hotel in the heart of the city. The anti-establishment faithful were enthralled when the thirty-three-year-old Singer ridiculed the "few dozen of Chicago's most powerful people" who had just pleaded with Daley to run. The Singer folks roared when their grinning young man referred to the "spontaneous" outpouring of devotion to Daley. Milking dry an obvious cow, Singer provoked laughter with his explanation of how, simultaneously, so many important people had been seized by a desire to visit Mayor Daley. "I guess they all waked up at ten A.M. and said, 'Eureka! I've got to go to City Hall.'" On a grimmer note, Singer added: "I want to caution Mr. Daley and those men of wealth and power: We have too much planning without people, too much government by decree instead of by consent." As expected, Singer was making things a little sticky—but in no way did he have a bearing on Daley's ultimate decision.

As he contemplated his options at the close of 1974, Daley must have indulged in some satisfaction that he had been, as many said, The Greatest Mayor Chicago Ever Had. Conditions had changed. The hog-butcher-of-the-world stuff belonged to another age. Yet Chicago was a vibrant place; this was the city of clout, to be sure, but this was the city that had inspired the creation of sky-scrapers. The world's gifted artists sing as well in Chicago's Lyric as anywhere else, the grains that feed millions of people in the western world are traded in Daley's city, and for reasons of sewage disposal, the Chicago River has been made to flow backward.

At year's end, 1974, the business community remained enthralled by the kind of government Daley had provided for two decades. Chicago, having been prevented by state statute from getting itself dangerously in debt—Daley not taking advantage of the freedom to borrow heavily, which first Senator Lynch and then the revised State Con-stitution of 1970 had made possible—was an economic jewel among municipalities. Chicago could boast a dramat-ically lower per capita bonded debt than any other major city of the nation ($298 as compared to $784 for New York, $688 for Dallas, $564 for San Francisco and Boston, and so on). Taxes consequently were comparatively rea-sonable, with a long-term likelihood that they would remain relatively low. In late 1974, Chicago was granted an enviable Double-A rating on its bonds by the New York financial community; Moody's Investors Service rated O'Hare Airport bonds at A-1, the only airport in all fifty states to enjoy this distinction. Chicago had a diversification of commerce and a good work force and a better than average public transit company, The Chicago Transit Authority, admitting that the CTA was almost constantly in a state of financial distress—hard put to find operating money, 87 percent of its fare box dollar required to meet the payroll. On balance, Chicago was financially sound and it was understandable that a mayor who took undue credit for all of this was reluctant to surrender control of the place to someone else.

Especially when the mayor was Richard J. Daley, son of an Irish immigrant, who has risen above the Congress-man Dawsons, the Harry Sains, the Al Horans and the Joe Gills, the Charlie Webers, and, oh, so many old gray cats, most of them now dead, whom he had fought to sit in the seat of power. Having attained such preeminence, greatest of all the big city bosses, it was torture to face the thought of giving it up. This was Daley's torment at the end of 1974.

Part of Daley's indecision was the question of whether, in seeking to retain prominence in the changing climate of the Democratic party's approach to the problems of national affairs, the scabs might be torn off the old 1972 and 1968 convention wounds, with the result that Daley would once again get bloodied up. Amid speculation of whether he would run again or step aside, Daley decided to put his vulnerability to the test at the party's unique mini-convention in Kansas City, Missouri. The mini-convention had been called to reevaluate the old controversy of proportional representation of delegates to the party's presidential nominating conventions; on the one side were the "regulars," resentful of change, and, on the other side, a mixed bag of plain folks who wanted to beef up the role that the various minority blocs of the party could play in choosing presidential candidates and setting party policy on controversial issues. It was an unlikely setting for Chicago's Mayor Daley to test his acceptability, but he was delighted to discover on his December 6-8 participation in the convocation at Kansas City that he was gently and respectfully treated, applauded even by the reformers who hated him when he said, in an address to the mini-convention: "The people are counting on Democrats to solve current problems and restore confidence and spirit in government. We come here not to look inward or backward, but to look forward to 1976."

Daley was pleased that Governor Walker had cancelled his plans to attend the mini-convention. The Illinois legislature had just mortified Walker by voting to override his vetoes of numerous appropriation bills—creating a fiduciary crisis for Walker that the usually taciturn Victor deGrazia decried as "Just chaos!" The governor, in scratching his intention to see what political hay he could rake up for himself in Kansas City, charged that he had been stabbed in the back by Daley's people. A press aide of Walker snarled, "We won't be part of any phony show in Kansas City when they have just done us in on the governor's 1975 budget." Advised that Walker was refusing to show up, Daley mildly remarked, "Boycotting the mini-convention will not achieve anything. You do not boycott—you participate and try to change things." This was on Saturday, December 6. On Monday, December 8, Daley, back in Chicago, formally accepted the call to run for an unprecedented sixth term.

Daley made his announcement at a luncheon for the fifty Democratic ward committeemen in the Illinois Room of the La Salle Hotel. Escorted into the private luncheon by Lieutenant Governor Neil Hartigan, Alderman Vito Marzullo, the First Ward's John D'Arco (the crime syndicate's man), and fifteen other prominent members of the clan, Daley sat with hands folded in his lap as almost a dozen of his ward bosses—Congressman Dan Rostenkowski presiding—gushed extravagant praise of his political virtues. No reference was made to the opposition that there would be to Daley's getting elected again—no mention of Alderman Singer; the discredited ex-state's attorney, Ed Hanrahan; the handsome and articulate State Senator Richard Newhouse, sole hope of the blacks; the Democratic ward bosses were devoid of interest as to whom the Republicans would turn to in seeking a candidate (nor would they have cared had they known that a Republican search committee, headed by Alderman John Hoellen, who had served twenty-eight years in City Council, badgering Mayor Daley for the last twenty of them, would wind up selecting Hoellen for the hopeless assignment of running against Daley).

In an atmosphere so heavy with synthetic adulation as to be sickening, Daley made an acceptance speech that was as vigorous as it was weighted with platitudes. He loved Chicago. The city had much to be proud of. There were challenges to be faced but, thank God, "We have people who can meet these challenges. And that's why I'm proud to say that I'm ready to join with you today in continuing this fight."

There were cheers aplenty, and a couple of standing ovations, but little sign on the faces of his ward committeemen that they held their leader in anything that approached genuine affection. Inwardly, many of those present might have been wondering—particularly those under investigation by District Attorney Thompson—what the next four years would bring. Even Daley had reason for reflection as to whether—having thus far escaped unscathed in the vicious carnage of Chicago's political battles—he might be staying too long in the combat zone. His next four years, if he survived, might well establish him as the nation's most prestigious Democrat; yet he could not tell in changing racial and economic times what the price of this might be.

If Daley had had to answer the question of whether he had had a full life, his answer could only have been yes. Faithful husband of a decent woman, father of seven children, feared by some people of influence and respected by many—what else could he ask of the Father to whom each morning at mass he prayed? One more taste, only, of the fruits of power, one more term as mayor. Time to deal with his enemies and search further for a solution to the social problems that haunt those in charge of such urban centers as Chicago. That would be enough.

Richard Daley had said that every man must answer for himself. He believed without question that every mortal must finally stand at the judgment seat of God, to be welcomed, he hoped, into paradise—and his daily prayer was that he would make it. His earthly ambition had been to be a great man; his desire for eternity was that he had been a good one. Whatever the final judgment might be, God knows that Richard J. Daley had tried to be both.

Index

266